INTERIOR ACTS

Teleology, Justice, and Friendship in the Religious Ethics of Thomas Aquinas

Steven Anthony Edwards

UNIVERSITY
PRESS OF
AMERICA

LANHAM • NEW YORK • LONDON

Copyright © 1986 by
Steven Anthony Edwards

University Press of America,® Inc.

4720 Boston Way
Lanham, MD 20706

3 Henrietta Street
London WC2E 8LU England

All rights reserved

Printed in the United States of America

Library of Congress Cataloging in Publication Data

Edwards, Steven Anthony.
  Interior acts.

  Bibliography: p.
  Includes index.
  1. Thomas, Aquinas, Saint, 1225?-1274—Contributions.
in ethics.   2. Ethics, Medieval.   I. Title.
B765.T54E34   1986   241'.042'0924   85-29530
ISBN 0-8191-5212-9 (alk. paper)
ISBN 0-8191-5213-7 (pbk. : alk. paper)

All University Press of America books are produced on acid-free
paper which exceeds the minimum standards set by the National
Historical Publications and Records Commission.

In Memoriam
Alene Love
ἄλλουσ ἔσωσεν

ACKNOWLEDGMENTS

Many of the ideas in this book appeared first in my Stanford doctoral dissertation. I would therefore like to take this opportunity to thank the members of my dissertation committee--Professor Lawrence V. Berman, the late Professor William A. Clebsch, Professor David S. Nivison, and Professor Diana Y. Paul--for their advice and criticism. I am especially grateful to Professor Berman, principal advisor and midwife extraordinaire, who somehow knew at each turn how best to aid the birth. And Professor Clebsch's standards for knowledge worth having made him a challenging presence as I sat at my desk; many parts of the book that I like best first found formulation because of that challenge. Professors Nivison and Paul, although less immediately involved in the emergence of the dissertation, were readers whose ranges of expertise at once extended and focused my own inquiries. I am someone for whom the sense of audience or readership matters greatly, and in these four readers I was very fortunate.

The Giles R. Whiting Foundation made the early research of this project possible through a generous fellowship.

A grant from the Faculty of Arts and Sciences Grants Committee, University of Pittsburgh, gave me the free time to work more deeply into double bind theory and its applications to religious ethics.

Special thanks go to John Bell of the Pitt Computer Center, and also to Michael Spring of the Pitt External Studies Program, for their help in formatting the book on the Pitt computer.

I would also like to thank my parents, George and Anne Edwards, and my late grandmother, Ruth Partridge, for the advice and support they have given me in my work. I am also grateful to many good friends, among them Pat Barry, Wendy Smith, Henry Levinson, Kim Miller, Rich Jacks, William E. Coles, Jr., David Halperin, John Imhoff, Ned Spofford, Rick Maddox, David Barnhill, Jean Lee, Bob Leach, Sharon Traweek, Jack Fernandez, and Anne Schwarzkopf.

TABLE OF CONTENTS

1. An Ethics of Spiritual Change	1
2. Teleology	24
3. Justice and Love	46
4. Some Problems of Justice	63
5. Action	85
6. Sin	119
7. Epilogue	132
Bibliography	135
Index	166

PREFACE

In this book I interpret Thomas Aquinas's theory of responsibility by placing it in the wider context of his religious ethics. Aquinas held what I call here an "introvert conception of responsibility." In his view, human action had two sides or faces: an inner face by which the individual was related to God, and an outer face by which he was related to other human beings. Aquinas gave greater emphasis to the former. Interior acts of the intellect and will, he believed, were causally prior, more truly one's own, more readily controlled, more directly determinate of the soul's condition, and more accurately expressive of it than external behavior or speech. They therefore had a larger role in deciding the ultimate status of the individual as saved or damned. Yet exterior acts were important too. The need to act in the external world and to associate with other human beings could only be met by exterior acts, and these in turn could only be brought about by <u>actus interiores</u> that would also alter the condition of the soul.

It was as if the individual lived two lives at once. Born with a will oriented both inwardly toward God and outwardly toward the external world, a human being existed in the tension between the inner and outer sides of his life. On the one hand, the individual was eternally responsible to God for the condition of his soul; on the other, he was temporally answerable to other human beings for his physical behavior. Aquinas believed that the individual should be aware of both faces of action, and, just as he should place God above all other things, and spiritual goods above temporal ones, so he should also have more regard for the events and conditions of his inner life than for those of his external affairs. Yet because the individual acted daily and intensively in the world, and thus involved himself with it, he all too easily allowed this priority to become reversed, and thereby sinned. Thus, Aquinas's conception of human action reflected the difficulty of the human condition as a pilgrimage through life, a transitional phase in which it was necessary for the individual to be "in the world, but not of it."

Aquinas's reasons for holding an introvert conception of responsibility followed from very basic ideas in his system of thought: his doctrine of God; his unique adaptation of Aristotle's concepts of teleology, justice, and friendship; his hierarchical conception of the universe and its subsystems; his characteristically Christian skepticism about our moral knowledge of other minds. As with so many other of Aquinas's views, his view of personal responsibility can be understood properly only by setting it in its systematic context.

The language of responsibility belongs to the wider language of justice, and "justice" is without a doubt one of the major conceptions governing this ethics. Yet "justice" does not stand alone. Aquinas was a Christian ethicist, alert always to what was for him the basic fact of the human condition: "Man is ordained to God as to an end that exceeds his reason." Whatever "justice" might mean as a norm governing human interaction, it could not be so construed that it entailed that a just God could not become incarnate, call sinners, and "give up his life for his friends." "Justice" must have a meaning that was consistent with "divine justice," and "divine justice" must be compatible both with the attainment by sinners of a supernatural end in God, and with their transformation into friends who returned his love for them. In other words, in a systematic moral theology, "justice" had not only to be mapped onto "teleology," but so defined that loving friendship toward God could suffice for salvation.

Aristotle had shown that "teleology," "justice," and "friendship" could be effectively and coherently interwoven, but Thomas's architectonic problems were different and, in a sense, more severe. Thomas needed to distinguish and relate (1) the end in God, (2) the reward of his eternal presence, and (3) the eternal friendship with him. Since for Aquinas end, reward and friend were combined in God, the problem of achieving a synthesis of teleology, justice, and friendship was intensified. This was nothing new, really: Paul had faced similar problems; so had Augustine. Each had left paradoxes in his religious ethics. Aquinas does not criticize them for this, but unlike them he made a special effort to show that these paradoxes were not falsidical but veridical. Ultimately, in the mind of God, there was no difficulty, and the strength of human reason was sufficient to refute all those who would claim to have shown that salvation in Christian terms was logically impossible.

My strategy in this book has been to emphasize that, although these paradoxes may be veridical, nevertheless they are problematic, and existentially problematic for those who would try to live out the ethics that Aquinas proposes. Thus, unlike most of Thomas's present-day followers, I try to deepen our sense of both the theoretical and practical difficulties of the ethics he proposes before going on to display the solutions he offers.

To help me bring into focus the practical significance of this problematics, I have drawn upon the language and theory of the "double bind." For many people, I know, the phrase "double bind" carries negative connotations. And it is true that double bind theory first appeared as an interpretation of schizophrenia, and even today the popular usage of "double bind" carries the implication that a double bind is something perpetrated by a binder against a victim. Yet those who developed the original theory--Bateson, Jackson, Haley, and Weakland--had already recognized other applications by the time "Toward a Theory of Schizophrenia" was published. They saw, too, that "binder" and "victim" were equally bound by the paradoxical structure of their relationship. Most importantly, they noted even in "Toward a Theory of Schizophrenia" that paradoxes could function therapeutically as well as pathogenically. In their view, a paradox might temporarily be pathogenic, but in the long run therapeutic; temporarily therapeutic, but in the long run pathogenic; or therapeutic for one person and pathogenic for another. Bateson in particular was interested in the paradoxes of learning, especially where the change in the learner was so radical that it also involved profound changes in roles and relations to others.

I suggest here that the fundamental paradoxes of classical Christian ethics are a direct function of the deep learning required for salvation and the profound changes in role that go with it. The intuition that informs the argument is simple: if paradoxes are involved in human learning and in concomitant changes in human relationships, then they will certainly be involved in the far deeper transformation that occurs in Christian salvation and in the relationship between the individual and God. And in fact they are; moreover, seeing where they are placed in the ethics of a particular Christian thinker helps us to see in a new way how the ethics of this tradition works to effect the changes it describes.

CHAPTER 1
AN ETHICS OF SPIRITUAL CHANGE

I

One of Aquinas's gifts as a theologian was a guiding sense of how things in the universe fit together and worked as a whole. "<u>Ordo</u>" and its cognates appear constantly in his work, as do "<u>conveniens</u>" (suitable or fitting), "<u>aequalis</u>" (equal), "<u>commensuratus</u>" (commensurate), "<u>debitus</u>" (due), and "<u>proportionatus</u>" (proportionate). These ways of talking about fitness carry mathematical connotations; to Thomas, the <u>ordo universalis</u> was like a society, but it was also like an economy kept in balance by an unseen intellect. He used "<u>ordo</u>" and kindred words to indicate arrangement and ongoing equilibrium in the universal process, and he employed "<u>proportionatus</u>" and like terms to suggest the particular equations by which God maintained his design through change.

This language of fitness appears throughout Aquinas's theology, but it is especially prominent in his discussions of salvation and damnation, for salvation and damnation raised major questions about the consistent maintenance of divine order. Thomas turned therefore to "<u>proportionatus</u>," "<u>conveniens</u>," "<u>debitus</u>," and the rest in order to argue that, in saving some and damning others, God preserved the order that he governed.

Aquinas understood the individual's fitness for salvation as a type of relation to God; and, "Since fitness (<u>conveniens</u>) is based upon a relation, it depends on each extreme of the relation." The human soul was one term, with principal emphasis on intellect, will, and their cooperative interaction; the second term was God (or "in God," as Aquinas preferred to put it). Accordingly, he distinguished the modes of fitness by the distinct ways in which he spoke of the soul's ultimate activity and its ultimate mode of subjection in God.

Three modes were basic. Those in a state of grace were (1) fit for their ultimate <u>end</u>, the vision of God (teleology), (2) fit for their eternal <u>reward</u>, the enjoyment of that vision (justice), and (3) fit for eternal <u>friendship</u>, the mutual indwelling of the lover and the Beloved (charity). Of course, end, reward, and friendship were attained fully only after death. In the present life, each person was faced with the problem of how to become fit for God in each of these ways.

It is worth noting, in passing, that the overlap of these modes was not due simply to their analogical adaptation to theological usage. The soul's proportion to God might be compared to that of a medical student to different aspects of his future work:

1. If you complete your medical studies here, you will be fit to practice medicine. (end/teleology)

2. If you complete your medical studies here, you will deserve a good start in your practice. (reward/justice)

3. If you complete your medical studies here, you will have men like John and Matthew as your colleagues. (friend/charity)[1]

Fitness for the <u>activity</u> of beatitude, then, was analogous to the fitness of a doctor to practice medicine: the intellect had become capable of a high order of activity. Fitness for the <u>enjoyment</u> of the vision was like deserving a good start in medical practice: prior performance and present skill merited a favorable situation. Fitness for friendship with God was comparable to the shared activity and mutual respect of colleagues.

II

Among the modes of fitness, fitness for the ultimate end had a privileged status. Justice and charity could be mapped onto teleology more easily than teleology could be enfigured in them. Accordingly, in the first article of the <u>Summa Theologiae</u>, Aquinas did not say, "When life is over, man gets his due," nor did he say, "You shall love the Lord your God"; rather, he said, "Man is ordained to God as to an end that exceeds the grasp of reason."[2] This was one of Thomas's "he-who-has-ears-to-hear" remarks, foreshadowing the major and problematic role that teleology would play in the questions to follow.[3] By mentioning it at the first available opportunity, he underscored its importance. Ordination to an end belonged to every species, and therefore represented a deeper layer of reality, a more abiding and extensive actuation of potentiality, than justice or charity.

Aquinas laid the groundwork for his teleological model, and hence for the rest of his ethics, in his philosophical theology. In the fifth argument for the existence of God, he reasoned that since there were beings without intelligence that nevertheless acted for ends, there therefore had to be an intelligence who directed them to those ends, "as the arrow is shot to its mark by the archer." This intelligence was God.[4]

As with each of his other proofs, Thomas made the most of the Fifth Way in subsequent articles of the <u>Summa</u>. He found that the God of the proof corresponded to the traditional Christian conception of God as a ruler or king, and that the work of the divine intelligence in directing things to their ends could therefore be understood as a form of government, the practical wisdom (<u>prudentia</u>) or providence (<u>providentia</u>) of God.[5] Accordingly, he attached the analogical name "ruler" (<u>gubernator</u>, <u>rector</u>) to the Deity, and thereafter spoke of "the whole community of the universe" as the realm God administered through his laws.[6]

Aquinas explained in his discussion of analogy that "ruler" and other names that implied relation to creatures, such as "father," "lord," and friend," were predicated temporally of God. That is, they applied to God only because creatures had come into existence and had become related to him in various ways:

> Thus, though God is prior to the creature, still, because the signification of "lord" includes the idea of "servant" and conversely, these two relative terms, "lord" and "servant," are simultaneous by nature. Hence, God was not "lord" until he had a creature subject to himself.[7]

To forestall the inference that there were accidents and change in God, Aquinas argued that the relation of creatures to God did not imply that he in turn was really related to them:

> Since therefore God is outside the whole order of creation, and all creatures are ordered to him, and not conversely, it is manifest that creatures are really related to God himself; whereas in God there is no real relation to creatures, but a relation only in idea, inasmuch as creatures are referred to him.[8]

To Aquinas, relation was an accident, and accidents presupposed potentiality in their subject. God, however, was perfect, a pure actus in whom there was no potentiality, and hence no accidents. There were, therefore, no relations in God. Consequently, to define any relation between God and the creature was actually to define a relation of the creature to its "principle of being and government."[9]

Thomas denied that this interpretation of temporal attributes left them vacuous or distorted. Since the perfections of all things pre-existed in God, whatever perfections belonged to such roles as ruler, lord, or father belonged preeminently to God as causa universalis; and, since only the perfections were attributed to God, Aquinas saw a gain in intelligibility, not a loss, in the exclusion of imperfections entailed by relationship. Also, despite the one-sided character of the relationship, he held that an expression such as "God is lord" was not merely metaphorical:

> Since God is related to the creature for the reason that the creature is related to him, and since the relation of subjection is real in the creature, it follows that God is lord not only in idea but in reality; for he is called "lord" according to the manner in which the creature is subject to him.[10]

The theory of temporal attributes thus equipped Aquinas with an interpretation and justification for the traditional language of divine roles. The theory was bound to have an important place in his theology, for he was explicating a religious tradition in which temporal attributes were central: God was conceived as the ruler of the universe, prayed to as "Our Father," and understood to have expressed his love in "giving up his life for his friends." Using temporal attributes, Thomas could argue that a creature was subject to God as end, specify the mode of that subjection according to the type of creature, and analyze any changes that might occur in the creature's mode of subjection.

Since rational animals were the creatures that changed their modes of subjection through divine grace and human choice, and since some of those changes were decisive for salvation or damnation, the doctrine of temporal analogy had direct bearing on moral theology, and particularly on the ethics and psychology of human change. Moreover, since "mode of subjection" referred at once to the relation to the end and to the relationship to a person, Aquinas found that the analogy of temporal attributes enabled him to shift between the language of ultimate end and means and the language of relationship and interaction, depending on the analytic and rhetorical needs of the moment.

The theory of temporal attributes, therefore, provided the theoretical basis for a two-pronged approach to any state, change, or problem of the human spirit: it could be examined intrapersonally, as a matter of the soul's condition, or interpersonally, as a matter of the soul's relation to God. Mortal sin, for example, could be diagnosed both as a disorder of the will and as a breach of friendship with God. Changes in the soul and changes in relationship to God, therefore, were different ways to conceptualize the same events. And, since God played many roles in relation to rational creatures--lawgiver, judge, father, lord, teacher, friend, and lover--interpretation could be closely fitted to specific shifts in the individual's mode of subjection. By moving the focus back and forth between individual soul and interpersonal relationship, Thomas found that he could use the analogy of temporal attributes to give a more complete picture of the human soul, its condition, and its patterns of change.

Yet given the theory of temporal attributes, the relationship of the soul to God and the interaction within that relationship remained one-sided. Although an act of the will affected the relationship to God, God never "responded," strictly speaking, since in God himself there was neither a real relation to the creature nor any change of attitude toward it.[11] As <u>actus purus</u>, God had no potentiality for new, responsive acts. Hence, although Aquinas used the language of roles, relations, and interaction in his religious ethics, he did so with the proviso that real relation to the soul could not be predicated of God.

III

Because "mode of subjection" referred both to the soul's relation to its own ultimate end and to its relation to a superordinate Other, in Aquinas's religious ethics the self-regarding and other-regarding elements were related to one another like the surfaces of a Möbius strip: in a sense there was only one side, but in another sense there were two. Aquinas had to sustain this double perspective, not just in principle, but throughout his moral theology. He did so in four ways. (1) He qualified his self-regarding model, teleology, in an other-regarding direction, by arguing that the telos of the self was the vision of an Other. (2) He qualified his other-regarding model, justice, in a self-regarding direction, by arguing that the relation to the Other was determined by the inclinations of the self. (3) He combined and coordinated the self-regarding and other-regarding elements of the other two by expanding on Augustine's idea that charity was a form of friendship. Finally, (4) he found that an introvert conception of responsibility was needed to complete the synthesis.[12]

(1) Thomas grounded his teleological conception of the soul's return to God in the idea that the human will was naturally inclined to its own perfection or happiness.[13] Determinate acts of the will presupposed this natural inclination and moved toward the fulfillment of it as their term.[14] The attainment of this end, the full realization of the soul's potential for "doing well and faring well,"[15] was an activity of the soul, and actuations of internal powers were the only means strictly necessary to its attainment. Although often the psychological potencies or powers were actuated in the effort to attain external objectives, actus interiores, not their outward manifestations, were principally responsible for changes in internal moods, dispositions, and habits, and thereby for the perfection or imperfection of the person.

As acts critical to the attainment or loss of salvation, moral acts were indeed interiores:

> [S]ome acts pass into external matter, e.g., to cut and to burn; and such acts have for their matter and subject the thing into which the action passes: thus the Philosopher states in III Physic., that "movement is the act of the thing moved, caused by a mover." On the other hand, there are acts which do not pass into external matter, but remain in the agent, e.g., to desire and to know: and such are all moral acts, whether virtuous or sinful.[16]

By actuating the powers of the soul in various ways, moral acts affected its habitus, and therefore its mode of subjection to the ultimate end. In doing so, they either aided or hampered the movement toward that end.

A further reason for emphasizing the inner life followed from the notion of a hierarchy of being. In Aquinas's hierarchical conception of the universe, causation was the affect of something higher on something lower. This, at least, was the general rule; exceptions in human action were due to the disorder caused in the internal hierarchy by original sin. Thus, except where the consequences of original sin played the major role in causing an action (e.g., in a sudden movement of passion or anger), something lower in the hierarchy could not affect something higher except by the act or omission of the higher: "The higher mover is not directly moved by the lower; but in a manner it can be moved by it indirectly."[17] Since in the rational animal "higher" was "more inward," events in the external world, body, or lower powers of the soul could not act upon the higher, more inward powers without their acquiescence.[18] And unless the higher powers were involved in an action by commission or omission, the mode of subjection to the ultimate end remained substantially unchanged. The higher, more inward powers, therefore, were the principal means by which the soul contributed to or obstructed its own transformation and perfection.

The position described would be one of pure self-determination, were it not that the perfection of the individual was the vision of God, an activity beyond the power of any finite creature to perform on its own. "Nothing can by its operation bring about an effect that exceeds its active force, but only such as is proportionate to its active power."[19] Since the vision of God was infinite, and natural power finite, there could be no question of attaining the ultimate end without supernatural aid. There was no possibility of the soul lifting itself by its bootstraps, and human teachers could not directly affect the will, and could only make a modest contribution through the intellect: "the teacher only brings exterior help, as the physician who heals: but just as the interior nature is the principal cause of healing, so the interior light of the intellect is the principal cause of knowledge. But both of these are from God."[20] The self-regarding model of perfection in eternal happiness was qualified, therefore, by the fact that this happiness was the vision of God, who was also involved in the means to this end as an indispensable aid and guide. In the movement to the end, the individual had to do what he could through actus interiores to cooperate with the inward stimulation and direction of divine grace.

(2) Just as Aquinas gave teleology an other-regarding emphasis, so he gave justice a self-regarding or inner-regarding turn. Justice for Aquinas was a mean in external operations between self and other, but this norm, though relevant in an analogical form to the sinner's debt of eternal punishment, did not hold for eternal reward.[21] The divine distributive justice that governed the reward of eternal happiness presupposed the fulfillment of legal justice under the divine ruler, but it was not the office of the ruler to reward obedience to his laws.[22] Reward belonged rather to the context of more immediate relationships, such as servant-lord, child-parent, and monk-abbot. In such asymmetrical relationships, said Thomas, a strict mean could not be upheld, for there was no equitable quid quo pro between a subordinate and a superior: a subordinate could never give a superior more than his due, and a superior as such owed nothing to his subordinate.[23] This held a fortiori for the infinitely asymmetrical relationship between the individual and God; indeed, the individual could not even render to God the full reverence and obedience that were his due. Fortunately, Aquinas noted,

> Virtue is praised because of the will, not because of the ability; and therefore if a man fall short of equality which is the mean of justice through lack of ability, his virtue deserves no less praise, provided there be no failing on the part of the will.[24]

As Aristotle had observed, the will in the act of wishing could have something impossible as the object of its desire.[25] By centering his ethics on the interior act of the will, Aquinas could argue that even wishing that one could render to God his due would be imputed to the individual as a virtuous activity in its own right.

This additional qualification of justice helped to counterbalance the radical inequality of the relationship between finite and infinite persons, but it presupposed a unique conception of God's presence to the human soul. God's superiority to the rational agent was defined in a manner analogous to that of other persons who are "principles of being and government," such as the superiority of a parent to a child.[26] Yet God was unique, a principle of being and government who operated differently than any other. As a principle of being, God was ontologically present to the soul, for God was pure being, and being was "innermost in each thing and most fundamentally inherent in all things"; "therefore," Thomas concluded, "it must be that God is in all things and inwardly (intime)."[27] As a principle of government, on the other hand, God was intentionally present to the will of the individual as its ultimate end.[28]

God's presence to each creature, therefore, depended on its mode of being, which in turn determined its mode of subjection. And God's presence to the rational animal was greater ontologically because it was made in his image and therefore had greater being, life, and self-possession.[29] Because the rational creature had greater self-possession than other creatures, God's intentional presence to it was subject to variation through changes of intellect and will.[30] Thus, God was more intimate as a father to his children under the divine law than to those whom he merely ruled through the natural law; he was more intimate still with those who were his friends, for in them he was present through the additional sharing of his goodness and love; and to mystics and to those who would enjoy the beatific vision itself, his intimacy was like that of a lover.[31] These variations in the intentional presence of God were determined by interior acts, moved either by God working inwardly on the soul, by the individual cooperating inwardly with God's interior stimulation and guidance, or by the individual unilaterally diminishing God's presence through sin.

(3) Thomas's conception of charity as at once a habit infused in the soul and a kind of friendship uniting the soul to God was designed to combine and surpass the self-regarding emphasis of teleology and the other-regarding emphasis of justice; charity, Aquinas believed, was continuous with both.[32] Like teleology, charity had to do with the individual's relation to God as an end. Indeed, unlike all other acts and virtues, the act and virtue of charity had the ultimate end as the immediate object of the will.[33] On the other hand, like justice, charity had to do with the individual's relation to God as a person. Whereas justice implied a somewhat distant give-and-take between the two parties, involving the exchange of possessions, friendship was a more intimate reciprocity of love and good will.[34] Thus, charity could be construed either as a disposition of the self toward its ultimate end, or as a relationship between

self and Other; in either case, its supernatural form and power coordinated the self-regarding and other-regarding aspects of Aquinas's ethics. Through the habitus infusus of charity, the divine Other became a friend, and, as Aristotle had said, "a friend is in a sense another self."[35]

Since charity involved the mutual indwelling of the loving friend and the Beloved, the shared activity that characterized friendship between the soul and God was exercised through interior acts:

> Man's life is twofold. There is his outward life in respect of his sensitive and corporeal nature: and with regard to this life there is no communication (communicatio) or fellowship (conversatio) between us and God or the angels. The other is man's spiritual life in respect of his mind (secundum mentem), and with regard to this life there is fellowship between us and both God and the angels, imperfectly indeed in this present life, wherefore it is written Phillipp. 3: "Our fellowship is in heaven."[36]

The individual therefore began, carried on, and, in the case of mortal sin, broke off the friendship with God through the interior actuation of the soul's powers.

(4) Under each of these three ethical models, Thomas saw the modes of subjection to God as adjusted through internal interaction, for what was in question in each case was the fitness (proportio) of the soul for salvation.[37] Thus, conceived under the teleology of perfection, the soul became fit for the contemplative activity of the vision of God through actus interiores that gave it the habitual inclinations necessary to this, the highest order of activity.[38] Under the justice of reward, likewise, the soul became fit to enjoy that vision through interior acts that made it deserving of an infinite joy. Finally, under the friendship of charity the soul became fit for the union of the vision through actus interiores that rendered it eternally compatible with the Deity.[39] Each ethical model, and each corresponding mode of fitness, characterized the soul's mode of subjection in a different way, but each model presupposed interior acts as the process by which the soul succeeded with God's help or failed on its own to close the infinite distance to its ultimate end.

IV

Three features of Aquinas's interweaving of teleology, justice, and friendship are especially noteworthy: he viewed each of the three models as necessary to a complete ethics; he used a conception of God and his temporal attributes as a basis for the models; and, in combining them, he confounded his own, usually parallel distinctions between inner and outer, self and other.

In juggling all these ideas at once, Thomas seems to have had two chief problems that he wished to solve. First, the attempt to balance self-regarding and other-regarding ethical conceptions was part of his effort to demarcate the boundaries between the legitimate interests of self and others. Second, the parts played by God, supernatural virtue, and the inner life in that effort indicate that he was at the same time thinking through the traditional Christian problem of the proper attitude to take toward "the world" of human culture, social relationships, and other mutable goods.

Aquinas approached both problems through an analysis of the human will. God, he believed, had designed the will with a dual orientation, allowing a wide-ranging adaptability within the world, yet directed beyond it to an otherworldly goal. As naturally inclined to the good in general, the will had the potentiality to turn to any particular good.[40] This openness enabled the rational animal to deal with a variety of situations, accepting as good on some occasions ends or means that it would reject if circumstances were otherwise. The contingencies of life could be met, therefore, because the natural necessitation of the will was not narrowly specified, but was inclined to anything that could be affirmed as good.

Yet as inclined to the good in general, the will was frustrated even in the attainment of particular goods, for the scope of its inclination remained largely unsatisfied. The individual could have wealth, fame, power, health, honor, friends--no matter: the will went on wanting, restless for something more.[41]

Given the nature of the will, the attempt to balance the interests of self and others without grace could at best result in an uneasy truce, more often in a kind of trench warfare. Even in theory there were difficulties in resolving the self-regarding desire for happiness with the other-regarding exigencies of justice and friendship, though Aristotle, he seems to have thought, had shown that these could be solved. The deeper and more persistent problems, however, were practical and personal. The natural and fallen propensities of the will made it extremely difficult to negotiate a balance between the desires of the self and the demands of others.

Aquinas was not concerned that people would be unduly attentive to the interests of others, and consequently take inadequate care for themselves and their own. On the contrary, he believed that the major problem lay in excessive self-love--expanding the limits of one's own desires outward to encompass more and more of what belongs to others, in the vain hope of fulfilling the natural inclination of the will with particular goods. His deprecating treatment of natural friendship is telling. Thomas had great respect for Aristotle's analysis of friendship in the <u>Nicomachean Ethics</u>, but he appropriated it in a way that would have surprised Aristotle. In discussing friendship based on mutual usefulness or pleasure, Aquinas undercut Aristotle's emphasis on mutuality:

> When a friendship is based on usefulness or pleasure, a man does indeed wish his friends some good: and in this respect the character of friendship is preserved. But since he refers this good further to his own pleasure or use, the result is that friendship of the useful or pleasant, insofar as it is connected with love of concupiscence, loses the character of true friendship.[42]

The operative motivations in natural friendship, as he saw it, reduced to usefulness-for-me, pleasure-for-me. True friendship, by contrast, was not a natural phenomenon, but a gift of God's grace.

In Aquinas's view, natural curbs to self-love were insufficient: the problem created by the dual orientation of the will was too deep in the human spirit, and required a more radical remedy. Directed toward a world of mutable, particular goods, the will remained unsatisfied and insatiable. The solution, therefore, must be to direct it away from the world and toward an otherworldly good that would answer to the inclination to the good in general. In order to satisfy the natural inclination, such an object would have to be good from every point of view, and singular so that the will would not go unsatisfied in moving from one good to another. The requirement, therefore, was for a good that was universal yet singular: there was such a good, said Aquinas; it was God.

Conversion to God was the solution, therefore, but it involved problems of its own, for it required that the individual be "in the world but not of it." The dual orientation of the will, in other words, amounted to a double bind. If the natural inclination to the good in general drew the individual into contact with and accomodation to a world of mutable goods, yet could be fulfilled only by an immutable good that exceeded both the grasp of reason and the power of the will, then a paradox was built into the human condition: "Be independent, but return to me with my help." The paradox was not falsidical, but few could discriminate successfully the injunctions against inappropriate dependence, on the one hand, and those against inordinate independence on the other.[43] Failure resulted in damnation. In order to direct a finite creature to an infinite end, God had defined the post-lapsarian condition of the human species as radically problematic.[44]

Thomas believed that the solution of this problem could be achieved through the theological virtues of faith, hope, and charity; and for him, as for Paul, the greatest of these was charity. Charity had the ultimate end of the self as the immediate object of the will, and thereby directed human action more effectively toward that end. Moreover, through charity, the worldly assumption that the inclination to happiness must be self-regarding was overcome; the object of the will in charity was not the good-for-me, but the good <u>sans phrase</u>. The universal good was good not merely from a limited perspective, but from every point of view, and the basic response to it in charity was an acceptance and affirmation that went beyond the desire for possession.[45]

In charity, therefore, the love of the good-for-me was fulfilled and surpassed in the love of the good for its own sake. Aquinas indicated this in interpersonal terms by implying that, in the friendship of charity, God became "another self."[46] Aquinas meant this figuratively, but used it to point to the power of charity in confounding natural and conventional distinctions between self and other: God became "another self"; the self, now loved "in God," befriended itself as if it too were "another self"; and family, neighbors--even enemies--became "other selves."[47]

This paradoxical language of love expressed and promoted a transformation of human relationships through the power acquired in the friendship with God. Having given up its life, the self gained it back again; but life was no longer the same. The self was now seen in God, as a particular good partaking of God's universal goodness; God was now seen in the self, as present particularly through the grace of the infused virtue; and God and self were now seen in others, as actual and potential friends of God. To borrow a term from Victor Turner, the language of charity was in this respect a language of "liminality," a confusion of the individual's previous conceptions of identity and role that reflected and fostered radical psychological change.[48] Yet Thomas held that only the figurative language of charity was expressly paradoxical, and that its implications were not uncontrolled or antinomian. In his view, grace did not destroy nature, but perfected it. The natural law, with its emphasis on care for one's own, was respected, not obliterated, by the infusion of charity. Consequently, there was an order to charity that defined the chief priorities to be followed in adjudicating the proper interests of God, self, family, neighbors, and enemies. This order went beyond the priorities that followed from the natural law, but remained continuous with them. The will gave up its life, then, but received it back again; neither conformed to the world nor in opposition to it, the will in charity operated "voluntarily, readily, with delight, and firmly," in the world but not of it.

Thus, Aquinas met the paradoxical injunctions of the double bind with a counterparadox conceiving self, Other, and others as "other selves," pointing the way out of the bind, toward union with the Deity. In Aquinas's conception of charity, then, the combination of self-regarding and other-regarding conceptions provided a perspective on the happiness of the self, the just treatment of others, and proper love and good will toward them that was not only a theoretical synthesis but also a conceptual framework that promoted personal change.

In reworking the boundaries of self, others, and Other, Aquinas blurred the distinction between what was internal to the self and what was external to it, creating a controlled confusion of identities. But in the context of the double bind and its resolution, his emphasis on the inner life had another significance that may be noted here in passing. For part of the answer to the problem created by the dual orientation of the will was to withdraw the will from undue attachment to the world of mutable goods, and this solution was reinforced by the belief that the more real and important life of the self was the inner life. The introversion of responsibility, therefore, was salutary in its own right, on this view, so long as it was recognized that external acts were a strong index of the soul's condition. By withdrawing primary attention from <u>actus exteriores</u>, the individual also withdrew attention from the field of mutable goods, God's principal rival for the inclination of the will.

Thus, Thomas's introvert conception of responsibility, like many of the ideas in this closely-woven system, had more than one function in his moral theology. He emphasized interior acts because they affected the soul's condition and mode of subjection to God, but also used his introvert position to coordinate teleology, justice, and friendship, for the self-regarding and other-regarding aspects of these conceptions were neatly meshed in the notion that the divine Other was within the soul and needed no external evidence to decide the individual's fitness for salvation. Finally, Aquinas's introvert conception of responsibility encouraged the individual to withdraw the will from the mutable goods of the world and turn it toward the immutable good that was God.

V

Each of the paradoxes that are central to Aquinas's religious ethics have familiar counterparts in the relations between parent and child, and in three basic functions that the parent can perform: judge, teacher, and friend. Aquinas did not draw sharp distinctions between these divine roles and the modes of subjection they represent, but he seems to have seen fatherhood as God's most important role in any history or biography of salvation. As a judge, God was related to the individual in a way that could result only in punishment, not in reward; at the other extreme, as a friend from whom spiritual gifts and favors were appropriate, God was related to the individual in a way that presupposed some previous relationship out of which the friendship grew. Judging from the use he made of Aristotle's account of friendship between unequals, Thomas's comments on the relation between the old and new forms of the divine law,[49] and his view of baptism as effecting a share in the sonship of Christ,[50] Aquinas seems to have seen divine fatherhood as the role that mediated the change from the distance of "ruler" to the intimacy of "friend." God, after all, was not only the ruler of the community of the universe, but also the father of the children of Israel and Jesus of Nazareth. This Deity of many roles became a friend to those of his children who grew to a mature and loving relationship with him.[51]

With God as father and the individual as his child, the relationship was radically asymmetrical; the upbringing, demanding and intense. For, having ordained the human species to the vision of himself as end, God had established that those who attained that state of friendship with him would have to be "deiform" in intellect, sufficiently like him to see him face-to-face.[52] Accordingly, the parent-child relationship between God and the soul analogically reproduced the paradoxes that arise in the maturation of a child.[53] In a parent-child relationship, distinctions proper to an early stage in the relationship, such as a distinction between self and other, lose their sharp outlines when they are used to define a later stage. In particular, the boundaries between proper dependence and proper independence can easily become confused in adolescence as the maturation of the child calls for a new set of boundaries.[54] Thomas's task as theologian was to communicate the need for a shift in boundaries, yet to argue that the paradoxes thus generated were not falsidical. The metaphors of charity created a controlled confusion of identities, thereby answering to both needs.

Specific stages in the relationship between the soul and God display further connections between the problems that arise in human roles and relationships and the problems that arise in their divine analogues. With God as father-judge, the soul's relationship to him under original sin was characterized in double-bind terms. The "Be independent" paradox was paramount, and its solution was the habitus infusus of charity. Accordingly, God issued the first precept of charity, "Thou shalt love the Lord thy God with all thy heart, and all thy soul, and all thy strength."[55] But the commandment to love, although liberating when viewed from the perspective of a person in charity or ready for it, was painful to the mortal sinner. To the sinner it said, "Love me or I will damn you." Such an injunction is a double bind, for a sinner will perceive a conflict between the spontaneity of the will's act and the coercive character of the precept. To someone in a sinful frame of mind, then, the liberating potential of the precept was obscured, leaving only a sense of entrapment.

In Aquinas's view, of course, God was neither cruel nor thoughtless in promulgating a commandment to love, although he admitted that this precept, like other precepts that enjoined interior acts, was especially hard to fulfill.[56] Because the divine father deserved love, the precept was just; and because the sinner might have a change of heart in his distress, even the anguish the precept caused might be beneficial in the long run. The sinner had no hope of leaving the field of the bind, and would come to view the commandment differently if the fear of punishment broke his resistance.[57]

If the will did become more malleable--and sometimes even if it did not-- God taught the sinner to love by instilling the virtue of charity. But with God the father functioning as a teacher, paradoxes in the child's relationship to him remained. God's bind was to find a way to induce voluntary change. Like other paradoxes of the will, however, the divine attempt to induce voluntary change was not only a form of "Be independent" paradox, but was also, more specifically, a form of the "Be spontaneous" paradox. To command a spontaneous reaction would seem to preclude its spontaneity at the time, for it seems that an act done on command cannot be spontaneous. God's solution was possible to him only because he was intimus. He worked through the inherent structure of the will, since he, as the proper object of its natural necessitation, was part of that structure.[58] He therefore operated through the spontaneity of the will, not against it.

Yet here again a problem arose, in this case the paradox of denying a parallel between the distinctions of self and other, inner and outer. The statement, "The teacher is within the learner," seems either to be a figure of speech or nonsense. A response was ready to hand:

> Although corporeal things are said to be in another as in that which contains them, nevertheless spiritual things contain those things in which they are; as the soul contains the body. Hence also God is in things as containing them: nevertheless by a certain similitude to

corporeal things, it is said that all things are in God; inasmuch as they are contained by him.[59]

Aquinas also suggested that when God taught the individual to love by infusing the virtue of charity, he was actually initiating a friendship with the individual; and, because a friend was another self, "what we can do through our friends, we can in some sense do ourselves."[60]

With God the Father acting as a friend, a new range of problems arose. Former enemies could sometimes be friends, but, it seemed, a teacher and his student could not, just as a parent and child could not. Friends were equals, but the learner or child owed more than he could ever repay. Creditor and debtor were not equals, and this, it appears, was the same type of case.

God's problem, therefore, was to remove the inequality. Yet it seemed every offer of grace that might be made in the effort to do so would merely compound the debt of the sinner to God, and thereby increase the inequality. And the individual's bind, on the other hand, was no less severe, for every act of repayment would fall short, when there was nothing that he did not owe to God. In presenting the solution to this bind, Thomas followed Aristotle's analysis of friendship between unequals, but with the qualification that God would accept the will in lieu of the deed. The individual might have nothing of his own to give, but he did control the turning of the will, and this left him with the personal dignity that derived from doing all he could.

VI

The paradoxes mentioned above were not merely pitfalls into which the Christian tradition had stumbled accidentally, embarrassments which Aquinas had to labor to disguise or remove. On the contrary, what is remarkable about these paradoxes is that, precisely as paradoxes, they make an odd sort of sense. When we think of God as a parent who must find a way of responding to a strong-minded child, or as a teacher who must leave the student a sense of personal ownership of what has been learned, we see the significance of the nature and position of these seams in Aquinas's system. Each paradox marks a stage or transition in the soul's relationship to God, and these shifts are analogous to the stages and transitions in human relationships. How to make someone love you; how to respond to a request for love; how to induce voluntary change; how to appropriate as your own a change induced by someone else; how to befriend an unequal; how to receive such an offer of friendship--all of these are problems of personal interaction that are quite real. The paradoxes of Christian ethics have been powerful and appealing, then, largely because they trade on the language and problematics of everyday binds.

In Aquinas's ethics, these problems appear as critical moments in the individual's relationship to God. To be sure, Aquinas did not stress the turbulence of the relationship to the same degree as Augustine or Luther; but for Aquinas too, the soul was imperiled if it presumed for a moment on its good relationship with the Deity. In this life the relationship remained unstable. Paradoxes pointed up the distance to be covered if the soul was to move from imperfection to perfection; the apparent contradictions they posed merely evinced in various ways the disparity between a temporal perspective on the divine intention and the eternal vision of his essence.

In Aquinas's moral theology, therefore, the problematics are as definitive of his system as the solutions he offers. More important, perhaps, is Thomas's recurrent assurance that the problems can be resolved. If one of the binds were simply falsidical, then there would be no way out of it unless one or both of the injunctions could be dropped. Aquinas, however, was firmly committed both to logical consistency and to the view that God's perfection and simplicity precluded impossible demands on the human soul. God did not ignorantly or maliciously trap the soul; he defined for it a narrow and difficult path that led back to him.

As a theologian Aquinas saw it as his job to find the interpretation that charted this path and to propose to his readers a way of thinking about the problems that the soul was likely to encounter. Although his immediate aim was not pastoral, his exposition was not only analytic and architectonic in its balance, but rhetorical as well: now touching on the favorable and hopeful aspects of the human condition, now stressing its dangerous and fearful side.

Some religious thinkers prefer to emphasize the paradoxical features in religious change, since to them this captures more accurately the impasses and reversals of the soul's journey through the world. Aquinas, however, thought it more important to emphasize the underlying consistency in Christian ethics. Not only did he believe that it was spiritually advantageous to see clearly and consciously the path of salvation that led through the stages of spiritual development, but also, as evidenced in his articles on extremes of religious affect (e.g., despair, presumption), he distrusted the unstable lows and highs that come with an ethics of complete entrapment and complete release.[61] To Thomas the return to God was a sustained tension, not a story of a change that occurred once and for all, needing no improvement and threatened by no backsliding. He was trying to draw together a tradition in which life itself was conceived as one long rite of passage, a transition in which spiritual maturation was possible, but never final. Paradoxes marked the difficulties of the lifelong trial, and paradoxes marked the most profound changes in the soul.

If we try to determine the consistency or inconsistency of Aquinas's position, we find that it takes a major effort of interpretation to do so. We are led from problem to problem, distinction to distinction, on and on. This theoretical movement of analysis and interpretation has a practical counterpart. If we interpret some of these same problems and distinctions as belonging to an ethics of religious change, we find that many of them correspond to junctures in the transformation of the soul. Aquinas's solutions are not just a regress of questions in an elaborate system, but also the markers for spiritual passages: doors that open, but onto other doors; binds that loosen, but into other binds;

paradoxes that are resolved, but by implicit reference to other paradoxes. As Thomas presents them, none of these passages is inherently impassable, but only the last passage ends the journey of the soul.

Thus, the commandment to love God was arguably the most important bind, but Aquinas diminished its significance by denying that the individual could know whether he or she possessed the habitus infusus. And, for those who thought that they had indeed advanced to a state of friendship with God, Aquinas counselled further spiritual growth through vows.[62] Each vow was to be fulfilled both out of the dependence and discipline of obedience and out of the independence and spontaneity of love.[63] The controlled spontaneity of the will could thus be increasingly refined and perfected.

It is arguable, of course, that in all of this Thomas was a master of mystification, representing an incoherent tradition with a labyrinth of subtleties. Paradox, it might be said, was as often multiplied as removed when Aquinas drew his distinctions. This is not the place to pursue that issue. But the interpretation offered in the preceding pages suggests that his acts of mystification were no different than those of parents, teachers, and others in roles of authority. For just as he deliberately modelled the roles and relationships between the soul and God on the roles and relationships of subject and ruler, child and father, student and teacher, and friend and friend, so the paradoxes that obtained between the soul and God were inadvertently patterned after those that often occur in those same roles and relationships.[64] And, just as the paradoxes of human interaction are commonly masked, so the paradoxes of divine-human interaction can be masked as well.

More specifically, the paradoxes that Aquinas tried to disarm in his ethics would, on this view, have the following features in common with others in roles of teaching authority: (1) there is a hierarchy or asymmetry of superordinate and subordinate; (2) the superordinate figure teaches the subordinate; (3) part of the content of the teaching is how to be subordinate, i.e., unlike the superordinate; but (4) another part of the teaching is how to be like the superordinate; and (5) the subordinate is principally responsible for his or her progress and bears the burden of proof for shifting responsibility to the superordinate.

In regard to (5), the subordinate is thought to be able to learn only because he or she is held responsible, and this responsibility, in turn, is thought to be suitable only if the subordinate cannot point to incoherence in the complex of claims and directives that are received in the context of learning. Contradictions and confusions naturally arise in learning, and are just as readily mystified in order to continue the onus of responsibility on the learner.

The most general form in which paradox is likely to be perceived by the learner may be expressed by the injunction, "Do what you can't." This paradox has been frequently remarked of moral theories in the Augustinian tradition--as reflected in Augustine's own supplication, "Grant what you command, and command what you will"--but it is in fact common to all contexts in which the learner is held responsible for a level of behavior beyond his or her present known capacity. Mystification occurs, then, when the teacher tells the learner that the injunction can be fulfilled even though that is by no means certain; and it occurs, therefore, not in the interest of truth or justice, but in the interest of learning. Of course, the language of justice and responsibility can be manipulated in this way for ends other than those of learning. But I emphasize learning here both because it exhibits moral ambiguity in a way that should be familiar, and because it really is the analogical counterpart to teleology in Aquinas's ethics.

Thomas's implication that his moral theology was internally consistent was a mystification in the way described. God and the individual were related as superordinate to subordinate; God taught the individual through reason, revelation, and grace; the individual was to become like God, so that he might see him as he was and enjoy eternal friendship with him; and, although the individual was independently capable of imitating God only in the perversity of pride, he was nevertheless held responsible for success or failure in completing the learning necessary to become godlike, "deiform." The paradoxes, falsidical or not, that arose in this relationship were played down in order that the learning might occur through pressure on the learner, focused in responsibility for mental acts. The spontaneity binds placed on the individual through enjoining such acts could be overcome only through a transformation of mind, an advance in learning that brought a momentary freedom from the burden of responsibility for interior acts, and sometimes brought also a palpable sense of release and grace.

Through the theory of temporal attributes, then, Aquinas adapted to his moral theology familiar modes of asymmetrical relationship. In his account of how the individual developed in the context of those relationships, he replicated the aporias and paradoxes that characteristically arose in such contexts. Whether his arguments are to be interpreted as displaying the coherence of his ethics or as masking its incoherence, his interest was not only theoretical but practical as well, aimed paternalistically at the health of the soul.[65]

NOTES

[1] The example is borrowed from Eric D'Arcy. See his "'Worthy of Worship': A Catholic Contribution," in Religion and Morality, eds. Gene Outka and John P. Reeder, Jr. (Garden City, New York: Anchor, 1973), pp. 190-191.

[2] Summa Theologiae, I, 1, a. 1.

[3] See pp. 43-44.

[4] S. T., I, 2, a. 3; cf. I-II, a. 5.

[5] S.T., I, 22, prologue.

[6] S.T., I-II, 21, a. 4; cf. 21, a. 3.

[7] S.T., I, 13, a. 7 ad 6.

[8] S.T., I, 13, a. 7.

[9] S.T., I, 13, a. 8; II-II, 101, a. 1; 102, aa. 1-3; 103, aa. 1, 3, 3 ad 1; 104, a. 3, a. 3 ad 1.

[10] S.T., I, 13, a. 7 ad 5.

[11] S.T., I, 13, a. 7: "Thus there is nothing to prevent these names which import relation to the creature from being predicated of God temporally, not by reason of any change in him, but by reason of the change of the creature; as a column is on the right of an animal, without change in itself, but by change in the animal."

[12] Cf. Anthony Kenny, Will, Freedom and Power (New York: Barnes and Noble, 1976), pp. 12-28.

[13] S.T., I, 82, aa. 1, 2; I-II, aa. 4-7; 5, aa. 1, 8.

[14] Cf. Robert P. Sullivan, "Natural Necessitation of the Human Will," Thomist, 14 (1951), 351-399, and Frederick Crowe, "Complacency and Concern in the Thought of St. Thomas," Theological Studies, 20 (1959), pp. 1-39, 198-230, 343-395.

[15] Aristotle, Nicomachean Ethics, 1095 a19; 1176 b7.

[16] S.T., I-II, 74, a. 1.

[17] S.T., I-II, 77, a. 1 ad 2.

[18] See Chapter 5.

[19] S.T., I-II, 109, a. 5.

[20] S.T., I, 117, a. 1 ad 1.

[21] S.T., I, 21, a. 1, a. 1 ad 3.

[22] S.T., I-II, 92, a. 2 ad 3.

[23] S.T., II-II, 80, ad 3.

[24] S.T., II-II, 81, a. 6 ad 1; cf. 80.

[25] Aristotle, Nicomachean Ethics, 1111 b19-30.

[26] See note 6.
[27] S.T., I, 8, a. 1.
[28] S.T., I, 8, a. 3; I-II, 9, aa. 4, 6.
[29] S.T., I, 8, a. 3.
[30] Cf. Sullivan, op. cit.
[31] Cf. S.T., I-II, 28, aa. 1-6.
[32] S.T., II-II, 23, aa. 3-6. Cf. Sententia Libri Ethicorum, ed. Leon. p. 456, ll. 93-116. In Litzinger's translation: "[F]riendship is a kind of union or association between widely separated persons; but they must approach equality. Hence it pertains to friendship to use an equality already uniformly established, but it pertains to justice to reduce unequal things to an equality. When equality exists the work of justice is done. For that reason equality is the goal of justice and the starting point of friendship." Thomas Aquinas, Commentary on the Nicomachean Ethics, 2 vols., trans. C. I. Litzinger (Chicago: H. Regnery Company, 1964), pp. 737-738.
[33] S.T., II-II, 23, aa. 1-5.
[34] S.T., II-II, 23, a. 1.
[35] Aristotle, Nicomachean Ethics, 1166 a32; Aquinas, De caritate, 7; S.T., II-II, 44, a. 7.
[36] S.T., II-II, 23, a. 1 ad 1.
[37] S.T., I-II, 4, aa. 3, 4; 5, aa. 1, 7; II-II, 109, a. 5; III, 4, a. 1 ad 2.
[38] S.T., I-II, 3, aa. 2-8.
[39] De caritate, 11; S.T., II-II, 23, a. 1 ad 1.
[40] See note 9. S.T., I-II, 10, a. 2.
[41] S.T., I-II, 2, aa. 1-8.
[42] S.T., I-II, 26, a. 4 ad 3.
[43] W. V. O. Quine, "Ways of Paradox," in his Ways of Paradox and Other Essays (New York: Random House, 1966), pp. 3-20.
[44] Since the phrase "double bind" is now part of everyday language, I should note that I have in mind the technical meaning of the phrase, as originally given by Gregory Bateson, Don D. Jackson, Jay Haley, and John Weakland in their article, "Toward a Theory of Schizophrenia." They state their conception of the double bind as follows:

> The necessary ingredients for a double bind situation, as we see it, are:
>
> 1. *Two or more persons.* Of these, we designate one, for purposes of our definition, as the "victim." We do not assume that the double bind is inflicted by the mother alone, but that it may be done either by mother alone or by some combination of mother, father, and/or siblings.
>
> 2. *Repeated experience.* We assume that the double bind is a recurrent theme in the experience of the victim. Our hypothesis

does not involve a single traumatic experience, but such repeated experience that the double bind structure comes to be an habitual expectation.

3. *A primary negative injunction.* This may have either of two forms: (a) "Do not do so and so, or I will punish you," or (b) "If you do not do so and so, I will punish you." Here we select a context of learning based on avoidance of punishment rather than a context of reward seeking. There is perhaps no formal reason for this selection. We assume that the punishment may be either the withdrawal of love or the expression of hate or anger--or most devastating--the kind of abandonment that results from the parent's expression of extreme helplessness.

4. *A secondary injunction conflicting with the first at a more abstract level, and like the first enforced by punishments or signals which threaten survival.* This secondary injunction is more difficult to describe than the primary for two reasons. First, the secondary injunction is commonly communicated to the child by nonverbal means. Posture, gesture, tone of voice, meaningful action, and the implications concealed in verbal comment may all be used to convey this more abstract message. Second, the secondary injunction may impinge upon any element of the primary prohibition. Verbalization of the secondary injunction may, therefore, include a wide variety of forms; for example, "Do not see this as a punishment"; "Do not see me as the punishing agent"; "Do not submit to my prohibitions"; "Do not think of what you must not do"; "Do not question my love of which the primary prohibition is (or is not) an example"; and so on. Other examples become possible when the double bind is inflicted not by one individual but by two. For example, one parent may negate at a more abstract level the injunctions of the other.

5. *A tertiary negative injunction prohibiting the victim from escaping from the field.* In a formal sense it is perhaps unnecessary to list this injunction as a separate item since the reinforcement at the other two levels involves a threat to survival, and if the double binds are imposed during infancy escape is naturally impossible. However, it seems that in some cases the escape from the field is made impossible by certain devices which are not purely negative, e.g., capricious promises of love, and the like.

6. Finally, the complete set of ingredients is no longer necessary when the victim has learned to perceive his universe in double bind patterns. Almost any part of a double bind sequence may then be sufficient to precipitate panic or rage. The pattern of conflicting injunctions may even be taken over by hallucinatory voices.

From Gregory Bateson, Steps to an Ecology of Mind (New York: Chandler, 1972), pp. 206-208.

In subsequent writings, this group of researchers dropped the term "victim," stopped assuming that the mother was the chief perpetrator, and recognized the importance of contexts of reward seeking. They were thus able to see that double binds which are the same as or similar to those that are pathogenic are also capable of being therapeutic and contributing to learning and creativity as well. For an intriguing exploration of the "Be independent" paradox in this regard, see Carlos E. Sluzki and Eliseo Veron, "The Double Bind as a Universal Pathogenic Situation," in Carlos E. Sluzki and Donald C. Ransom, eds., Double Bind: the Foundation of the Communicational Approach to the Family (New York: Grune and Stratton, 1976).

In the study of religious ethics, perhaps the most promising areas of application for double bind theory are spiritual disciplines which include injunctions to perform certain types of mental acts or to possess certain types of mental attitudes. Given the spontaneous character of many such acts and attitudes, the double binds that are involved in enjoining them are often of the sort Paul Watzlawick has called the "Be spontaneous" paradox. Enjoined spontaneity in the interest of spiritual perfection seems to be the source of many paradoxes of religious language.

[45]Cf. Frederick Crowe, "Complacency and Concern in the Thought of St. Thomas," Theological Studies, 20 (1959), 1-39.

[46]Aristotle, Nicomachean Ethics, 1166 a30-32, 1170 b6; cf. 1161 b27.

[47]S.T., II-II, 25, aa. 1-12; 26, aa. 1-13.

[48]Victor Turner, "Betwixt and Between: The Liminal Period in Rites de Passage," in William A. Lessa and Egon Z. Vogt, eds., Reader in Comparative Religion: An Anthropological Approach (New York: Harper and Row, 1972), pp. 338-347, and his The Ritual Process (Chicago: Aldine, 1969). See also Gregory Bateson, "A Theory of Play and Fantasy," in his Steps to an Ecology of Mind (New York: Chandler, 1972), pp. 177-193.

[49]S.T., I-II, 107, a. 1: "[T]he new law is distinct from the old law: because the old law is like a pedagogue of children, as the Apostle says in Galatians, whereas the new law is the law of perfection, since it is the law of charity, of which the Apostle says in Colossians that it is 'the bond of perfection.'"

[50]De caritate, a. 2 ad 15.

[51]S.T., II-II, 27.

[52] S.T., I, 12, aa. 1, 4, 5.
[53] Here I use the present tense, "arise," because these general judgments are not based on medieval documents, but on contemporary research. I assume, however, not that they hold for every culture, but for those cultures and periods in the West which subscribe to αὐτάρκεια, autonomy, self-sufficiency, self-reliance, or independence as an ideal for male adults.
[54] Sluzki and Veron write:

> According to [Ronald Fairbairn], the child passes through the following three evolutional states: (a) <u>infantile dependence</u>, marked by a relative lack of differentiation between the self and the non-self and a preponderance of the incorporation or "taking" of objects; (b) <u>transition</u>; and (c) <u>mature dependency</u>, characterized by "relations between two independent beings who are completely differentiated" and by a predominance of "giving" in object relations.
>
> The transitional stage ushers in the core dilemma of all mental development: <u>dependence</u> <u>versus</u> <u>independence</u> .... [T]his process is a complex one, as the parents will have to redefine to their child almost daily, avoiding any overlap of boundaries, the respective areas of dependency (where action, except within a frame of compliance, is bad), of independence (where action based on compliance is bad), and a third, "experimental" one (which could be called one of 'supervised experience in independence').

From Sluzki and Veron, op. cit., p. 254.
[55] S.T., II-II, 44, aa. 4, 5.
[56] S.T., I-II, 107, a. 4.
[57] S.T., III, 85, a. 5.
[58] Cf. Sullivan, op. cit.
[59] S.T., I, 8, a. 1 ad 2.
[60] S.T., II-II, 81, a. 6 ad 1; II-II, 57, a. 1 ad 3.
[61] S.T., II-II, 19-22.
[62] S.T., II-II, 88.
[63] S.T., II-II, 104, a. 3
[64] Jay Haley:

> When we acknowledge that all learning creatures are compelled to organize (they cannot not organize, just as they cannot not communicate as Bateson pointed out many years ago) and that organization is hierarchical, then we must expect confusions in the hierarchy. At times conflicting levels of hierarchy will be defined, and at times the structure will simply be ambiguous. (For example, when a therapist assumes the posture of an expert and puts the patient in charge of what is to happen, the hierarchy is confused.) When the hierarchy is not clearly established, the creatures within it will struggle with one another.

Jay Haley, "Development of a Theory: A History of a Research Project," in Sluzki and Ransom, eds. Double Bind , p. 78 n. 1. My point here and in what follows is much the same as Haley's except that I stress the shifting status of the learner rather than the shifting status of the teacher or therapist. See also René Girard, Deceit, Desire, and the Novel (Baltimore: Johns Hopkins, 1965), and Violence and the Sacred (Baltimore: Johns Hopkins, 1977).

65

> [A]lthough among the philosophical sciences one is speculative and another practical, nevertheless sacred doctrine includes both; as God, by one and the same science, knows both himself and his works. Still, it is more speculative than practical, because it is more concerned with divine things than with human acts; though it does treat even of these latter, inasmuch as man is ordained by them to the perfect knowledge of God, in which consists eternal happiness.

S.T. , I, 1 a. 4.

CHAPTER 2
TELEOLOGY

I

In the initial article of the <u>Summa Theologiae</u> Aquinas described the relation between man and his ultimate end: "Man is ordained to God as to an end that exceeds the grasp of reason."[1] From one standpoint, this ordination to God could be seen as a good thing, the loftiness of the human calling; and, as such, it deserved gratitude, reverence, and even love in response. Yet from another point of view, God's intention seemed less attractive. For unless a person did become fit for his end in God, he would experience eternal suffering. To make matters worse, by natural endowment alone, he could know little about the means or the end, and was incapable of effecting the former or attaining the latter. Divine aid might prove sufficient for salvation, but there was no guarantee of it. High stakes for success or failure were combined with uncertainty and weakness.

This was Aquinas's conception of the human condition--at once a gift of life and an all but untenable situation. Thomas explained that, in a sense, God had no choice but to define human existence in this way. God was perfect, and therefore, if he was to create at all, his creation had to be perfect as well. A paradox of independence followed from this:

> [P]erfect goodness would not be found in created things unless there were an order of goodness in them, in the sense that some of them are better than others. Otherwise, all possible grades of goodness would not be realized, nor would any creature be like God by virtue of holding a higher place than another. The highest beauty would be taken away from things, too, if the order of distinct and unequal things were removed. And what is more, multiplicity would be taken away from things if inequality of goodness were removed, since through the differences by which things are distinguished from each other one thing stands out as better than others; for instance, the animate in relation to the inanimate, and the rational in regard to the irrational. And so, if complete equality were present in things, there would be but one created good, which clearly disparages the perfection of the creature. Now, it is a higher grade of goodness for a thing to be good because it cannot fall from goodness; lower than that is the thing which can fall from goodness. So, the perfection of the

> universe requires both grades of goodness. But it pertains to the providence of the governor to preserve perfection in the things governed, not to decrease it. Therefore, it does not pertain to divine goodness, entirely to exclude from things the power of falling from the good. But evil is the consequence of this power, because what is able to fall does fall at times. And this defection of the good is evil, as we showed above. Therefore, it does not pertain to divine providence to prohibit evil entirely from things.[2]

As a consequence of the first fall from goodness, virtually everyone, at one time or another, was in a state of mortal sin, and therefore was unfit by his own powers for the ultimate end in God.

But God had not created the human race only to see it fall and suffer. His hands were tied by perfection in another sense as well. The perfection of God's order required not only that there exist creatures who can fall from good, but also that the natural inclination of every species of creature be fulfilled. In the case of the human species, there was a natural inclination toward the perfection of the intellect:

> For there resides in every man a natural desire to know the cause of any effect which he sees; and thence arises wonder in men. But if the intellect of the rational creature could not reach so far as to the first cause of things, the natural desire would remain void.[3]

If God were to maintain the perfection of his order, it was necessary that some should attain the vision of the divine essence. A parallel argument held for the will. As naturally inclined to the good in general, and insatiable by particular goods such as wealth, fame, honors, and power, the will could be truly satisfied and perfected only by the universal good, which was God. Thus, again, it would have implied an imperfection in the creation if there had been no members of the human species who attained the fulfillment of their wills. In both respects, then, the human race had a natural orientation to God that God himself was committed to fulfill, even though those he aided had previously shown contempt toward him through their sins. As often occurs in a double bind, the problem for the one bound was merely the obverse of the problem for the one binding.[4]

Yet if God was committed to helping some souls to their end, he was not thereby committed to helping all. The general outlines of God's solution of the paradox were made known to the individual through reason and revelation, but the ultimate implications for any one individual remained unclear. One might be predestined to salvation, or might not. The uncertainty continued throughout the individual's time in the world.

Aquinas could not be fully reassuring, therefore, but he could present a course of life that allowed independence consistent with human dignity, yet disallowed independence that would cost the individual his ultimate happiness. In doing so, Aquinas did not see himself as clearing a path for the soul, but rather as reporting the path that God had kept clear for it from eternity. If an individual found his way to God, it was because God had helped by operating on and cooperating with him. A theologian merely provided a spiritual map on which an individual case could be located. Aquinas's theological writings did not have an immediate pastoral purpose, but they did have a mediate one, for theology had a practical as well as theoretical side.[5] And hence Thomas's task of resolving the apparent theoretical difficulties in Christian doctrine was often at the same time a task of resolving the outstanding spiritual problems that would face a believer seeking to attain the vision of God. Central among these was the double bind, "Be independent, but return to me through my help."

Aquinas found that the problem and solution could be formulated by combining predominantly Aristotelian conceptions of happiness, self-sufficiency, and habituation with primarily Augustinian conceptions of God, the need for grace, and the importance of charity. Human independence had to be acknowledged and defined, but in a way that not only allowed but fostered the attainment of the end in God; divine aid, on the other hand, had to be characterized as an immeasurable contribution to the life of the soul, yet given in a manner fully respectful of the autonomy of the individual.

II

Central to Aquinas's solution was his conception of the end.

For Aristotle an end was a product or an activity, and if a product, then it was ordered beyond itself, to some activity as its end. For Augustine, on the other hand, an end was conceived as a thing or a person, a "beloved" (amatum); activities were undertaken in order to attain or possess the amatum. The two views, therefore, were apparently incompatible; what was intermediate for Augustine was ultimate for Aristotle, and conversely.

Yet Aquinas found little difficulty in reconciling these positions. Following Aristotle, he held that man's ultimate end was happiness, and that happiness was an activity of the soul in keeping with excellence or virtue; following Augustine, he held that the object of this activity was a person, God. Both conceptions of an end were therefore evident in the phrase, "visio dei." "Visio" referred to knowing, an activity of the soul in keeping with excellence or virtue; "dei" to what was known in that activity. With this solution in mind, Aquinas found that he could move comfortably between Aristotelian and Augustinian modes of expression, for they simply referred to the subjective and objective aspects of the same union of the soul with God. And if the question were pressed, "Which of the two is really ultimate?", Aquinas had an answer: the goodness of the activity was secondary, for it derived from the goodness of its object: "absolutely speaking, the ultimate end is the thing itself, for [e.g.] the possession of money is good only because there is good in the money."[6] In the beatific vision, the mode of "possession" was that of speculative knowledge or contemplation, the penultimate good, while the good possessed was God, the highest good.

Thus, for Aquinas, both Aristotelian and Augustinian expressions might be used for the ultimate end, and each complemented a deficiency in the other. On the one hand, Aristotle's conception of happiness as θεωρετική did not satisfactorily answer the question, "Contemplation of what?" To it, Augustine provided the complement. On the other hand, Augustine's position was also incomplete: his emphasis on the beloved Other did not stress sufficiently that the end for man must be a perfection of man, a full actuation of the intellect, man's noblest and most distinctive power. Accordingly, Thomas combined the autarchic, self-regarding accent in Aristotle's position with the dependent, other-regarding emphasis of Augustine. In the final union, act and object could be distinguished only analytically; the self was perfected, completed, and fulfilled through rapt contemplation of the Other. "Happiness itself, since it is a perfection of the soul, is a good inhering in the soul. But that in which happiness consists, which makes man happy, is something outside the soul, as we have said."[7]

Since Thomas's God was a simple unity, distinctions between end, reward, and friend were to be drawn from the human, subjective side of the beatific vision, focusing on aspects of the activity of the soul rather than implying composition in its object. Fitness for the ultimate end in this sense was fitness for an activity, the contemplation of the divine essence. Yet, as Aristotle had said, this activity was "an activity in conformity with excellence or virtue."[8] Therefore, although the fitness of the soul for this end was primarily a fitness of the intellect, it was secondarily a fitness of the will, for the will was the seat of most of the virtues, and particularly of charity, the virtue by which the soul was bound in love to God. Thus, in addition to arguing that happiness was an activity of the speculative intellect, Aquinas also argued that it presupposed and perfected the right ordering of the will:

> Rectitude of the will is required for happiness both antecedently and concomitantly. Antecedently, because rectitude of the will consists in being properly ordered to the ultimate end. Now the end is compared to what is ordered to the end as form to matter. Hence just as matter cannot attain form unless it is disposed in an appropriate way for form, so nothing attains the end unless it is rightly ordered to it. Consequently no one can attain happiness unless he has rectitude of the will.
>
> Concomitantly because, as has been said, ultimate happiness consists in the vision of the divine essence, which is the very essence of goodness. Thus the will of one who sees the essence of God necessarily loves whatever he loves under the common notion of the good which he knows. Now this is precisely what makes the will right. Hence it is clear that happiness is not possible without rectitude of the will.[9]

In developing his conception of this twofold fitness, Aquinas needed to combine not only Aristotle's and Augustine's conceptions of the end, but also their conceptions of man's orientation to it. Aristotle's belief that all people desire happiness was to be coordinated with Augustine's view that "You have made us for yourself, and our hearts are restless till they rest in you."[10] Aquinas effected this synthesis by arguing that the natural desire for truth and happiness that God had built into the human species could be fully satisfied after the fall only in the enjoyment of the supernatural end in God. The intellect's broad orientation to being in general was also an orientation to Being Itself; the will's inclination to the good in general was also an inclination to the Universal Good. In Thomas's view, God provided the way to solve the "Be independent" paradox even as he established it in the human soul, for by the dual orientation of intellect and will he was able to give man the independence proper to his place on the hierarchy of being, yet by the very nature of that independence to draw man back to himself as end.

God operated in all things through their forms, and their forms included a natural inclination to the ultimate end.[11] In this way, the divine ruler could govern the community of the universe without being related to it. Man was a special case of this governance, for his form, or soul, was less instinctually determined than the forms of other creatures. "The rational creature is subject to divine providence in the most excellent way, inasmuch as it partakes of a share of providence by being provident for itself and for others."[12] God did not simply direct the individual to his end; he directed him to it via the individual's own capacity for self-direction.

There were no innate ideas in man, only the seeds of the first principles of reason, actuated when the concept-forming function of the intellect, the agent intellect, ordered the sensation which it received from the bodily senses.[13] Thus, although "swallows build their nests alike" and "bees have skill at making nothing but honeycombs," human beings had a broader orientation in thought and action.[14] The human intellect had "an operation extending to universal being," and, because the intellect specified the object toward which the will was exercised, the will had an inclination to the good in general. Just as the object of the intellect was being, the object of the will was the good; and both objects were open-ended. Good in general, then, was one necessary object of the will, but this necessity implied only a broadly defined bearing; not a "turning" of the will, but the presupposition of every turning. Aquinas identified this object with happiness and thus with the manifold objectives in which people of all kinds sought the repose of their wills.

The natural indeterminacy of human thought and action went hand-in-hand with a greater capacity for self-determination. A rock was highly determined by nature, and, if it was moved at all, it was moved by something else. Further up the hierarchy, this was not the case. A bee was characteristically self-moved, and the principle or ordering cause of its self-movement was its soul. (In Aquinas's view, if something was self-moved, then it was necessary to posit in it both a motive principle and a part that was moved; to draw this distinction was the same as to distinguish soul and body.) Yet even in a bee the inclinations imprinted in the soul were highly determined, though less so than the inclinations natural to a rock. And too, the inclinations determining the bee's operation were imprinted in the soul of the bee, not by the bee itself, but by God, its creator.[15]

Man was self-moved in a higher sense. A human being moved himself, and did so in part by inclinations that belonged to his soul as part of his lower appetite. These inclinations were not uncontrolled, however, but operated in voluntary acts only as they were moved by the higher powers of intellect and will. The interface between the higher and lower powers was distinctive to man, his unique characteristic and problem as a being located on the boundary between the spiritual and material levels of the cosmic hierarchy. Man was the highest animal, therefore, in the sense that he was not only self-moved, but could decide how to move himself. The ordered relation of the powers of intellect and will enabled him to reflect upon his possibilities of action, order them as means to end, and thereby exercise free choice:

> It is accordingly apparent to anyone who considers the matter aright that judgment about what is to be done is attributed to brute animals in the same way as motion and action are attributed to inanimate natural bodies. Just as heavy and light bodies do not move themselves so too brutes do not judge about their judgment but follow the judgment implanted in them by God. Thus they are not the cause of their own decision nor do they have freedom of choice. But man, judging about his course of action by the power of reason, can also judge about his own decision inasmuch as he knows the meaning of an end and of a means to an end, and the relationship of one with reference to the other. Thus he is his own cause not only in moving but also in judging. He is therefore endowed with free choice--that is to say, with a free judgment about acting or not acting.[16]

Thus, in lieu of the narrowly defined inclinations of the irrational animals, man had an inclination to the good in general, and a capacity for practical reasoning as the medium through which he determined his own behavior.

This natural inclination to the good in general was God's providential means for directing man to himself as the universal good.[17] What the individual discovered, if he reflected on his experience, was that no particular good available to him, nor any set of particular goods within his ability to attain, would satisfy his natural inclination to the good in general. His rational appetite for the good would therefore remain frustrated in this life, just as his natural desire to know universal being would go unrequited. By instilling in the will a stereoscopic view of the end as general in inclination yet single in consummation, God not only allowed for variety and adaptability in temporal thought and action, but enabled the individual to move toward a single, eternal activity that was the vision of his own essence. Man's urge toward the good was general enough to allow for human freedom in the selection of particular goods, therefore, but demanding enough to direct some people back toward God as the only good that would answer fully to that urge. The vaguely defined desire for happiness corresponded to the vaguely known Deity whose presence alone brought true happiness.

Thus, Aquinas reconciled Aristotle's and Augustine's views by arguing that the natural inclination to the good in general, obscurely pursued as "happiness," was at the same time an inclination to the supernatural "rest in you." In doing so, Thomas posed the "Be independent" paradox and provided a first-approximation solution to it. Indeed, in his view, any thoroughgoing presentation of this problem pointed directly to the way to solve it. The very same inclinatio that caused some people to become lost in a forest of particular goods caused others to turn to the source of all good as the one object that could fulfill and perfect them.

III

Yet for this conversion to God to be complete, and for what I am calling the "Be independent" paradox to be fully resolved, the conditions for attaining the end had to be met. It was Thomas's job to show that they could be, and he therefore had to argue that several subordinate paradoxes could be given a consistent reading.

The correct means to the ultimate end (ea quae sunt ad finem) were not ways of affecting God, since he was immutable, nor were they ways of influencing the mutable, temporal goods of the external world, since these were not the soul itself and did not have any direct impact upon its salvation. Because fitness for the ultimate end was the fitness of the soul to the beatific vision, the means to this end could only be events affecting the soul. Just as "the activity [of the vision was] a perfection and actuation of the agent,"[18] so also the means to arriving at this activity were actuations of the agent, actus internal to the soul and private to external observation. Hence Aquinas wrote, "[T]hese are acts which do not pass into external matter but remain in the agent, e.g., to desire and to know: and such are all moral acts, whether virtuous or sinful."[19] Aquinas used examples to clarify his meaning: "to desire" and "to know" were not internal merely in the sense of "belonging to body or soul," but in the stronger sense of "belonging to the soul's highest powers," the intellect and will.

Any empirically observable behavior, therefore, was Janus-faced. Whether it was a meritorious action informed by the love of God or a mortally sinful action done in contempt of him, it could be viewed either in light of its internal impact upon the condition of the soul or in light of its external impact upon the world at large. In regard to the first, the individual was responsible before God, for his internal actions affected the mode of his soul's subjection to God. Throughout his life, the individual was engaged in an ongoing process of defining and redefining his relation to God through his actus interiores. In regard to the second, the individual was responsible before his fellow human beings, for his external actions affected his relations to others, defining and redefining them. Thomas distinguished the two faces of human life into distinct actus, since distinct powers of the person were reduced from potency to act. The internal aspect was related to the external as cause to effect, but each aspect had distinct effects of its own--the actus interior upon the soul and its inward relation to the Deity, and the actus exterior upon other people and upon the external world. Among the interior acts, two were central in their consequences for the soul's mode of subjection to God: the movement of the will in appropriation of the infused habit of charity, and the movement of the will against charity, the mortal insult of contempt shown inwardly to the divine friend.

As actus interiores, the means contributing to the soul's fitness for the ultimate end were primarily actus intellectus or actus voluntatis--acts of the intellect or acts of the will. In the intellect there had to be a "connaturality" of the knower and the known, a correspondence between the form of the intellect and its object, the divine essence. In the will, on the other hand, there had to be a "rectitude," a due ordering of the will to the ultimate end in God. Aquinas argued that man was capable of both:

> Happiness means the attainment of the perfect good. Accordingly, whoever has a capacity for the perfect good can attain happiness. That man has a capacity for the perfect good is evident from the fact that his intellect apprehends the universal and perfect good, and his will seeks it. Hence man can attain happiness.[20]

"Man is ordained to God as to an end exceeding the grasp of reason," therefore, can be read as a double bind that is analyzable into subordinate paradoxes of intellect and will. Each paradox could be resolved only if God helped the soul, and only if he helped it in ways that respected its independence. In effect, God had to exercise the skills and sensitivity that we associate today with parenthood, teaching, and therapy. Much of the appeal of Thomas's position as well as many of its difficulties lie in this commitment to the belief that God could help the soul to its very depths yet respect its autonomy. It was a strong assumption, but salvation was impossible if it could not be upheld.

IV

The bind on the intellect may be defined as the paradox of "seeking to know." It appears in Plato's Meno as the second horn of a dilemma:

> Do you see what a captious argument you are introducing--that a man cannot inquire either about what he knows or what he does not know?

> For he cannot inquire about what he knows, since he knows it, and in that case is in no need of inquiry; nor can he inquire about what he does not know, since he does not know about what he is to inquire.[21]

Seven centuries later, the second horn appeared again at the beginning of Augustine's <u>Confessions</u>. To Augustine's way of thinking, it was less important to show the seeker the correct logic of "seeking to know" than to tell him that he could find help in his seeking--that the paradox was theoretically resolved by the notions of divine grace, the incarnation, and the authoritative preaching of Paul, and that it was practically mediated by the realities that corresponded to those notions:

> You arouse [us] to take joy in praising you, for you have made us for yourself, and our heart is restless until it rests in you. Lord, grant me to know and understand which is first, to call upon you or to praise you, and also which is first, to know you or to call upon you? For one who does not know you might call upon another instead of you. Or must you rather be called upon so that you may be known? Yet "how shall they call upon him in whom they have not believed? Or how shall they believe without a preacher?" "And they shall praise the Lord that seek him," for they that seek him find him, and finding him they shall praise him. Lord, let me seek you by calling upon you, and let me call upon you by believing in you, for you have been preached to us. Lord my faith calls upon you, that faith which you have given to me, which you have breathed into me by the incarnation of your son and through the ministry of your preacher.[22]

Here Augustine's problem of how to begin his book becomes his way of beginning it: he finds in the problem of how to put first things first an important and revealing instance of the problem of seeking to know God. The theme dominates the <u>Confessions</u>. Like a nearsighted man looking for his glasses, the soul seeking God needs to have what it is looking for in order to begin looking. God's solution, Augustine implies, is to give the soul direction in its seeking.

Aquinas's aim was to show the limits within which such help must fall in order to respect the freedom and dignity of the rational creature. A nearsighted man will be grateful if we direct him to his glasses, but only if the direction is offered in the right spirit, without mocking his disadvantage or humiliating him. Thomas had much the same problem; he wanted to show not only that God provided grace, but that God's grace was graciously respectful of man's proper independence.

The basic outline of Aquinas's approach to the fitness of the intellect can be given briefly. Natural reason could attain to the knowledge of God's existence, due to its natural desire or "<u>capax</u>" for answers to all "why" questions. But this, although it implied "some proportion between the knower and the known,"[23] did not provide the proportion sufficient in this life for vision in the next. The habitus infusus of faith, which directed the intellect toward God in this life, had first to be bestowed upon the individual; after his death it would be superseded by the light of glory (lumen gloriae). By this light, the intellect was made "deiform," and thereby sufficiently connatural with God to allow and indeed bring about the attainment of the vision.[24] In describing this moment in the soul's career, Thomas cited Psalm 35 and I John 2:2: "In thy light we shall see light," and "When he shall appear we shall be like to him, and we shall see him as he is."[25] This similarity or congruence in form between the intellect and the divine essence was crucial to the final vision. Without it, said Aquinas, the soul would be like a bat trying to look at the sun.[26]

The fitness of the soul for the vision of God, therefore, was similar to the fitness of the medical student to practice medicine--a full capability for a high level of activity. In this narrow regard, no question of justice or love arose in connection with salvation and damnation: it was a simple question of whether the individual "had what it took" to contemplate the divine essence. The image of the bat is instructive here. Thomas recurrently likened God to the sun, and therefore compared the damned soul's awareness of God to the bat's awareness of the sun. Though indirectly the beneficiary of the sun's activity, the bat had, and could have, no vision of the sun itself. Justice and love were beside the point: a bat was simply incapable of looking at the sun, a beginning medical student was simply untrained for surgery, and, by the same token, an ungraced soul was simply disproportionate in power to the act of seeing God.

In moving toward fitness, the intellect was gradually educated to its final actus by progressive increases of divine illumination, each illumination adding to the last and presupposing it. Each step in the process obeyed the rule that "the known is received in the knower according to the mode of reception of the knower."[27] As a teacher of the intellect, God invariably met the seeker more than halfway, increasing his grace as the seeker appropriated it and used it well.

In objection to this solution, it might be argued that instead of solving the paradox of "seeking to know," Aquinas's gradualist theory merely broke it up into a series of stages, each of which embodied a more fine-grained variant of the same paradox. If the intellect was fully disposed to receive further illumination, what need was there for God to intervene? If the intellect was not fully disposed to receive further illumination, how could God's intervention fail to violate its antecedent condition?

Thomas's theory included at least two responses to this objection. First, the increase of learning about God through grace simply followed the natural orientation of the intellect to universal being, merely realizing its already existent natural potency. At no point, therefore, was the intellect overwhelmed by an advance, even if there might occasionally occur moments of powerful and surprising insight.

Second, God was in the peculiar position of being both the teacher and the subject taught. In a passage reminiscent of Augustine's "credo ut intelligam," Aquinas wrote,

> [M]an's ultimate happiness consists in a supernatural vision of God: to which vision man cannot attain unless he be taught by God, according to John 6:45: "Everyone that has heard of the Father and has learned comes to me." Now man acquires a share of this learning, not indeed all at once, but little by little, according to the mode of his nature: and everyone who learns in this way must believe, in order that he may acquire knowledge in a perfect degree; thus also the Philosopher remarks that "it behooves a learner to believe."
>
> Hence, in order that a man arrive at the perfect vision of heavenly happiness, he must first of all believe God, as a disciple believes a master who is teaching him.[28]

This is more than an argument for docility--though it is that. Since God knew both the teacher and the subject taught, the paradox of "seeking to know" was resolved in an unusual way. On the one hand, it appeared to be resolved in a manner similar to telling a nearsighted man where his glasses were. But on the other hand, it was as if only the man, his glasses, and the light were involved in his discovery--as if, as he was about to walk past them, the man noticed a reflection, and, turning toward it, found that it was caused by the light striking his glasses.

In Aquinas's view, God's teaching might be characterized in both ways. The help God offered was immensely powerful, and in this respect intervened in the relation of the learner to what he was trying to learn. By analogy to human teaching, then, it was natural to represent God as a third party, mediating learning to the learner. But this analogy had to be qualified, for in this type of learning the teacher was also the subject taught. In this respect, the process was more closely analogous to the man being drawn to his glasses by their reflection, as if by an attractive power of their own. As teacher and subject taught, then, Thomas's God could be seen as a teacher who was never invasive in his teaching, but who at every stage drew the learner toward the subject taught, and could not possibly stand between them. Yet, as we have seen in the closing analysis of the previous chapter, this very fact--that the teacher is also the subject taught--could with equal ease be taken problematically. The typical self-referentiality of the paradox makes for the ease of shifting from passage to impasse, or, to use again the image of the Möbius strip, to move from one side to the other.

V

Like the intellect, the will had to become fit for the ultimate end. Aquinas saw the fitness of the will for the ultimate end as a rectitude (rectitudo), a due order to the end (ordo debitus ad finem).²⁹ This proportionality held if and only if the individual loved whatever he loved in subordination to God; in turn, love of this sort was possible if and only if the will was informed by the habit of charity.

Accordingly, in the will's final fitness, hope gave way to attainment, and charity was fulfilled in the mutual indwelling of the lover and the Beloved. Of the theological virtues, therefore, only charity remained and increased in the beatific vision. Indeed, Thomas believed that the degree of charity in the will decided the greater or lesser degree of knowledge in the intellect:

> Hence the intellect which has more of the light of glory will see God the more perfectly; and he will have a fuller participation of the light of glory who has more charity; because where there is greater charity, there is more desire; and desire in a certain degree makes the one desiring apt and prepared to receive the object desired. Hence he who possesses the more charity will see God the more perfectly, and will be the more beatified.³⁰

In the vision of God, then, the lumen gloriae in the intellect and the habitus infusus caritatis in the will combined to establish the proportion of the soul to its end in God.

For the will to reach this state of fitness, however, God had to help the individual through still another form of the "Be independent" paradox. Again the problem could be stated as a "captious argument": it seemed that the will could neither order itself nor be ordered by another; it could not improve itself any more than a man could lift himself by his bootstraps; and it could not be improved by another without suffering an infringement of its autonomy.

Aquinas had several reasons for denying that the human will had the ability to change itself for the better. First, he made a tacit appeal to personal experience. Attempts at self-reform met with the stubborn resistance of current priorities habituated in the will. Second, his conception of will and habit provided theoretical support for his view. How could a new idea, reason, or resolution weigh more heavily with the will today than it did yesterday? If the change occurred by the will's own power, then it seemed that the priorities seated in the habitus voluntatis had mysteriously denied themselves; if the change occurred by some other power, then the change did not take place through the initiative of the will after all. Finally, Aquinas's notion of hierarchy ran contrary to the bootstrap theory. The human will could not independently act above the proportion of its natural power, and the will of an individual could not independently act above the proportion of its present condition. In the hierarchy of being, activity was possible to a creature at levels equal to or lower than its own status. Since the human species was largely self-determined, different individuals occupied different positions on the spiritual scale, and those who had reduced themselves to a low position had thereby given up the power to function at a higher level. A mortal sinner could no more lift himself to a state of charity than a horse could discuss logic.

Matters were barely improved in relation to other human beings. In natural moral education, for example, a moral teacher could perhaps succeed in helping his student attain the teacher's own upper limit, and that limit might even be equal to the highest development possible for fallen man. But this would constitute only minor repair work on the disordered will, and could prove deceptively cosmetic. In any case, it would be entirely inadequate to raise the will to proportionality to its ultimate end in God.

Could the angels help? Thomas rejected the possibility:

> Every creature is subject to the laws of nature, since each has limited power and action; therefore, whatever exceeds created nature cannot be brought about by the power of a creature. Hence if anything needs to be accomplished that is beyond nature, it is done directly by God....[31]

If the will was to be put in order, therefore, only God could do it. But could he? The rectitude of the will included the ability to function correctly and independently; how could God, or anyone else, for that matter, help someone to function independently? If the teacher was human, the problem was delicate, but surmountable: although in human teaching, help became harm when the autonomy of the learner was violated, the threshold of individual autonomy could be observed and respected. Problems arose only when the change sought was radical and abrupt. Yet if the teacher was God, and the change desired was the deep and sudden transformation from unfitness for the ultimate end to fitness for it, violation seemed to be inevitable. Not only was the teacher more powerful than any human being, but "learning" seemed to take the form of a forced reordering of the dispositions of the will. It seemed, at least, that God could not transform the will beyond its natural and fallen proportions without violating personal autonomy.

Yet God wanted their agreement to be uncoerced. To resolve the double bind, therefore, he had to bring the will to agreement with him in a manner agreeable to the will as it was.

Thomas said, in effect, that God met this problem by distinguishing paternalistically between what the individual thought he wanted and what he really wanted. The current dispositions of the will might be turned away from the ultimate end, but the most fundamental inclination of the will--indeed, its natural necessitation[32]--was to God himself. The will might be disordered, therefore, in seeking its happiness in temporal goods, but it was still ordered toward happiness, and this it could find only by enjoying the vision of God. In other words, although God violated the autonomy of the individual in respect to his current dispositions, he respected and fulfilled that autonomy in respect to the individual's most fundamental and important work. God's intervention in the interior life of the agent followed the natural inclination of the will to its ultimate end and good. Even the most radically disordered will since Adam remained oriented toward the good in general. If God had respected all dispositions of the will, therefore, he would have responded to its accidental propensities rather than its deepest needs. Instead, God acted in the true interests of the individual. He knew best, and taught accordingly. When the will was "converted," therefore, it was not turned in an entirely new direction, but was given a new impetus toward its oldest and deepest objective.

Thus, the will retained its autonomy, not in the sense that it remained disordered, but in the sense that God carefully observed its basic inclination even as he changed some of its dispositions radically. The continuity of its independence throughout this process of conversion can be traced in the following passage:

> Every movement of the will towards God can be termed a conversion to God. And so there is a threefold turning to God. The first is by the perfect love of God; this belongs to the creature enjoying the possession of God; and for such conversion, consummate grace is required. The next turning to God is that which merits beatitude; and for this there is required habitual grace, which is the principle of merit. The third conversion is that whereby a man disposes himself so that he may have grace; for this no habitual grace is required; but the operation of God, who draws the soul toward himself, according to Lament. 5:21: "Convert us, O Lord, to you, and we shall be converted." Hence it is clear that there is no need to go on to infinity.[33]

If we reverse the order of the conversions as presented here, the three "turnings" may be seen as transitions between four distinct stages of the will:

1. The will in mortal sin:

    a. Profoundly disordered, but with its natural inclination to the good intact;

    b. In other respects the same as in a., but the inclination has now become a movement, for God has operated upon the will unilaterally, turning it toward himself. However briefly and confusedly, the will now identifies God more closely with what it seeks in its pursuit of the good in general, or happiness. God and the ultimate end are one, and God is the object of the act of the will.

2. The will in a state of charity:

    a. As in 1.b., God is conceived as ultimate end and proximate object of the will, but now habitually as well as actually. The will is not only inclined or turned to God, but united to him in love;

      b. In other respects the same as in 2.a., but in the actual vision, the love of God includes both desire and possession.

    The pattern was cumulative. In the first stage, the ultimate end was conceived as happiness; in the second, as happiness and God; in the third, as happiness, God, and object habitually loved; in the fourth, as happiness, God, and object desired and possessed in love.

    Each stage represented a more complete reduction of the will from potency to act. In the first, the will was merely broadly oriented toward the good in general, and happiness was vaguely conceived. The will, therefore, was at odds with itself, for it embodied priorities inconsistent with its own natural inclination. In the second stage, the will was specified to God as end and object, but this more determinate specification and actuation was temporary, not habitual. In the third, the will was specified to God as end and object habitually loved; God was now that good for the sake of which the will willed other goods subordinately. Yet at this stage, the individual was still in transition. The inclination to God had become increasingly determinate and actual, but, since God was not yet seen, the will was not yet fully reduced to actuation, and therefore remained in potency. Finally, in the fourth stage, the will actually enjoyed what it had sought, more or less unwittingly, all along—the end for which God had created it, the Deity himself. Man, having been ordained to God as to an end beyond the reach of his powers, found those powers fully actualized in the attainment of the beatific vision.

    Thus, although Aquinas used the notion of "turning" to describe the will's movement toward God, "foreshortening" might have been a more accurate metaphor. In rejecting a proposed argument for the existence of God, he had said,

> To know that God exists in a general and confused way is implanted in us by nature, inasmuch as God is man's beatitude. For man naturally desires happiness, and what is naturally desired by man must be naturally known to him. This, however, is not to know absolutely that God exists; just as to know that someone is approaching is not the same as to know that Peter is approaching, even though it is Peter who is approaching; for many there are who imagine that man's perfect good which is happiness consists in riches, and others in pleasures, and others in something else.[34]

In the first stage, then, the individual was directed toward God only "in a general and confused way," but in the second and third stages he arrived at a firmer sense of "who was approaching"; finally, in the fourth stage, they were face to face, and embraced in friendship. At every stage God fulfilled the natural inclination of the will to the good in general.

    God's conversion of the will respected its antecedent condition in another way as well. "Love," said Thomas, "is the most basic movement of the will and of every appetitive faculty,"[35] and love was the principal act of charity as well.

Thus, in reducing the will from its natural potency and inclination to its consummate act in the vision and love of himself, God not only respected the fundamental inclination of the will but also its characteristic type of movement. This feature of conversion could be spelled out in detail:

> [T]he appetible object gives the appetite, first a certain adaptation to itself, which consists in complacency in that object; and from this follows movement towards the appetible object. For "the appetitive movement is circular," as stated in De Anima iii. 10; because the appetible object moves the appetite, introducing itself, as it were, into its intention; while the appetite moves towards the realization of the appetible object, so that the movement ends where it began. Accordingly, the first change wrought in the appetite by the appetible object is called "love," and is nothing more than complacency in that object; and from this complacency results a movement towards that same object, and this movement is "desire"; and lastly, there is rest which is "joy". Since, therefore, love consists in a change wrought in the appetite by the appetible object, it is evident that love is a passion: properly so called, according as it is in the concupiscible faculty; in a wider and extended sense, according as it is in the will.[36]

The circular movement Aquinas described was never more fully upheld than in the love of, desire for, and joy in God. For whereas it was natural to the will that the appetible object "introduce itself, as it were," into the will's intention of the end, in the movement of the will toward God this "introduction" had been established beforehand, built into the very structure of the will by divine design. Since God was the universal good that fulfilled the will's inclination to the good in general, the movement of the will toward God was shown to be the most general and encompassing of all circular movements of the rational appetite. Other circular movements of the will merely replicated the circle that the movement toward God instanced more perfectly and preeminently. In both inclination and movement, therefore, Aquinas argued that God's conversions of the will to himself observed and perfected the basic character of the will.

Nevertheless, the solution that God provided remained an act of paternalism; the autonomy of the will was not so respected in conversion that it was allowed to remain in mortal sin. Much as we might intervene to stop someone from committing suicide, thinking we know his interests better than he currently knows them himself, so God intervened to reorder the dispositions of the will. With the infusion of the habit of charity, the will was so directly and intimately bound to the ultimate end that all fundamental priorities of the soul's powers were brought into line as a consequence. Charity was thus the "form" of the other virtues, for their end was its immediate object.[37] In a sense, then, there remained an infringement of independence, but, in Aquinas's view, God simply did what a good man would do in similar circumstances, and in respecting the deepest inclination of the will, he might be conceived as responding benevolently to the desperate situation of the sinner. Like many suicides, the mortal sinner really <u>wants</u> to be helped against his will, and this, in a sense, was what God recognized in helping the soul to fulfill its natural inclination. Aquinas put it as follows:

> There is not always a movement of violence when what is passive is changed by its active principle, but only when this is done against the interior inclination of what is passive. Otherwise all alterations and generations would be unnatural and violent. They are natural, however, because of the natural interior aptitude of the matter or of the subject to such a disposition. In like manner, when the will is moved to what is desirable by its own inclination, the movement is not violent, but voluntary.[38]

With this remark Aquinas argued that even though a conversion of the will marked a crucial event in the life of the soul, and unquestionably disregarded some of the present aptitudes and proclivities of the will, it was a divine act performed in the interest of the agent not only in the sense that it was what he should have wanted, but also in the sense that it was what he already wanted most of all, even if he did not know it.

Yet God's intervention, it seems, remained radically invasive, and if the believer maintained this impression of divine grace, he would find it difficult to appropriate the change wrought within him. Of course, in the case of the infusion of charity, the sacrament of penance provided a subsequent ritual process which functioned to encourage the appropriation of the new identity.[39] But Aquinas's concern to show the compatibility between divine help and human freedom took him still further.

VI

In the preceding chapter, I suggested that Aquinas's introvert conception of responsibility was reinforced by the belief that God was within the human soul, just as he was "in all things, and intimately." This, I argued, enabled him to move the will without violating it. It is easy to see how this doctrine provided further support for the line of argument explored above. Yet problems with this interpretation are not far to seek, for Thomas often spoke of God's movement of the will as movement "by an exterior principle," and this seems to contradict the view that God operated from within the soul. Of course, since God was everywhere, it might appear obvious that he was both inside and outside the soul, and therefore moot to decide which was the more appropriate way of speaking in a particular case. Yet not only theodicy and the ethics of salvation, but also the spirituality defined by a theologian, depends upon the way the parties are distinguished in divine-human interaction. God was "in" all things, and all things were "in" God: very well; but how? Certainly all things were not in God in the sense that the lover was in the Beloved; for then not only the individual but everything else would already have been enjoying the vision of God. In order for the individual to place himself on the spiritual map, the language of inner and outer had to be given a more regular function.

Aquinas spoke of God's existence in things in three ways:

> Therefore, God is in all things by his power, inasmuch as all things are subject to his power; he is by his presence in all things, as all things are bare and open to his eyes; he is in all things by his essence, inasmuch as he is present to all as the cause of their being.[40]

To this he added that God is sometimes present by grace:

> He is in things as the object of operation is in the operator; and this is proper to the operations of the soul, according as the thing known is in the one who knows; and the thing desired in the one desiring. In this second way God is especially in the rational creature, which knows and loves him actually or habitually. And because the rational creature possesses this prerogative by grace, as will be shown later, he is said to be thus in the saints by grace.[41]

The question to be asked of these passages is not whether "in" was being used in the same general sense in each; clearly it was not. Yet Aquinas, by using "in" in several ways, did mean to suggest a continuity between God's presence in the soul in one of the first three ways, and God's presence by grace.

Aquinas's solution was subtle. First, God was internal to the will as its original cause, as causa universalis and creator; but he was external to it as a subsequent moving cause. Yet, secondly, he could move it subsequently only because he had been its creator, and in moving it he operated not upon the will directly, nor upon any of the lower, "outer" powers, but upon the very essence of the soul. The flow of grace moved inside-out, not from the will itself, but more inwardly still, from the center of the individual's being.

In regard to the first, Aquinas argued that God's status as cause of the will enabled him to operate upon it afterwards without violating its nature:

> The movement of the will is from an intrinsic principle, just as natural movement is. Now although something can move a natural thing which is not the cause of the nature of the thing, still it cannot cause a natural movement in it except as it is in some way the cause of the nature. For man can move a stone upward though he is not the cause of the nature of a stone, but this movement is not natural to a stone; its natural movement is caused only by that which causes the nature. Hence it is said that whatever brings things into existence moves light and heavy things according to place. Therefore man, as having a will, can be moved by something which is not his cause, but it is impossible that his voluntary movement be from an extrinsic principle which is not the cause of the will.
>
> Now the cause of the two can be none other than God. This is

> evident for two reasons. First, the will is a power of the rational soul, which is caused by God alone through creation, as we have said. Second, the will is ordered to the universal good. Hence nothing else can be the cause of the will except God himself, who is the universal good. For every other thing is called good by participation and is some kind of particular good, and a particular cause does not produce a universal inclination.[42]

In this respect, then, God remained an exterior principle of the will's movement, for although he was what the will sought in all its inclinations and movements, he was not part of the will as belonging to its proper definition.

It might seem to follow, therefore, that God's operation and cooperation with the will had no special characteristics, but simply obeyed a rule that might be more broadly stated for all created things as they were moved naturally. But the fact that God did not belong to the will as properly defined did not entail that he worked from further outside the human soul. This would have meant that God acted at a distance, and Aquinas denied that this was possible:

> No action of an agent, however powerful it may be, acts at a distance, except through a medium. But it belongs to the great power of God that he acts immediately in all things. Hence nothing is distant from him, as if it could be without God in itself. But things are said to be distant from God by the unlikeness to him in nature or grace; as also he is above all by the excellence of his own nature.[43]

God did not act upon the soul through any medium, then; rather, his grace entered the will through the very essence of the soul--even further off the stage of public action than the will itself. Thus, God was "exterior" in that he was substantially distinct from the will, but "interior" in that he operated upon it and the other powers through the essence of the soul, not through any lower, more external powers.

With the arguments considered above, then, Aquinas tried to show that the "Be independent" paradox that defined the individual's orientation to his ultimate end could be resolved. He argued, first, that no contradiction was involved. This argument was crucial not only to the consistency of Aquinas's system, but also to the believer's hope that he might be able to attain the ultimate end. Second, God not only helped the soul toward its end, but provided it with a built-in inclination toward it, an inclination that could be trusted and followed. Third, Aquinas argued that God's help did not violate the autonomy and dignity of the creature, but respected it. This was important, again, both for the consistency of Aquinas's theory and for the believer's practical perspective on his own condition. God in his wisdom recognized that help invading the soul from without did not influence individual autonomy but damaged it, and Aquinas, in portraying the divine concern, depicted God, not as invading from the outside, but as working from within, offering and reaffirming the possibility of an independent but cooperative interaction between the individual and himself.

Throughout the pilgrimage of the soul, from its birth into the "Be independent" paradox to its ultimate end in God, the interaction between the soul and its spiritual Teacher was a process that Aquinas conceived as occurring at the internal interface between the soul and God. Thomas maintained his usage of the self/other and inner/outer distinctions, but their logic became increasingly complex as theoretical and spiritual difficulties were disarmed. Paradoxes and infringements remained, but Aquinas kept them at or below the level analogous to those that arise between human beings. God's involvement in the life of the soul and the soul's movement toward God were intimately but neatly meshed. Aquinas drew the analogy to human teaching and parenthood in such a way that the divine roles were not more problematic than those in human life, but less so. If the language used to describe them was stretched beyond its ordinary usage, then this was merely a measure of God's advantage as a teacher.

NOTES

[1] S.T., I, 1, a. 1.
[2] S.C.G., III, 71, a. 3.
[3] S.T., I, 12, a. 1.
[4] Of course, Aquinas denied that these limitations on God's action constrained him. They were merely the consequences of his perfection. No coercion was implied: in the act of creation, God foresaw the need for grace and made provision for it.
[5] See Chapter 1, n. 58.
[6] S.T., I-II, 16, a. 3. Cf. also 1, a. 1 ad 2; 1, a. 8; 2, a. 7; 11, a. 3 ad 3.
[7] S.T., I-II, 2, a. 7 ad 3.
[8] Aristotle, Nicomachean Ethics, 1098 a16.
[9] S.T., I-II, 4, a. 4.
[10] Augustine, Confessions, trans. John K. Ryan (Garden City, New York: Image, 1960), p. 43.
[11] S.T., I, 19, a. 2.
[12] S.T., I-II, 91, a. 2.
[13] For contrasting views of Aquinas's conception of the agent intellect, cf. Etienne Gilson, The Christian Philosophy of St. Thomas Aquinas, trans. L. K. Shook (London: Victor Gollancz, 1957), pp. 207–222, and Peter Geach, Mental Acts (New York: Humanities Press, 1957), pp. 130–131.
[14] Q.D.V., 24, a. 1. Cf. also S.T., I, 18, a. 3. References here to Aquinas's Disputed Question on Truth are based on S. Thomae Aquinatis Opera Omnia iussu Leonis XIII edita, 22 (Rome, 1972–75). The translations are from Thomas Aquinas, Truth, 3 vols., trans. Robert W. Mulligan, James V. McGlynn, and Robert W. Schmidt (Chicago: H. Regnery Company, 1952).
[15] Q.D.V., 24, a. 1.
[16] Ibid.
[17] Cf. Robert P. Sullivan, "Natural Necessitation of the Human Will," Thomist, 14 (1951), 351–399.
[18] S.T., I-II, 3, a. 2.
[19] S.T., I-II, 74, a. 1. Cf. also II-II, 23, a. 1 ad 1.
[20] S.T., I-II, 5, a. 1.
[21] Plato, Meno, in Plato: Laches, Protagoras, Meno, Euthydemus, W. R. M. Lamb, trans. (London: William Heinemann, 1924), p. 301. My treatment of the issues in this section is informed by Kierkegaard's Philosophical Fragments (Princeton: Princeton University Press, 1962). I am grateful to Lee

H. Yearley for pointing out the usefulness of the Fragments for the interpretation of religious thought. Also, since drafting this chapter I have been happy to discover John Schwartzman's "Symptoms and Rituals: Paradoxical Modes and Social Organization," Ethos 10 (1982), pp. 3-25, a synthesis of Turner, Bateson, Haley, Sluzki and Veron, and others on the problems of paradox, change, and pathology.

[22] Augustine, Confessions, p. 43.
[23] S.T., I, 12, aa. 1, 4.
[24] S.T., I, 12, aa. 4, 5.
[25] S.T., I, 12, aa. 2, 5.
[26] S.T., I, 12, a. 1.
[27] S.T., I, 12, a. 11.
[28] S.T., II-II, 2, a. 3.
[29] S.T., I-II, 4, a. 4.
[30] S.T., I, 12, a. 6.
[31] S.T., I-II, 5, a. 6; I, 111, a. 2.
[32] Cf. Sullivan, "Natural Necessitation of the Will."
[33] S.T., I, 62, a. 2 ad 3.
[34] S.T., I, 2, a. 1 ad 1.
[35] S.T., I, 20, a. 1.
[36] S.T., I-II, 26, a. 2, a. 2 ad 2.
[37] Q.D.C., 10; S.T., II-II, 23, a. 8.
[38] S.T., I-II, 6, a. 4.
[39] S.T., III, 84-91.
[40] S.T., I, 8, a. 3.
[41] Ibid.
[42] S.T., I-II, 9, a. 6.
[43] S.T., I, 8, a. 1 ad 3.

CHAPTER 3
JUSTICE AND LOVE

I

Although in the text of the Summa Theologiae fitness for the ultimate end is closely intertwined with fitness for eternal reward, the two are distinct conceptions. To say that an individual is capable of a high order of intellectual activity is not to say that he deserves the enjoyment that goes with it; nor is someone deserving therefore capable. Moreover, teleology is a self-regarding conception, whereas justice is an other-regarding one. And teleology is forward-looking, incorporating the end intended in the action willed now, while justice is backward-looking, invoking past actions to decide future deserts. Finally, intention of an end is proper to the pursuit and attainment of that end, yet intention of reward sometimes disqualifies an agent from receiving it.

These differences between teleology and justice make it inherently difficult to construe salvation as at once a goal and a reward. This has complicated ethics in the Christian tradition, even as it has helped to give it its distinctive character. Aquinas's strategy was to allow the teleological model to predominate, thereby enabling the seeker to aim directly at the salvation to be sought. The price of doing so was an accomodation of the notion of justice. In consequence, fitness for eternal reward was more remote in meaning from "iustitia" in the strict sense than fitness for the ultimate end was from "perfectio." As Aquinas saw it, if God rewarded an individual with salvation, then this presupposed a unique relation between the individual and God, and this relation was only partially covered by the norms of legal and distributive justice. Indeed, the other modes of propriety involved were not included among the "principal parts" of justice at all, but belonged with its "potential parts." These "potential parts" were not part of justice proper; they were "annexed" to it (iustitiae annecti).[1] And to apply to man's salvation, the potential parts, like distributive and legal justice, had to be extended in keeping with the doctrine of temporal analogy, and further modified in light of the introvert character of the individual's relation to Deity.

With regard to personal salvation, then, the modifications of "iustitia" by "divina" were both more numerous and more substantial than those of "finis" by "ultima." For Aquinas, the form of justice was equality, a mean in external operations toward an other. All told, then, Aquinas had to depart from this more obvious meaning of "iustitia" in five ways in order to extend its application to the individual's fitness for salvation or damnation: (1) equality was an impossible norm for the individual's transactions with God; (2) the relevant media of operation were spiritual, not material goods; (3) the parties were not external to each other; (4) their operations were likewise internal; and (5) the grounds for eternal reward were not operations themselves, but the residual effects that internal operations had upon the soul and upon its mode of subjection to God.

To some readers of Aquinas, it may come as a surprise to hear that the discussion of the potential parts of justice was important to Aquinas's understanding of divine retribution. The potential parts seems at first to be a place where Aquinas could address questions that were of peripheral interest. Also, Aquinas appears to have contradicted outright the interpretation just given, when he stated explicitly and early in the Summa that divine justice was distributive justice[2]--for distributive justice was one of the principal parts.

There is a case, then, for seeing little or no relevance to the subject of divine justice in the ideas presented in the section on the potential parts.

This reading, however, cannot stand. God's justice was distributive, to be sure, but distributive justice required a basis for distribution. The "distributive" act of creation, of course, could presuppose nothing in creatures as a basis for distributive justice, but Aquinas believed that subsequent acts of divine justice did respect the integrity of a universe already in place, and therefore held that God responded in distributive proportion to any primary or derivative rights or deserts of the rational creature.

A human being had some claims simply as a person; he or she had others based on principalitas, or standing in the community.[3] Standing, in turn, was settled by the individual's mode of subjection to the ruler of the community, and "mode of subjection" in this context was merely another way of indicating the virtuous or vicious condition of the soul. That is, Aquinas did not view the community of the universe as one in which birthright wholly determined the standing of the subject; some strata of the universe were analogous to "aristocratic communities" in which the status of each member was decided by virtue and its free exercise.[4] Nor were the standards of virtue left a matter of tacit convention: the divine ruler legislated them outright. God's distributive justice, therefore, presupposed his legal justice as its basis--his lex aeterna, lex naturalis, and lex divina.

If Aquinas had held that God's justice consisted in damning all rational animals for their lack of virtue, he might have completed his account of divine justice merely by adding legal justice to distributive justice. But Aquinas believed that God did save some sinners, and that he was as just in doing this as in damning the rest. And therein lay a problem that could only be resolved by adding a further kind of justice. For eternal reward could not be a matter of distributive justice as determined by legal justice: just as subjects earned no reward for obeying the law, so Aquinas's rational animals earned no reward for fulfilling the legal justice of the divine ruler.[5] Thus, if eternal reward was an act of divine distribution, the individual must be related to God under some other mode of subjection than that of a subject to his ruler. Accordingly, there must be some other mode of propriety involved in divine justice toward human beings. Commutative justice was out of the question; the need for a third type had to be met by the potential parts of justice.

The line of thought supporting this conclusion can be reconstructed here briefly. In Aquinas's view, the relationship between a ruler and his subject was never direct. The individual subject, per se, was only one of many members of the community, and his ties to the ruler were mediated by law. If a subject did enjoy immediate access to his ruler, then it was not qua subject, but qua something more: as servant, perhaps, or as child. Without some such direct relationship to his sovereign, the individual had no reason to expect a reward, certainly no claim to one.

Thus, eternal reward became possible only on the assumption of some closer relationship to God. Aquinas believed that all people under the divine law had such a relationship to the Deity: Jews while the old law was in effect, Christians once the law of grace was instituted.[6] Under the divine law, God was not to be understood merely as the ruler of the universe--as he was for all creatures--but as the father of his children, and therefore as their teacher in wisdom and virtue. Of course, this closer relationship did not provide any guarantee of reward, but it did establish a necessary precondition of it. God's children were closer to him; he was more intimately concerned with their well-being; he asked more of them; and he cooperated with them in their efforts toward full spiritual maturity.

Reward was actually merited, however, only when the relationship took on a still more intimate character. For, through the rearing and maturation of the child, resistance to paternal regulation decreased; the father's norms came to be shared fully by the son or daughter. Under these conditions, and with mutual good will and affection between the child and parent, the relationship developed into a fragile but vital friendship. By infusing the habitus of charity, God granted the spiritual maturity necessary to friendship even as he established a friendship within which further maturation could be nurtured.[7] Aquinas could speak of the individual's merit of eternal reward only at this point, for only here was the distance and inequality of the divine-human relationship sufficiently reduced for human merit to be possible.[8] This was another way of saying that infused virtue was necessary if the intellect and will were to have the power to see and enjoy God. The friendship remained fragile until death, but if, with God's help, the individual persevered through death, then a stable friendship was established eternally.

Hence the importance of the section on the potential parts: each of the immediate relationships between God and man was an analogue of a relationship discussed there.[9] To understand fitness for eternal reward, therefore, it is necessary not only to consider Aquinas's basic theory of justice, but also to examine the modes of propriety that he annexed to justice; for Aquinas believed that God brought the individual to salvation in keeping with these modes. Through the inequality of the relationships in the potential parts of justice, the individual soul was raised toward the equality (deificere) of actual justice and perfect friendship.

It is important to recognize how profoundly all types of moral proportionality were altered when God was introduced in one of the roles. In Aquinas's theory, the modification of "iustitia" by "divina" turned justice outside-in: instead of being related to an external other through the media of external acts and objects, the individual was related to an internal other through the media of actus interiores and spiritual goods. With the introversion of the relationship came an introversion of justice; the introversion of responsibility was a direct and logical consequence.[10]

These modifications of "justice" will occupy our attention for the rest of this chapter. Since distributive and legal justice provide the basic framework for Aquinas's conception of fitness for eternal reward, we begin with the principal parts of justice.

II

Aquinas's classic statement on divine justice came early in the Summa Theologiae:

> There are two kinds of justice. The one consists in mutual giving and receiving, as in buying and selling, and other kinds of intercourse and exchange. This the Philosopher in Ethic. v. 4 calls commutative justice, that directs exchange and the intercourse of business. This does not belong to God, since, as the Apostle says in Rom. 11:35: "Who has first given to him, and recompense shall be made to him?" The other consists in distribution, and is called distributive justice; whereby a ruler or a steward gives to each what his rank deserves. As then the proper order displayed in ruling a family or any kind of multitude evinces justice of this kind in the ruler, so the order of the universe, which is seen both in effects of nature and in effects of will, shows forth the justice of God. Hence Dionysius says in Div. Nom. viii. 4: "We must needs see that God is truly just, in seeing how he gives to all existing things what is proper to the condition of each; and preserves the nature of each one in the order and with the powers that properly belong to it."[11]

Later in the Summa, in his treatise on justice, Aquinas defined the virtue of justice as a disposition to render to each his own with a constant and perpetual will. Distributive justice, then, was distinguished by the feature that "his own" was determined by "his principalitas," or rank. The basis of distributive justice was a hierarchical ranking of persons; its outcome was a hierarchically differentiated apportionment:

> As stated above, in distributive justice something is given to a private individual, in so far as what belongs to the whole is due to the part, and in a quantity that is proportionate to the importance of the position (principalitas) of the part in relation to the whole. Consequently, in distributive justice a person receives all the more of the common goods, according as he holds a more important position in the community.[12]

Aquinas did not put forward a single principle to explain the gradations of status in all communities; in his view the norms of status-gradation differed from one type of community to another:

> This importance (principalitas) in an aristocratic community is gauged according to virtue, in an oligarchy according to wealth, in a democracy according to liberty, and in various ways according to various forms of community.[13]

To return, then, to the subject of divine justice: which kind of community was the most analogous to the community of the universe? If the grounds for deserving eternal reward were rank or importance in the cosmic community (and this would seem to follow from the claim that divine justice was distributive justice), then the particular type of community would dictate the ways of living necessary for membership and rank. Oligarchy was excluded: "wealth" would differentiate creatures, to be sure, but would not distinguish people in a way that corresponded to their fitness for the vision of God. The community of the universe, therefore, was an aristocratic community.

The life of the aristocratic community was a life of virtue, and shares in its common good were therefore distributed according to virtue. In order to guide members of the community in virtue, laws were instituted:

> Now it is evident that all who are included in a community stand in relation to that community as parts to a whole; while a part, as such, belongs to a whole, so that whatever is the good of a part can be directed to the good of the whole. It follows therefore that the good of any virtue, whether such a virtue direct man in relation to himself, or in relation to certain other individual persons, is referable to the common good, to which justice directs: so that all acts of virtue can pertain to justice, in so far as it directs man to the common good, as stated above, it follows that the justice which is in this way styled general is called "legal justice," because thereby man is in harmony with the law which directs the acts of all the virtues to the common good.[14]

To say this was also to say that the law aimed at happiness:

> As stated above, the law belongs to that which is a principle of human acts, because it is their rule and measure. Now as reason is a principle of human acts, so in reason itself there is something which

is the principle in respect of all the rest: wherefore to this principle chiefly and mainly law must needs be referred.--Now the first principle in practical matters, which are the object of the practical reason, is the last end: and the last end of human life is bliss or happiness, as stated above. Consequently the law must needs regard principally the relationship to happiness. Moreover, since every part is ordained to the whole, as imperfect to perfect; and since one man is a part of the perfect community, the law must needs regard properly the relationship to universal happiness.[15]

In other words, the individual could seek the ultimate reward by obeying the divine law.

As noted above, Aquinas's conception of divine justice cannot be fully described as an analogical extension of distributive justice, not even as combined with an analogical extension of legal justice. For the full account, we must look to his discussion of the potential parts of justice, the virtues "annexed to justice"; for there Aquinas showed how God deserved the reverence, honor, and obedience to which he was entitled, and how man in turn could merit salvation from God.

A "potential part" of justice was a modality of justice that was similar to true justice, but which fell short of it either in equality or in obligation.[16] Justice to one's father, for example, failed in the first way, for an individual could never repay his father fully for having given life and support. By the natural asymmetry of the relationship, the son could neither repay in kind nor offer an equivalent return. Friendship, however, failed in the second way, for acts of friendship were certainly appropriate behavior, but they were not obligated (<u>debita</u>) in the full sense; they therefore fell under the notion of "<u>debitum</u>" only by extension. The potential parts of justice, then, were "annexed to justice" in that they bore a strong resemblance to legal, distributive, and commutative justice: two or more parties were involved, orders were given, shares of good and evil were dispensed, and there was mutual give-and-take. Nevertheless, the potential parts were only <u>annecti</u>; they did not fully actualize <u>aequalitas</u> and <u>debitum</u>, the criteria central to the notion of justice.

Although Aquinas implied that the potential parts were relevant to the subject of divine justice, he did not indicate their bearing precisely. Throughout this section of the <u>Summa</u>, Aquinas remained terse and suggestive, implying analogies more often than stating them. The most basic question for divine justice was whether God, whose power and title to rule the universe Aquinas took for granted in this context, also <u>deserved</u> to have that power and title.[17] A theology that acknowledges this question as appropriate and offers an answer to it commends a different piety than a theology that rejects it as prideful or impious. Aquinas wanted to encourage a piety of "loving obedience" and to do so found it necessary not only to affirm God's sovereignty, but also to affirm the legitimacy of that sovereignty: its basis in God's supreme goodness. In Aquinas's view, obedience to God would have been mismotivated unless it were based on an affirmation of God's goodness, and such an affirmation could be reasonably commanded only because God did indeed deserve it, was indeed good. Among other things, therefore, the potential parts addressed aspects of divine justice that were not covered by legal entitlement, but instead belonged to personal desert. God was not only entitled to reverence, honor, and obedience by law, he also deserved these responses from his rational subjects.

It was just, therefore, that God ruled the universe, but the justice of his worthiness to rule lacked the equality of strict "iustitia". The relationship between God and his creation was an asymmetrical relationship; he was its "principle of being and government," not the other way around.[18] In Aquinas's view, therefore, God deserved more reverence, honor, and obedience than a creature could ever repay. Moreover, the justice of his worthiness to rule also fell short of obligation or debitum. "Debitum" in the full sense held only under established institutional conditions or contractual relations. To ask why God was worthy to rule the universe or deserved obedience was not the same as to ask why God was entitled to rule or had a right to obedience. To Aquinas, God had the title because he deserved it; he deserved it because his excellence surpassed that of all other beings.[19] Roughly speaking, excellence is the basis for deserving reverence, which is then expressed in internal or external acts of honor and obedience.[20] God's worthiness or desert to rule was thus the basis of his right to rule. His title, "ruler of the universe," implied in him the power to command the reverence, honor, and obedience he deserved, as well as to promulgate laws and distribute goods in the interest of the common good. (Again, the "common good" of the community of the universe was God himself, in his aspect as ultimate end and universal good.) The notion of God's institutional authority as ruler of the cosmic community was the basis, therefore, for Aquinas's theory of law, and, by extension, for his theory of eternal reward and punishment. In Aquinas's view, the eternal law, the natural law, the divine law (in both its old and new forms), and the human right to establish positive law, were all institutional actualizations of God's fundamental, non-institutional worthiness to rule.[21]

As subject to the divine ruler, the individual was related to God mediately, as a member of a community governed by law. But to be related to God mediately, as subject to ruler, was to be related to someone whose office was not to reward those who obeyed the law, but to punish those who disobeyed it:

> To reward may also pertain to anyone: but to punish pertains to none but the framer of the law, by whose authority the pain is inflicted. Wherefore to reward is not reckoned an effect of the law, but only to punish.[22]

If the law was not the basis of reward, and the relation of ruler to subject was not one within which reward was merited, then the individual had to be related to God in a more direct and immediate way in order to receive reward from him.

For most people a closer relationship to God was virtually impossible, but not for those under the divine law. Aquinas said that under the old law, and again under the new, closer relationships to God had been established. He was not only a distant figure, the majestic ruler of the community of the universe; he was also the father of his children. The new law, "the law of grace," did not merely govern the external acts of the child, but expressed God's more intimate concern that internal acts be well-ordered.[23] This concern was analogous to that of a good father who wanted his son, born in his image, to grow to be like him in character as well. God's demands upon his children were made in their best interest, for attainment of the highest end required this similarity between them: "friends have the same likes and dislikes."

Fatherhood, therefore, was the second asymmetrical relationship that was relevant to divine justice, and it was supported on the same grounds. Fathers had their role and their rights as principles of being and government; since God was the preeminent principle of being and government, he was preeminently a father. As such, he deserved reverence and honor from his children. Religion was instituted to fulfill that obligation:

> [I]t belongs to religion to show reverence to one God under one aspect, namely, as the first principle of the creation and government of things. Wherefore God himself says in Malach. 1:6: "If...I be a father, where is my honor?" For it belongs to a father to beget and to govern [and these are the grounds for honor].[24]

Children, on the other hand, had no rights of their own. In parent-child relations, as in other asymmetrical relations analyzed in the potential parts, all rights and claims belonged to the superordinate party, while all obligations belonged to the subordinate. Hence Aquinas said, "one is under no obligation to watch over inferiors."[25] And of the father-son relationship in particular, he said, "A son belongs to his father, since he is part of him somewhat."[26] Thus, the propriety that governed God-man relations under the divine law was a one-way street. There was no basis from which the child could exercise claims against the father. This closer, more direct mode of subjection therefore only created the possibility of ultimate reward; it did not ensure it.

III

In effect, the shift from rulership to fatherhood replicated the limitations of the former, but at a more personal and intimate level. Just as it was not the office of the ruler to reward those who obeyed the law, so it did not belong to a father, as such, to befriend his children at their maturity. Yet, as with rulership, fatherhood provided opportunity for further interaction and further development. Friendship with grown children was not a father's obligation, but in some cases it might emerge as an option.

Aristotle had said as much in the Nicomachean Ethics:

> But when children render to their parents what is due those who gave them life, and when parents render what is due to their children, the friendship between them will be lasting and equitable.[27]

With this and other remarks, Aristotle provided Aquinas with resources which he could use to expand the analogy of temporal attributes. Friendship might be built on justice between parents and children; if so, then some sinners might justly be saved.

Before looking at some of the other passages from the <u>Nicomachean Ethics</u> that informed Aquinas's solution, we should pause to consider a passage that was less favorable:

> Persons much inferior to [kings] in station do not expect to be friends with kings, nor do insignificant people expect to be friends with the best and wisest men. There is no exact line of demarcation in such cases to indicate up to what point [of inequality] men can still be friends. The friendship can still remain even when much is taken away, but when one partner is quite separated from the other, as in the case of divinity, it can remain no longer.[28]

On a surface reading, it seems to follow that if one chose to agree with Aristotle on this point, then one was obliged also to conclude that salvation was impossible. For the passage seems to say that no friendship between God and man could occur; and charity, which was necessary for salvation, was a kind of friendship. Salvation, it seems, could not occur.

This was a line of reasoning that Thomas wanted to close off. He dissented unobtrusively, merely clarifying the text with a paraphrase:

> If the persons are far apart, like men from God, then <u>the friendship we are discussing</u> does not survive.[29]

Not every friendship between God and man was impossible, then; only the friendship under discussion. Aristotle could not have known what had been revealed only through the prophets of Israel. His remarks were narrower than he realized.

In another important passage from his commentary, Aquinas pointed out the connection and continuity between the equality of justice and that of friendship:

> [F]riendship is a kind of union or association of friends that cannot exist between widely separated persons; but they must approach equality. Hence it pertains to friendship to use an equality already uniformly established, but it pertains to justice to reduce unequal things to an equality. When equality exists the work of justice is done. For that reason equality is the goal of justice and the starting point of friendship.[30]

As we have seen, the potential parts of justice set forth a propriety that achieved equality in the interaction between unequal persons. Again, parent-child relations are a relevant example of this: "[W]hen children render to their parents what is due those who gave them life, and when parents render what is due their children, the friendship between them will be lasting and equitable."[31]

But, as we have also seen, children could not fully repay their parents. A fortiori the children of God could not repay their heavenly Father the much greater debt that they owed to him both as their "principle of being and government" and as the Lord against whom they had sinned. Here also Aristotle's reflections on human relations seem to have offered an analogue for the way of salvation that Aquinas would develop:

> A debtor must pay his debt, but nothing a son may have done [to repay his father] is a worthy return for everything his father has provided for him, and therefore he will always be in his debt. But a creditor is free to remit the debt, and a father likewise. At the same time it seems unlikely that any father would break off relations with his son, unless the son were exceedingly wicked.[32]

Aquinas suggested that the Father would remit the debt if the child tried to repay as much as he could:

> Since justice implies equality, and since we cannot offer God an equal return, it follows that we cannot make him a perfectly just repayment. For this reason, the divine law is not properly called "right" (ius) but "allowable" (fas) because, to wit, God is satisfied if we accomplish what we can. Nevertheless justice tends to make man repay as much as he can, by subjecting his mind to him entirely.[33]

And again,

> And when I say "equality," I do not mean absolute equality, because it is not possible to pay God as much as we owe him, but equality in consideration of man's ability and God's acceptance.[34]

This equality, which Aquinas could not state in the potential parts with the same level of mathematical exactness he had found for distributive and commutative justice, seems to have been in this further, analogical extension a measure that existed in the mind of God, and was therefore to be trusted as belonging to him. The individual could only be assured that God's acceptance would come with his own full willingness to pay:

> Virtue is praised because of the will, not because of the ability: and therefore if a man fall short of equality which is the mean of justice, through lack of ability, his virtue deserves no less praise, provided there be no failing on the part of his will.[35]

But there's the rub: without charity there would indeed be a failing on the part of the will. Charity, a kind of friendship, had to be present in the will if justice to the Father was to be fulfilled. It appears, then, that friendship was a precondition for justice, but that justice was in turn a precondition for friendship. Yet "the goal of justice" was "the starting point of friendship": they might coincide in time. The starting point of friendship would then be the divine initiative of grace, which at the same moment that it was appropriated by the free choice of the will of the individual fulfilled the objective of justice: for "what we can do through our friends we can, in a sense, do ourselves." There was no vicious circle, for God's friendship to man was always prior to man's friendship to God, even if they occurred at the same instant.

In addressing this question, Aquinas pointed out that the human mind was essentially above time, accidentally subject to it; this meant that a double solution was necessary. As subject to time,

> [W]e must say that there is no last instant that sin inheres, but a last time; whereas there is a first instant that grace inheres; and in all previous time sin inhered.[36]

Aquinas's point here was that time (in this sense) was infinitely divisible, and therefore that there would be time between points or "instants" by which time might be divided, no matter what the intervening unit might be. Accordingly, it was coherent to say that there was no last instant that sin inhered, although there was a last time. In other words, the individual was in mortal sin throughout the whole of the time up to the first point or instant at which he was in grace, a moment not further divisible. This had the advantage of avoiding the difficulties that would arise from supposing that there was an intermediate time between mortal sin and charity. (E.g., what would become of someone who died during that interlude?)

As above time, the last instant of sin was immediately followed by the first instant of grace; hence, in this respect too there would be no problematic interlude. Of course, there were other problems in talking about the discontinuity of time for things above time, but those would take us beyond the scope of this discussion. Suffice it to say, then, that in the things that were above time, time was discontinuous or (as we might now say) digital; in the things that were subject to time time was continuous or (as we might now say) analogic. In neither case did Aquinas admit a "time" between the departure of mortal sin and the arrival of charity. In neither, therefore, was there a vicious circle of friendship prior to friendship or of a fulfillment of justice prior to a fulfillment of justice. As Aquinas quoted Aristotle, "what we can do through our friends we can, in a sense, do ourselves": God's first act of friendship was to empower the first movement of the free will by which justice (fas) was fulfilled to him and the reciprocal friendship of charity was established in the soul. There was, however, a natural or causal priority:

> [I]n their natural order the first in the justification of the ungodly is the infusion of grace; the second is the free-will's movement towards God; the third is the free-will's movement toward sin, for he who is being justified detests sin because it is against God, and thus the free-will's movement towards God naturally precedes the free-will's movement towards sin, since it is its cause and reason; the fourth and

last is the remission of sin, to which this transmutation is ordained as to an end, as stated above.[37]

In summary, then, the possibility that his heavenly father would become a friend was the individual's sole chance of salvation, analogous to the chance of a (medieval European) son to become friends with his father. The chance was slim, but it was much better than the chance of a subject to develop a friendship with a ruler, and was therefore a more positive way to characterize the possibility of salvation. Thus, if the father's child-rearing efforts proved successful, and the child matured to a spiritual adult, the inequality between parent and child was thereby reduced, and friendship became possible. Once the friendship was established it might be said that the enjoyment had less the character of a reward than the character of the good company of unequal but virtuous persons.

Fitness of eternal reward, therefore, came only when fitness for eternal friendship was established. Until the two parties were compatible for such a close and long relationship, friendship was impossible. And, unless friendship was indeed established, the exchange of affection between the two parties was likewise impossible. Thus, since the eternal reward was the enjoyment of reciprocal affection with the Deity, it presupposed eternal friendship. It was for this reason that Aquinas hesitated to speak of the vision as a reward. "Reward" (merces, premium) suggested a distant relationship and might be taken to allow a venality of motive inconsistent with the mutual affection of the lover and the Beloved; Aquinas preferred, therefore, to speak of "eternal happiness" as the object of merit. Friendship with God, then, was the basis for merit of eternal favor from him, and this was but another way of saying that the possession of the infused habit of charity was the essential condition of salvation.

IV

Fitness for eternal friendship may be conceived as a kind of compatibility between the soul and God; it was the deiformity of intellect and rectitude of will that made the individual someone suited for everlasting life with him. This compatibility, together with the mutual sharing of love between them, constituted the friendship of charity.

Aquinas's analogical appropriation of Aristotle's treatment of friendship took him further than is indicated by the passages cited above. Although Aquinas nowhere developed the analogy in an extended and systematic treatment, Leo M. Bond's work has shown that Thomas had thought through fully the scattered passages in which "amare," "amor," and "amicitia" combine Aristotelian and Christian conceptions of the role of friendship.

Aristotle gave two summary statements of friendship:

We conclude, therefore, that to be friends men must have good will for one another, must each wish for the good of the other on the basis of one of the three motives mentioned [i.e., usefulness, pleasure, goodness], and must each be aware of one another's good will.[38]

We count as a friend (1) a person who wishes for and does what is good or what appears to him good for his friend's sake; or (2) a person who wishes for the existence and life of his friend for his friend's sake.... We regard as a friend also (3) a person who spends time in our company and (4) whose desires are the same as ours, or (5) a person who shares sorrow and joy with his friend.... By one or another of these sentiments people also define friendship.[39]

From these two statements, Aristotle's basic conception of friendship may be described: friendship requires (a) two parties who are (b) mutually benevolent and know it, (c) communicate with one another or share a common activity, (d) have the same interests and values, and (e) base their affection on mutual usefulness, pleasure, goodness, or some combination of the three.

Aquinas opened his discussion of charity by applying this conception of friendship, and indicated that a friendship based on mutual goodness or virtue was the relevant type.[40] The individual and God were the two parties; they were mutual in their benevolence or love; this benevolence or love was based on communication or sharing between them; they had "the same likes and dislikes";[41] and both parties were virtuous.

Mutuality of affection presupposed a similarity between them, and in Aquinas's view this similarity was grounded in the fact that man was made in the image of God. This fundamental similarity, which he identified with the rational creature's powers of intellect and will, was further realized when intellect and will were assimilated to God by taking him as their object. This occurred in the intellect through natural reason and infused faith, and in the will through hope and charity. Charity was central, for its form provided a rectitude of will that established the same hierarchy of values in the human will as obtained in the divine will--"the same likes and dislikes"--and this was the desert base for deiformity of intellect.

God's benevolence was known to the individual through revelation and grace. Of course, the individual could not exercise reciprocal benevolence toward God, for God had no need of human assistance; but he could act to the greater glory of God through external actions that brought credit to God among human beings. Indeed, even his wishing that he could do more might be imputed to him as meritorious.

Communication was a special difficulty, since creatures were related to God, but he was not related to them.[42] Yet in establishing his providence, God made provision for communication with the individual; natural reason, natural law, and the revelation of knowledge about God and his divine law were all examples of divine communication toward man. The rational creature, in turn, could respond through prayer and acts of charity. These responses were known to the divine mind, and they affected the individual's relation to God by altering his mode of subjection to the Deity. Thus, Aquinas said,

> Man's life is twofold. There is his outward life in respect of his sensitive and corporeal nature: and with regard to this life there is no communication or fellowship between us and God or the angels. The other is man's spiritual life in respect of his mind, and with regard to this life there is fellowship between us and both God and the angels, imperfectly indeed in this present state of life, wherefore it is written (Phil. 3:20): "Our fellowship is in heaven."[43]

Through grace the individual was raised from the principalitas of subjection and childhood to the deiformity necessary for friendship with God. To the objection that there was too great an inequality between the parties for such a friendship to be possible, Aquinas pointed to the mediating sonship of Christ, for Christ had demonstrated this possibility by actualizing it himself:

> [I]t must be said that charity is not a virtue of man considered as man, but of man considered as becoming, through participation in grace, like God and the Son of God, according to which it is written (I John 3:1), "Behold what manner of charity the Father has bestowed upon us, that we should be called, and should be, sons of God."[44]

As noted in the previous chapter, Aquinas considered this diminution of the inequality between God and the individual a "deification" of the latter. Within the language of roles and their change, this diminution was another way of talking about the spiritual maturation of the son or daughter. (Thus, the new law could be characterized as "the law of a full-grown man," "a law of liberty.") The Father taught, recognized the effectiveness of his teaching, and justly raised his child to favored status--all in the instant in which charity was infused. Of course, the child still had to persevere in charity until death, but the shift from mortal sin to charity was instantaneous.

Aquinas seems to have been especially impressed with how, in Aristotle's conception of friendship, the communicatio, or shared activity of friends, overcame the separation of self and other. A friend was, in a sense, another self, and therefore what we could do through our friends we could in some sense do ourselves.[45] This idea was at the heart not only of Aquinas's theories of redemption and grace, but also of his conception of the love of enemies. In a typically ambiguous and suggestive passage, Aquinas addressed both possibilities at once:

> Friendship extends to a person in two ways: first in respect of himself, and in this way friendship never extends but to one's friends: secondly, it extends to someone in respect of another, as, when a man has friendship for a certain person, for his sake he loves all belonging to him, be they children, servants, or connected in any way. Indeed, so much do we love our friends, that for their sake we love all who belong to them, even if they hurt or hate us....[46]

Although chiefly written to develop the idea of the human individual's love for his enemies, these remarks applied analogically to God's love of those human beings who, as mortal sinners, were inimical to him. Indeed, in Aquinas's view, an individual's ability to love enemies was possible only because God's love of those who rebel against him was its energizing source.

As argued in Chapter 1, the notion of an "Other within" is a paradox central to Aquinas's religious ethics, a paradox that held for all three modes of subjection to God. In Chapter 2, we saw that this paradox was basic to Aquinas's characterization of the way God could at once help the individual and respect his autonomy. In the present chapter, we see how the idea of an "Other within" led Aquinas to an introversion of justice, and to a resultant introversion of responsibility. But the transition from justice to charity was a transition governed by roles and relationships. At each stage, roles and relationships changed for the better at God's initiative and the individual's cooperation. God was more than a ruler because he took the initiative to become a father, first by choosing a people, "the children of Israel," and then by sending his only-begotten son as a friend to his adopted children, thereby enabling them to become "deified" with him. By this initiative, and the initiatives of grace based upon it, the "Other within" appeared in the role of a friend, "another self" whose identification with his beloved children called for their identification in love with him. Charity, therefore, the friendship between God and man, was the highest and most inward temporal stage in the presence of Deity in the human soul, perfecting without abrogating the previous roles.

Thus, the virtue of charity had a central strategic function in Aquinas's ethics: in it the self-regarding and other-regarding aspects of teleology and justice combined and coalesced. When seen in connection with the teleological fitness for the ultimate end, charity made the ultimate end the proximate motive; the final cause of the will also became its immediate object. The will was thereby rectified, informed by a love from which its virtuous acts flowed "voluntarily, readily, with delight, and firmly."[47] When viewed in connection with justice, charity made the relation to another the relation to "another self." As an infused habit, therefore, charity might be seen primarily as the fulfillment of the other-regarding concern for justice in a more intimate and trusting <u>quid pro quo</u>, that of communication in friendship.

But ultimately the distinction between self-regarding and other-regarding virtues receded and dissolved--as I believe Aquinas wanted it to do. ,The duality that represented and reinforced the alienation of self from others was provisional, to be paradoxically reframed and confounded by the "form, mother, and root of the virtues." It returned again, in reconstituted form, in the order of charity--the priorities of love built into the <u>habitus infusus</u>. These priorities contained in microcosm the priorities of value in the divine mind. Thus, Aquinas tangled the distinction between self and other, but the result was not a simple conceptual snarl, but rather a liminal suspension of opposites.

NOTES

[1] S.T., II–II, 80.
[2] S.T., I, 21, a. 1.
[3] S.T., II–II, 61, a. 2.
[4] Ibid.
[5] S.T., I–II, 92, a. 2 ad 3.
[6] S.T., I–II, 91, aa. 4, 5, esp. 5 ad 1; 107,] aa. 1, 2.
[7] S.T., II–II, 23, a. 1.
[8] S.T., II–II, 114, a. 4.
[9] S.T., II–II, 80–85; 101–105.

[10] One might wish to say that this is a distortion even of the justice of the potential parts, but Aquinas did not formulate the criteria precisely enough for the question to be pursued to a conclusion.

[11] S.T., I, 21, a. 1.
[12] S.T., II–II, 61, a. 2.
[13] Ibid.
[14] S.T., II–II, 58, a. 5.
[15] S.T., I–II, 90, a. 2
[16] S.T., II–II, 80.

[17] See Joel Feinberg, "Justice and Personal Desert," in his Doing and Deserving: Essays in the Theory of Responsibility. Princeton: Princeton University Press, 1970.

[18] S.T., II–II, 101, a. 1.
[19] Ibid.
[20] Cf. S.T., II–II, 103, a. 1 ad 1, and a. 2.

[21] It is not clear why Aquinas did not make more of this position. Perhaps the reason was that, according to his analogy, even the ground for God's desert of reverence, honor, and obedience must have been instituted as laws from the beginning of God's rulership. As much as Aquinas might like some sort of desert/entitlement distinction, therefore, the circularity remains: God as ruler fixes the criteria for assessing his worthiness to rule.

[22] S.T., I–II, 92, a. 2 ad 3.
[23] S.T., I–II, 107, aa. 1, 2.
[24] S.T., II–II, 81, a. 3.
[25] S.T., II–II, 80.
[26] S.T., II–II, 57, a. 4.
[27] Aristotle, Nicomachean Ethics, 1158 b21–23.

[28] Aristotle, Nicomachean Ethics, 1159 a1-5.
[29] S.L.E., p. 465, ll. 140-145.
[30] S.L.E., p. 465, ll. 107-116.
[31] Aristotle, Nicomachean Ethics, 1158 b21-23.
[32] Aristotle, Nicomachean Ethics, 1163 b20-23.
[33] S.T., II-II, 57, a. 1 ad 3.
[34] S.T., 81, a. 5 ad 3.
[35] S.T., II-II, 81, a. 6 ad 1.
[36] S.T., I-II, 13, a. 7 ad 5.
[37] S.T., I-II, 13, a. 8.
[38] Aristotle, Nicomachean Ethics, 1156 a3-5.
[39] Aristotle, Nicomachean Ethics, 1166 a2-9.
[40] S.T., II-II, 23, a. 1
[41] S.T., II-II, 104, a. 3.
[42] Leo M. Bond writes:

> Aristotle often states that friendship is founded in κοινωνία (Latin, communicatione. The English word "communication," used in the sense which we have described above, is not an adequate translation of κοινωνία, in the sense in which Aristotle uses it, nor indeed of the Latin equivalent "communicatio." "Community" would be a better translation, community in the sense of common interests, common life, the participation of common goods, etc.; for the examples Aristotle gives of κοινωνία are "fellow-sailors who communicate in navigation and fellow-soldiers who communicate in military activity."

Bond, "A Comparison between Human and Divine Friendship," p. 70.

[43] S.T., II-II, 23, a. 1 ad 1.
[44] Q.D.C., a. 11.
[45] S.T., I-II, 156, a. 2 ad 1; cf. III, 48, a. 2, and Supplementum, 12-15, passim, where this idea controls the argument.
[46] S.T., II-II, 23, a. 1 ad 2.
[47] Q.D.C., a. 11.

CHAPTER 4
SOME PROBLEMS OF JUSTICE

I

It was one thing to say that those who got to see the Ruler of the universe were those who had the requisite power and status to do so. It may have been alright, too, to say that those who had those requisites were his relatives and friends; then as now, this must have had a familiar and realistic ring. But it was quite another thing to say that those with power, status, kinship, or other personal ties therefore <u>merited</u> this special access to their Lord.

Aquinas knew this, of course; he did not need to be told the difference between "gets" and "deserves." Yet his problem was not merely to distinguish them, but also to sustain this distinction even as he argued for the concomitance of justice with teleology and love, a concomitance that held not only in the ultimate conditions of salvation and damnation, but at every phase of personal development toward either. In this chapter I will concentrate on problems Aquinas faced in interweaving justice with the other two modes.

In Chapter 3, I argued that God's justice included application of the potential parts. In the following passage, Aquinas shows how he made use of the potential parts in his conception of merit, and how their relevance opens onto the question of how friendship with God can provide grounds for meriting salvation:

> Merit and reward refer to the same, for a reward means something given anyone in return for work or toil, as a price for it. Hence, as it is an act of justice to give a just price for anything received from another, so also is it an act of justice to make a return for work or toil. Now justice is a kind of equality, as is clear from the Philosopher in <u>Ethic.</u> v. 3, and hence justice holds simply between those that are equal simply; but where there is no absolute equality between them, neither is there absolute justice, but there may be a certain manner of justice, as when we speak of a father's or a master's right, as the Philosopher says at <u>ibid.</u> 6. And hence where justice holds simply, the character of merit and reward hold simply. But where no simple right holds, but only relative right, no character of merit holds simply, but only relatively, in so far as the character of justice is found there, since the child merits something from his father and the slave from his lord.

> Now it is clear that between God and man there is the greatest inequality: for they are infinitely apart, and all man's good is from God. Hence there can be no justice of absolute equality between man and God, but only of a certain proportion, inasmuch as both operate after their own manner. Now the manner and measure of human virtue is in man from God. Hence man's merit with God only exists on the presupposition of the divine ordination, so that man obtains from God, as a reward of his operation, what God gave him the power of operation for, even as natural things by their proper movements and operations obtain that to which they were ordained by God; differently, indeed, since the rational creature moves itself to act by its free-will, hence its action has the character of merit, which is not so in other creatures.[1]

"Man obtains from God, as a reward of his operation, what God gave him the power of operation for." In other words, God gave man the power of operation in order that man might attain the ultimate end, the vision of God himself. In this, the final stage of spiritual development, the deiformity of the intellect and rectitude of the will would find their reward in the pleasurable perfection of their potency. This perfection was not itself an operatio, not itself opus vel labor; these terms refer to means, and connote effort and anticipation. But in the end one rested, for in it activity was perfect, unencumbered, delightful. And this quality of its activity was its character as "reward." Eric D'Arcy has said it well:

> Here Aquinas' metaphysical bias becomes most plain. His theory of act and potentiality is involved in explaining the way that a morally good life in this world is a condition (necessary, not sufficient) of developing intrinsically into the sort of person capable (given supernatural elevation of his powers by grace) of enjoying the presence and sight of God in the next. The connection therefore is less of the nature, "If you graduate from medical school you can have a new Buick," than of the nature, "If you graduate from medical school you can become a good doctor."[2]

Virtue was not its own reward; the reward of virtue was the growth and increase of virtue itself.

Although D'Arcy's emphasis is accurate, there are passages in Aquinas that seem closer to the "new Buick" paradigm. Indeed, the very passage that concludes with the statement, "man obtains from God, as the reward of his operation, what God gave him the power of operation for," opens with a salary-like conception of reward:

> Merit and reward refer to the same, for a reward (merces) means something given anyone in return for work or toil, as a price (pretium) for it. Hence, as it is an act of justice to give a just price for anything received from another, so also is it an act of justice to

make a return (<u>recompensare</u>) for work or toil.[3]

Arguably, Thomas had qualified this sense of "<u>merces</u>" quite to death by the end of the article; yet this opening conception was the principal aspect under which he wished to regard eternal reward: he seems, therefore, to have seen some connection between the "new Buick" picture of reward and the "good doctor" picture.

The nature of the connection is not easy to determine. In fact, Aquinas appears to have been stuck on the horns of a dilemma. As to the first horn, if the salary-like conception of reward was the principal conception, then it is hard to see why Aquinas placed so much emphasis on the <u>habitus</u> of charity and its role in informing the will. Wages were paid, not for good will, but for good performance; and yet to Thomas the possession of the infused disposition of charity was the necessary condition for meriting some degree of the beatific vision in the next life. Of course, Aquinas mentioned a large number of conditions necessary for salvation, but these were collectively insufficient for salvation unless they were informed by charity. And charity sufficed for salvation because, given the <u>habitus</u> <u>infusus</u>, all other conditions of the soul's fitness for God either followed from it, were met by it, or were manifested externally as evidence of its presence.

Love of God was central. Yet love of God seems irrelevant to a conception of reward that was modelled on a worker's right to his wage; nor does it seem plausible that this difficulty would have escaped Aquinas. The performance of a contractually agreed-upon task established the right to wages. Affection for the person in charge of the crew or for the crew itself had a bearing only if it had a positive effect on performance; and, if it did have such an effect, then the performance itself, not the affection, was the basis of the right to the wages. One might ask whether Aquinas's point was that love was in some sense the "price" of salvation, a kind of inward "work" that would earn an infinite wage. But this recourse to metaphor would have run not only against the antecedent tradition, which rejected interior earning of salvation no less than exterior, but also against Thomas's own express rejection of commutative models of the individual's relation to God. Above all, "it is clear that between God and man there is the greatest inequality," and hence the assumption of equality of parties necessary for the commutativity of contractual agreement was removed from the beginning. Aquinas did not mean that love earned salvation as a wage.

But if the wage-like model is dropped, then the second horn of the dilemma seems to catch him. On this alternative, it was not that the individual became <u>entitled</u> to eternal reward as his right, but rather that he became deserving of it as an appropriate response from a just God. In general, desert reserves a large role for concepts of intention, motive, disposition, and attitude--concepts that have a lesser role in entitlement, if they appear at all. Desert seems to focus principally on the fitness between person and treatment, and on the fitness between action and treatment only insofar as it provides a warrant for the former: treatment befits action only insofar as action reveals and reflects character, and thus we care about voluntariness largely because "voluntariness" refers to a set of conditions that, if met, collectively assure us that an action did indeed reveal and reflect the agent's character. Similarly, because dispositions are conceived as "parts" of personal character rather than as emphemeral accidents of it, and because motives and intentions are thought to express character more directly than external actions, desert reserves a much larger role than entitlement for such notions as Aquinas's <u>inclinatio</u> and <u>habitus</u>, and for the power of a habit such as charity to "inform" an action. Perhaps, therefore, it would be more correct to see Thomas's conception of fitness for reward as closer to personal desert in our present sense, and to view the language of "reward," "recompense," and "price" as either an oversight of Aquinas or as a limitation of the terminology available to him.

But this alternative too is problematic. First, it supposes that the language of entitlement was not central to Aquinas's ethics. Second, it seems also to suppose that the logic of moral desert allows deserved reward and intended end to be the same. As to the first, Aquinas recurrently spoke of the universe as a hierarchically ordered polity structured throughout by the laws of God. <u>Sub lege</u> one is "entitled" or "bound," not "deserving," and this was true of Aquinas's description of the legal condition of man no less than of creatures on other rungs of the hierarchy. And, as to the second assumption, Thomas followed the rest of his tradition in saying that the person who sought salvation primarily for the sake of reward was not fit to be saved.

There seems to be no denying, then, that the language of entitlement was central to Aquinas's religious ethics. Yet, at the same time, he emphasized the fitness of the individual person for salvation--an emphasis proper to desert, not entitlement. The solution to his dilemma followed lines that have since been identified and criticized by Joel Feinberg: Aquinas wrote of personal desert as if it had been "an eccentric subspecies of entitlement,"[4] and therefore expressed his emphasis on dispositions, intentions, and love in a vocabulary that was in important ways misleading.

In doing so, he stood in two long traditions. Thinkers in the West since Plato had been criticizing their societies by projecting alternative, fuller institutionalizations of their view of justice--republics, kingdoms of God, heavenly cities. They thought through the implications of "desert" by envisioning its institutional realization in entitlement. What had not' been franchised and sanctioned was to be fully franchised, fully sanctioned; what had been marginal was to be legitimated. Although terms analogous to our "desert" were sometimes available (e.g., ἄξιος), they were often just as marginal as "desert" itself, and hence less fully developed and articulated than the language of entitlement. Accordingly, the Western philosophical and theological traditions have generally preferred to examine desert under the language of entitlement, favoring the complete, positive, and systematic picture of alternatives that this approach provided.

Aquinas shared this para-institutional approach to justice; in some ways he epitomized it. Although in the discussion of the potential parts of justice he displayed an awareness that such an approach could not fully account for all forms of human interaction traditionally evaluated as just or unjust, nevertheless most of his writing was controlled by the notion of the universe as a community operating according to the laws promulgated by a divine ruler. As a result, notions of justice that he might have characterized in non-institutional terms he instead presented as forms of institutionalized justice. For Thomas, the universe was a community with a ruler, laws, and subjects; human communities were lesser embodiments of this perfect type; and even the human person could be conceived--metaphorically, to be sure--according to the same institutional model. In keeping with the hierarchical ordering of the universe, the same language could be used for all three levels of "community."

Moreover, Aquinas stood also within the Christian tradition of world-renunciation. This reinforced his propensity to speak of the human person as a microcosm, a wee πόλισ. Christ's kingdom was not of this world, and temporal participation in that kingdom was possible only through the interior communication of the spirit. The individual's outward life, his sensitive and corporeal nature, might be relegated to Caesar, for "with regard to this life there is no communication between us and God or the angels." The inward life, however, was "man's spiritual life in respect of his mind, and with regard to this life there was fellowship between us and both God and the angels, imperfectly indeed in this present state of our life...."[5] Yet although the well-lived inner life was not of this world, it was modelled on it metaphorically, and so Aquinas selected juridical and other institutional conceptions to depict the ethics of the <u>forum</u> <u>internum</u>. The interior acts of the believer were governed by the new law, the law of grace. Arguably this manner of speaking was just as figurative as the language of interior agents and their transactions that Thomas employed in his discussion of metaphorical justice, but it was nevertheless the language that he used in writing his religious ethics. In short, because he spoke to the world-rejecting tradition of Christianity and to its predominantly introvert conception of responsibility, Thomas gave an inward turn to the para-institutional tendencies that he shared with other ethical theorists in the West.

The institutional language of entitlement, then, was indeed central; yet just as central was Aquinas's contention that the individual had no claim to eternal reward. If such a reward was forthcoming at all, it was granted not because of a claim of right, but because the individual deserved it for having shown the temporal friendship that befit him for the vision of the Beloved. Aquinas's theory of fitness for reward, therefore, should be seen as a case well-diagnosed by Feinberg's analysis: a case of a Western thinker whose basic working conception was closest to what we may now call "personal desert," but whose principal language for expressing that conception was closest to what we may now call "personal entitlement."

I do not believe that Aquinas was much misled by the language of entitlement that he used. He was careful in his choice of words, but careful also in qualifying them and in indicating the tentativeness of many of his formulations. Moreover, he did not share our current tendency to assume that a lack of clear and unambiguous means of expression betokens a lack of understanding. In his view, one could understand an idea and know its truth without having literal and univocal means to express it.

The passage on merit cited above exhibits well these differences between our own ethos of intellectual expression and his. He first presented the conception of <u>meritum</u> as it fell under justice simply, then pointed out that simple justice did not apply. He might then have referred his readers forward to the potential parts, but this was not his usual practice in the <u>Summa Theologiae</u>. He simply explained how things stood, and left it to his readers to go to the section on the potential parts to learn how, in his view, interaction between unequals was regulated. If he had played up the importance of the potential parts, he might more fully have disarmed the Feinbergian line of criticism that I have developed here, and might, for that matter, have more fully anticipated the objections of the Reformers. That difference in emphasis would have signalled more effectively that Thomas was not himself misled by the language of entitlement--that, in effect, Feinberg's distinction between desert and entitlement was anticipated by his own distinction between potential and actual parts of justice. Desert, then, would be, in Feinberg's terms, "a natural moral notion, prior to entitlement." Entitlement, in other words, actualizes the potential for justice in personal desert by giving it an institutional embodiment and codification.

II

What Aquinas had in mind, then, seems closest to our current conception of "personal desert." Here I will use this conception in order to show in greater detail how Aquinas spliced justice with teleology.

The individual's deserved reward and his intended end appear, at first, to have been identical: in each instance it was the beatific vision. But God could not reward salvation to someone whose principal intention was the enjoyment of reward; he could do so only to someone who had the proper motivation, someone with the infused virtue of charity. In other words, the soul would be rewarded if it loved God, provided that it did not love God primarily in order to be rewarded.

And yet, like many another concern for proper motivation, this one seems to be paradoxical, self-defeating. The individual, pursuing salvation (and avoiding damnation) out of self-love, tries in his own interest to fulfill the commandment to love--only to be told that the love he might be able to muster in this way will be insufficient for his purpose. Disturbed by the horrible implications of this for the quality of his afterlife, he tries harder--but, of course, fails again.

His problem, we might say, is that he has an ulterior motive for his love. Genuine or sincere love, we think, never has an ulterior motive, and thus, given Thomas's point of view, it would be understandable that only genuine or sincere love would suffice for salvation. To approach the difficulty from this angle, however, is to construe it as a relatively narrow form of the phenomenon of self-defeating egoism. Although this, I think, is how Aquinas himself understood the problem, I want to view it here from a wider perspective, as an analogical adaptation of a double-bind phase common in human moral development.

In deserts such as approval, our approval is diminished if we learn that a child or other person has performed a good action only in the interest of receiving approval. And our reaction is appropriate, for such a motivation indicates an important difference between the agent's values and our own: we think that his act is to be approved because it is good, while he thinks that it is good because it will receive our approval. Of course, he may still get our approval, but it will not be as strong and may be given grudgingly; we do not wish to communicate greater agreement than actually holds between us.

I want to linger on this issue here, for it is one of the many cases in which thinking through the problematics of Aquinas's ethics takes us into fundamental questions of moral psychology. In the above instance, it is not simply that we do not like to be manipulated, nor is it an ordinary instance of the way ends affect action-descriptions. Of course, whether we describe an action as "John rushed to the wounded man's aid" or as "John managed to keep blood off his rug" indicates a good deal of difference in what John deserves; and the correct description depends in turn on what end or ends John was trying to attain, what constraints he wanted to observe, as he returned quickly with the cotton and bandages. But the problem I want to pick out is a more specific case of the way ends make a difference in action-descriptions. I want to concentrate on the difference between "John rushed to his aid" and "John tried to win our approval."

If the first description is a correct interpretation of John's action, then John deserves approval, and gratitude as well. But if the second description is correct, then our approval and gratitude are diminished. Actions may have several motives, or may be "overdetermined," but the presence and salience of approval-seeking in such an instance will reduce approval even if other, nobler motives are also recognizably at work.

But why? As a first step toward explanation, we can say that according to the second description there is the difference already noted between the value John sees in his action and the value we see in it. For we approve of an action on the understanding that it is good; we do not think it is good because we have conferred our approval upon it. And this holds generally: runners are not fast because they receive trophies, but receive trophies because they are fast;

students are not intelligent because they receive good grades, but the other way around; murderers are not bad because they are punished, but are punished because they are bad. Aquinas makes a similar point himself. Although it is true to say that we may at times infer from trophies to speed, grades to intelligence, punishment to crime, and approval to good behavior, in doing so we assume that the actual bestowal of these deserts was made in the reverse order of inferring from speed to trophies, and so on.

In order to move beyond this observation to a more complete explanation, it is necessary to consider the communicative or symbolic function of deserved treatments. In approving the goodness of an action or the goodness of a person for an action, we approve the action or person as concretely embodying some value that we hold dear. Our express approval commends that value to the agent, to others, and to ourselves, and holds the agent up for imitation as an exemplar of that value. Thus, as Thomas says, and Feinberg and C.L. Stevenson would presumably agree, reverence is the communicative aim as well as the personal motive of honoring someone, "in so far as a person is honored in order that he may be held in reverence by others."[6]

Favorable and unfavorable treatments thus symbolically express and reinforce attitudes toward the specific action, the specific agent, the general type of action, and the general type of agent. Not only do we know "how to do things with words," as Austin told us, but also "how to say things with actions." Many actions have the function of commending the same sort of action to others, and this is especially true of actions we bring under the rubric of desert. Therefore, to approve of a person for an action is to commend that person to others, and the exact way we express our approval does a great deal to determine just how and how much we commend the person of whom we approve.

If an action does not represent the values we thought at first, we change our minds about the approval to be accorded. Thus, when we learn that John brought cotton and bandages primarily for the sake of approval, we conclude that he does not represent the values we normally wish to affirm and commend when a wounded man is given aid. For John either does not affirm those values in his action at all, or affirms them only in subordination to the values of receiving approval. And--to get to the heart of the matter--receiving approval, honor, gratitude and other basic deserts are rarely values that stand in need of commendation; rather, it is by virtue of approval and other basic deserts that we commend values that come less naturally. Hence, not only do we withhold from John the approval usual to someone who brings cotton and bandages to a wounded man, but we may not respond with approval at all; for it is not the function of approval to commend approval-seeking.

Deserts are bestowed as communicative behavior meant to commend the values exhibited by persons and actions, and as such they are crucial to the daily sustaining of a community's ethos. But approval-seeking is commended only at the peril of that ethos, and the same is true in general of the exclusive pursuit and avoidance of favorable and unfavorable deserts. People must have regard for them, to be sure, for if they did not, then deserts would lose their power to encourage the values they involve. Yet if deserts alone are regarded, then their purpose also fails; for just as the person who has no regard for the approval or disapproval of his fellow human beings subverts the mutual affirmation of values, so also does the person who is concerned only with their approval or disapproval. A society comprised entirely of either type of person would collapse. Although neither type of person is parasitic in the sense that he denies to his community actions in keeping with its values, still, neither type performs those actions in affirmation of the values of the community; and in that sense both get along by feeding off others' efforts to encourage and sustain the ethical life of the community.

It is extremely difficult and frustrating to deal with an approval-seeker. We cannot give him the full approval that he seeks--this would be unjust--and yet we are forced to admit that what he did (e.g., bring cotton and bandages) was the right thing to do. Striving earnestly for approval, approval-seekers find their efforts strangely, unaccountably unsuccessful, for what they seek by means of desert is denied to them on grounds of desert.

Suppose, then, that John asks, "Why don't you approve of my helping a wounded man?" What are we to say? No doubt we will try, in one way or another, to get across the points I have developed here; for they are common, if not conscious, knowledge. But whatever we say comes down to a paradoxical injunction: "If you want that kind of approval, you will have to give up seeking it--for only non-approval-seeking behavior receives that kind of approval." John may well be confounded when he hears this, and may even conclude that we are irrational. For if he seeks approval, he will not receive it; and if he avoids it in order to receive it, then he is seeking it after all. His only alternative is to give up seeking approval as his principal objective in acting.

It should be noted here that neither John nor ourselves are at fault for the double bind in which he finds himself. For example, if he is a child, adolescent, student, apprentice, or any other person undergoing a process of initiation or adaptation, then the bind is not entirely of his own making; his situation calls for it. And, in that situation with him, we want him to find, after awhile, a balance between total independence of our approval and excessive dependence upon it. He, for his part, wants clarification from us that tells where our approval will fall--clarification which he will receive only as advice on how to be a better approval-seeker.

This form of double bind is familiar not only to parents, teachers, and employers who sometimes struggle to avoid framing their directives as a "Be independent" paradox, but also to children, students, and employees who must puzzle over the meaning of such exhortations when they do occur. Independence and spontaneity binds are a problem in any form of learning in which independence, spontaneity, creativity, or innovation has a central place. If an ethics places emphasis on individual responsibility, in the sense that the behavior "cannot be traced back to starting points other than in ourselves," then education into that ethic will often give rise to binds similar to the one that John experienced. In moral education and maturation of this kind, dependence and independence are a special problem, for neither total dependence nor total independence of deserved treatments bestowed by others is the appropriate stance; the correct attitude effects a balance between the two, delicate at first, then habituated firmly as its viability continues.

The paradox of approval-seeking and the transition it marks is related to other, similar ethical paradoxes: transitions from egoism to altruism, from material to spiritual values, from heteronomy to autonomy, from self-love to the love of God. In each case, the individual in state B is encouraged to move on to the higher state, A. In B the priorities hold that a-type activities are subordinate to b-type activities, such that a-type activities are undertaken for the sake of b-type activities, but never conversely. In A, by contrast, the priorities hold that b-type activities are always subordinate to a-type. Hence the problem: what motivation could not only appeal to an individual in B but also lead that individual to A? For in B one can say, "Do a for the sake of b," but that will only be one more case of activity in B; and in A one can propose, "Do b for the sake of a," but since the individual is not yet in A, our appeal will fall on deaf ears. This is the structure of Aquinas's paradox of transformation.[7]

III

Just as the structure of desert was taken up analogically in Aquinas's system, so likewise with the structure and problematic of the paradox of approval-seeking. Eternal reward occupied the same position in Aquinas's ethics as approval in the discussion above.

Thomas avoided the falsidical form of the paradox of approval-seeking by distinguishing ultimate end from eternal reward, then by distinguishing the powers for which these were the objects (<u>obiecta</u>). In this way, Aquinas showed that it was logically possible for a person to aim for the vision of God without lapsing into reward-seeking. With this problem removed, Aquinas then tried to show how God could graciously intervene to loosen the bind. Powers were specified by their acts, and acts by their objects. Thus, as objects intended by the will, the activity of the beatific vision could be distinguished from ' the enjoyment that occurred in that activity. This distinction followed Aristotle's distinction between the activity of contemplation and the pleasure concomitant to it. Since highest happiness was the contemplation of the divine essence, Aristotle's distinction could be extended to it. The beatific vision was an end, therefore, in its aspect as an <u>operatio</u>, or activity; it involved a reward, on the other hand, in its aspect as <u>delectatio</u>, the enjoyment of the activity that accompanied the vision itself.

Aquinas distinguished these aspects as actuations of distinct powers, intellect and will. The ultimate end could not be an act of the will, since an act of the will was by nature purposive, inherently for-the-sake-of something else. As such, it could never be ultimate in the intention of the will. Rather, the ultimate end was an act of the intellect, the contemplative activity of seeing God face-to-face. This activity of the intellect, the operatio, was the end proper, while its side-effect was the passivity of the will--the fruitio of repose in the highest good. End and reward were thereby distinguished in object and potency:

> When a reward is given to someone the will of the one rewarded is at rest, and this is what delight is. Delight is therefore included in the very notion of a reward given.[8]

Thomas pointed out that although the will derived delight from the highest good, it did not desire that good simply for the sake of delight. The will of the individual who enjoyed the divine essence was informed by the habitus of charity; and

> Charity does not seek the good for the sake of delight; that it delights in the good it gains is correlative for charity.[9]

Thus, Aquinas had a ready and subtle solution to the paradox of approval-seeking, an answer that was consistent with the tradition and drew upon Aristotle's conception of happiness. The principal intention of the will, then, was the contemplative activity of the vision; its secondary and admissible interest lay in the reward of enjoying that vision. In effect, a clear-headed person in a state of charity might say, "Above all, I want to know God, but I look forward also to the joy of doing so." A person either less clear-headed or in a state of mortal sin might say, "Above all, I want the pleasure of the beatific vision, but I am also interested in contemplating the divine essence."

It is worth noting also that Aquinas provided a solution to the parallel paradox of "disapproval-avoiding." That is, the fear of God was a proper disposition or act of the will, but it too needed to be rightly ordered to the ultimate end. The correct fear of God was filial fear, the fear of being deprived of the Father's presence. Filial fear was informed by charity. Servile fear, on the other hand, though better than no fear at all, was a lower act or habit, the fear of being eternally punished by the Ruler. Servile fear was motivated by self-love. Thus, in the attraction and fascination that God stimulated, and in the awe and submissiveness that were his due, it was crucial that love of God take precedence over love of self. Paradoxes of reward-seeking and punishment-avoiding, therefore, were resolved accordingly. End and reward were distinguished, and corresponding distinctions were drawn in the powers of the soul or the acts of those powers. The principal object of the will was conceptually separated from the desert that accrued for that inclination or movement of the will.

These distinctions, however, only showed that the paradoxes were veridical;

they did not and could not guarantee that each believer would see this. A double bind remained, in the form of the first precept of charity: "Thou shalt love the Lord thy God with all thy heart, and all thy soul, and all thy mind." Failure to fulfill the precept resulted in the loss of eternal happiness. Yet love on command, although not impossible, was difficult; and when the command was backed by eternal punishment, love might well be blocked entirely for many believers. As one critic has posed the objection:

> [N]ote the addition--"with all thy heart, and all thy soul, and all thy mind." How can such a commandment be obeyed? The addition implies that it is not enough to think and act as if I loved God. I am not asked to pretend that I love. I am asked really to mean it, to be completely sincere. Jesus' whole condemnation of the Parisees [sic] was that they obeyed the law of God insincerely--with their lips and hands, but not with their hearts. But if the heart is the controller, how is it to convert itself? If I am to love sincerely, I must love with my whole being, with unhindered spontaneity. But this amounts to saying that I must be spontaneous, and controlled or willed spontaneity is a contradiction!^{10}

This statement of the objection is valuable, for it leads us to ask, "Did Aquinas think that controlled spontaneity was a contradiction in terms or falsidical paradox?" The answer is "no," as we will see in detail in the next chapter.

Aquinas was aware of the problem under this description:

> Further, charity, which is "poured forth in our hearts by the Holy Ghost" (Rom. 5:5), makes us free, since "where the Spirit of the Lord is, there is liberty (II Cor. 3:17). Now the obligation that arises from a precept is opposed to liberty, since it imposes a necessity. Therefore no precept should be given about charity.^{11}

But in his answer he seems unwilling to admit its full force:

> The obligation of a precept is not opposed to liberty, except in the one whose mind is averted from that which is prescribed, as may be seen in those who keep the precepts through fear alone. But the precept of love cannot be fulfilled save of one's own will, wherefore it is not opposed to charity.^{12}

It seems the precept was only opposed to the liberty of those who needed it. Unfortunately, they could not respond to it; in effect, they were in state B. Their previous sins had warped their perspective; it was something else they heard. Happily, it spoke clearly to those who already fulfilled it, for they were in state A. But what use was it to them? Would it not, if anything, have backfired, much as when we become irritated and stubborn toward those who tell us to do something we are already busy doing?

For one group, then, the precept seems to have been impossible; for the other, irrelevant. Yet one can ask whether this entrapment of the individual was conducive to his learning that there was one very narrow path to salvation. Perhaps, with this bind and others, the norms enjoining interior acts defined the human condition, not as an untenable situation, but as all but untenable. How, then, might the precept of charity function to direct the individual through the strait gate to the vision of God?

For those not yet in a state of charity, the commandment, "Thou shalt love the Lord thy God...," was backed by eternal punishment. Aggravating and pathogenic though it must have been for some, its beneficial reverse side was also there to be seen. Indeed, in Aquinas's view, by the time the full force of the injunction frightened the mortal sinner, God had already acted graciously in his behalf. The sinner, knowing this, had reason to hope, not to despair. As he said of the acts of penance--"whereby we cooperate with God operating"--

> the first principle...is the operation of God in turning the heart, according to Lament. 5:21: "Convert us, O Lord, to you, and we shall be converted"; the second, an act of faith; the third, a movement of servile fear, whereby a man is withdrawn from sin through fear of punishment; the fourth, a movement of hope, whereby a man makes a purpose of amendment, in hope of obtaining pardon....[13]

On this view, God was there, with the sinner, already showing his concern by bringing the sinner to an excruciating awareness of his condition. Servile fear was the unavoidable trauma of spiritual rebirth.

This pattern held throughout the conversions and convalescences of the will. If the sinner accepted responsibility for his condition, then he therefore had reason for hope, because his admission showed that God had drawn attention to his condition. The impetus to self-scrutiny that this perspective provided, especially as backed by the authoritative direction of the confessor, was extremely powerful. To see the bind as a context-marker for a rite of transition was already one step out of the fear conditioned by it. Moreover, this interpretation of the bind also provided considerable motivation to independent initiative on the sinner's part: it denied that such an initiative was entirely independent; if correct, it was moved and therefore sanctioned by divine grace. From the first interpretation of his servile fear, then, the individual could begin to move, actively and rapidly, out of the bind and toward his perfection in the vision of God.

Of course, a brief scare could only provide a temporary and superficial spiritual benefit. Yet fear did not end when charity was infused:

> ...the fifth, a movement of charity, whereby sin is displeasing to man for its own sake, and no longer for the sake of punishment; the sixth, a movement of filial fear whereby a man, of his own accord, offers to make amends to God through fear of him.[14]

The individual was never encouraged to stop fearing God. His fear was not terminated but trapped, transformed, then channelled into further spiritual activity and growth. The belief that the individual was moving increasingly away from the enclosing fear was matched by the knowledge that it could again close around him, as soon as he presumed upon his friendship with God. Movement toward the ultimate end, then, was always impelled also by a movement away from eternal punishment. A stage of spiritual "bottoming out" could result in an upward rebound toward God; the continuing element of fear would sustain the tension of the bind and the forward movement out and away from it. "Love me or I will damn you" was drastic treatment for a desperate condition. Its justification lay both in what it could save the sinner from and in what it could save him for.

But what of the individual who was already in a state of charity? His spiritual health seemed to make the precept otiose or worse. One friend did not order another to be friendly to him; a lover did not say to his beloved, "Keep loving me--or else!" Directives such as these occur when a relationship is in trouble, and might even generate trouble in a relationship that is otherwise sound. What place could they have, then, in temporal friendship with God?

Aquinas's answer to this question followed from his belief that the temporal friendship between the individual and God was inherently fragile. Spiritual progress could quickly give way to pride, then to active sin. This was one of his reasons for seeing filial fear as a proper effect of charity. By implicitly calling into question the friendship between the individual and God, therefore, the temporal instability of that friendship was underscored. Moreover, the individual in a state of charity had to increase in grace; any resting on spiritual laurels was presumption.

As mentioned earlier, this feature of the first precept of charity appears also in Thomas's discussion of vows. Thomas had little use for supererogation. It was better, in his view, for the individual to commit himself to an extraordinary practice beforehand than it was for him to do it without prior commitment. Surely there were risks in this position: in breaking a vow the failure was more serious than if no vow had been involved; and efforts to rationalize the failure would lead quite directly to contempt of God, and therefore to mortal sin. But the possible benefit of increased subjection to God overrode this consideration, and Aquinas in this instance, as always, preferred a clear commitment to a murky one, presumably because spiritual health required such clarity.

Aquinas saw spiritual progress as an increase in willing subjection, the goal of which was the complete humility of loving obedience, "with all thy heart, and all thy soul, and all thy mind." For action to be meritorious, therefore, it had to combine the obedience of subjection with the freedom of love. Hence he wrote,

> Among the moral virtues, the greater the thing which a man contemns that he may adhere to God, the greater the virtue. Now there are three kinds of human goods that man may contemn for God's sake. The lowest of these are external goods, the goods of the body take the middle place, and the highest are the goods of the soul;

and among these the chief, in a way, is the will, in so far as by his will man makes use of all other goods. Therefore, properly speaking, the virtue of obedience, whereby we contemn our own will for God's sake, is more praiseworthy than the other moral virtues, which contemn other goods for the sake of God.

Hence Gregory says (Moral. 35) that "obedience is rightly preferred to sacrifices, because by sacrifices another's body is slain, whereas by obedience we slay our own will." Wherefore even any other acts of virtue are meritorious before God through being performed out of obedience to God's will. For were one to suffer even martyrdom, or to give all one's goods to the poor, unless one directed these things to the fulfillment of the divine will, which pertains directly to obedience, they could not be meritorious: as neither would they be if they were done without charity, which cannot exist apart from obedience. For it is written (I John 2:4-5): "He who says that he knows God, and does not keep his commandments, is a liar...but he that keeps his word, in him in very deed the charity of God is perfected": and this because friends have the same likes and dislikes.[15]

Obedience was to issue from love and love from obedience. In Aquinas's view this was neither a vicious circle nor a vicious regress; ultimately, as Augustine had said, it rested on the divine will both to "grant what you command, and [to] command what you will."[16]

Nevertheless, this discipline of the spirit seems extremely demanding. Aquinas certainly thought so: God asked nothing less than perfection for and from his children. But Thomas believed also that the means God employed were proportionate to the end and necessary to it. And, as he saw it, there was neither contradiction in the norm of loving obedience, nor any demand in it that was incommensurate with the will. The will was at once spontaneous and controlled, and therefore capable of spontaneous control and controlled spontaneity in all its actuations.

Aquinas recognized, then, that charity was a unique and stringent demand: at once "the end of the law" and yet subject to it; at once the mode of the virtues and yet a virtue in its own right; at once a sacrifice by the will and a sacrifice of it.[17] Neither aspect of paradox gave way in the present life. Love and obedience remained in dialectical tension and alternation: now love informing obedience, now obedience informing love. Legality alone was insufficient, but so was undisciplined love of God. To advance spiritually, the individual had to submit his will to God again and again, ever narrowing the range and violence of the oscillations between control and spontaneity, obedience and love. In this perfectionist ethic, the soul on its journey could find comfort, not in the belief that "If I try, God will help," but in the belief that "If I try, God has helped."

IV

Fitness for salvation was only half the picture; fitness for damnation, the debt of eternal punishment, was the other possibility. There was no difficulty in this regard in distinguishing end and love from desert; the problem was rather to show that and how they were related. According to Aquinas, no one aimed at damnation, and anyone who thought he did was mistaken. The object of the will was an end, and an end was always a good; one's own damnation was an evil. Moreover, punishment was suffering, and no one suffered voluntarily.[18] Thus, whereas attaining the vision of God was never inadvertent and enjoying it never involuntary, ending in eternal punishment was always both. As Aquinas put it,

> Now it is evident that punishment is outside the intention of the sinner, wherefore it is accidentally referred to sin on the part of the sinner. Nevertheless it is referred to sin by an extrinsic principle, viz. the justice of the judge, who imposes various punishments according to the various manners of sin.[19]

In other respects, fitness for damnation was parallel to fitness for salvation, and was largely derivative in conception. An individual was fit for damnation because he was not fit for salvation. And, although the converse was also true--an individual was unfit to be saved because he was fit to be damned--it follows Aquinas's position more closely to say that damnation, an evil, was a privation of the good of salvation. For this reason, it seems, Aquinas characterized eternal punishment as principally derivative, an absence of the supreme good.

But surely more was involved in desert of eternal punishment than failure to merit eternal reward. Today, for example, capital punishment is not warranted by nondesert of good citizenship awards; indeed, few favorable and unfavorable deserts can be paired in a disjunctive, either/or polarity. Yet Aquinas's soteriology posed salvation and damnation as ultimate, either/or alternatives corresponding to the state of charity and mortal sin in the soul, and he maintained that this great divide was mediated by God's justice. If eternal punishment were only the loss of the beatific vision, the polarity might be sustained without further argument; but Aquinas believed that punishment involved the addition of hard treatment as well as the subtraction of the divine presence.

Moreover, just as the blessed were differentiated in reward according to their degrees of charity, the damned too had to be treated proportionately. As Dante later observed, the lovers Paolo and Francesca did not deserve the same treatment as Judas Iscariot. Lovers and traitors were not distinguished by, but rather shared, the fact that they were deprived of the vision of the Deity. For this reason too, then, some further features of punishment had to be involved if the justice of eternal punishment was to be evident.

Finally, there was the further objection that "the nature of punishment is to be against the will."[20] But in Thomas's view, a hardened mortal sinner had very little desire for God, and therefore the penalty of loss (poena damni) would be of little or no frustration to the will. To be sure, like everyone else, the sinner desired his own happiness, and his happiness--did he but know it--was the vision of God. But the will of the mortal sinner was so profoundly disordered that even his natural orientation to the good in general was corrupted. Only a vague sense of frustration, therefore, would remain, similar to the restless seeking and anxiety that he experienced during his time on earth. Indeed, it even seems that the individual who had tried to remain in a state of charity and failed would experience the loss of God more painfully than one who had never tried at all.

Each of these problems had to be resolved if Aquinas was to coordinate teleology and justice successfully. As noted above, Thomas's conception of reward and punishment was governed by his notion that the universal order operated according to a kind of economy. He therefore wrote,

> It has passed from natural things to human affairs that whenever one thing rises up against another, it suffers some detriment therefrom. For we observe in natural things that when one contrary supervenes, the other acts with greater energy, for which reason "hot water freezes more rapidly," as stated in Meteor. 1:12. Wherefore we find that the natural inclination of man is to repress those who rise up against him. Now it is evident that all things contained in an order are, in a manner, one, in relation to the principle of that order. Consequently, whatever rises up against an order is put down by that order or by the principle thereof. And because sin is an inordinate act, it is evident that whoever sins, commits an offense against an order: wherefore he is put down, in consequence, by that same order, which repression is punishment.[21]

Punishment, then, was a particular mode of the repression of activities that violated their proper order. The only difference between human beings and other creatures was the element of voluntariness in human behavior. A human individual, by his use or abuse of means-end reasoning, exceeded his proper order voluntarily, and therefore suffered a commensurate repression of his will in punishment. Retributive punishment, therefore, was the human counterpart of the forms God had built into every creature, even into inanimate elements such as water. The rational creature was provident for itself, and thereby could place itself in a bad relation to the economy of divine providence.

Punishment, then, was an instance of the tendency of everything and every order to preserve itself. And since every order included an inclination to its end, anything that worked against the perfection of an order worked also against the preservation of it. In this principle lay the metaphysical basis of the either/or disjunction of salvation and damnation as possession and loss of God.

If an individual did not work toward the perfection or realization of the end to which God has ordered the human species, he violated the divine order, which then reacted against him. Because the perfection of the human species required the infused virtue of charity, to work against charity was to incur loss of the end:

> As stated above, sin incurs a debt of punishment through disturbing an order. But the effect remains so long as the cause remains. Wherefore so long as the disturbance of the order remains, the debt of punishment must needs remain also. Now disturbance of an order is sometimes reparable, sometimes irreparable: because a defect which destroys the principle is irreparable, whereas if the principle be saved, defects can be repaired by virtue of that principle. For instance, if the principle of sight be destroyed, sight cannot be restored except by divine power; whereas, if the principle of sight be preserved, while there arise certain impediments to the use of sight, these can be remedied by nature or by art. Now in every order there is a principle whereby one takes part in that order. Consequently if a sin destroys a principle of the order whereby man's will is subject to God, the disorder will be such as to be, considered in itself, irreparable, although it is possible to repair it by the power of God. Now the principle of this order is the last end, to which man adheres by charity. Therefore whatever sins turn man away from God, so as to destroy charity, considered in themselves, incur a debt of eternal punishment.[22]

Because one act of mortal sin destroyed charity, it damaged the individual's connection to the ultimate end in a way that only God could repair.

The loss of charity explained the loss of the beatific vision, but it went no further; it specified no differentiating treatment for different sinners. The completion of the account of eternal punishment came from another direction of reflection. Mortal sin was an act in contemptu dei, in contempt of God. That is, God was contemned for the sake of something else, something lower. Again, the object of the will was an end and good--and therefore the will could not simply reject a good arbitrarily; it had to reject it in favor of another good which it held in higher esteem. Thus, the mortal sin of acting in aversion to God necessarily involved the attachment to a lower good. To indicate the gravity of this violation of the hierarchy of being and goodness, Aquinas stipulated a second aspect of eternal punishment, the pain of sense (poena sensus):

> Punishment is proportionate to sin. Now sin comprises two things. First, there is the turning away from the immutable good, which is infinite; wherefore, in this respect, sin is infinite. Secondly, there is the inordinate turning to mutable good. In this respect sin is finite, both because the mutable good itself is finite, and because the

movement of turning towards it is finite, since the acts of a creature cannot be infinite. Accordingly, in so far as sin consists in turning away from something, its corresponding punishment is "pain of loss," which is also infinite, because it is the loss of the infinite good, i.e., God. But in so far as sin turns inordinately to something, its corresponding punishment is the "pain of sense," which is also finite.[23]

In this passage Aquinas discussed the individual's fitness for eternal punishment in abstract terms; he seems to have planned a more detailed discussion for the Third Part of the Summa Theologiae.

In the Summa Contra Gentiles, however, he had said,

Those who sin against God are not only to be punished by their exclusion from perpetual happiness, but also by the experience of something painful. Punishment should proportionally correspond to the fault, as we have said above. In the fault, however, the mind is not only turned away from the ultimate end, but is also improperly turned toward other things as ends. So, the sinner is not only to be punished by being excluded from his end, but also by feeling injury from other things.[24]

The pain of loss, then, was simply the nondesert of infinite reward; the pain of sense, on the other hand, was not infinite but finite, a desert of punishment. Thomas described the fitness or proportion of the latter as a strict contrapassum:

For the sin of every rational creature grows out of this: it is not subject to God in obedience. Punishment, of course, should answer to fault proportionally, with this result: that in its punishment the will suffer an affliction which is the contrary of that for whose love it sinned. Therefore a befitting punishment to a sinning rational nature is this: to be subject somehow to the bondage of things which are its own inferiors, namely, bodily things.

Again, the sin committed against God deserves not only the punishment of loss, but the punishment of sense, as we showed in Book III, for the punishment of sense answers to the fault in regard to the soul's disordered turning toward a changeable good, as the punishment of loss answers to the fault in regard to its turning away from the unchangeable good. But the rational creature, and especially the human soul, sins by its disordered turning to bodily things. Therefore, its becoming punishment is affliction by bodily things.[25]

Here, then, was the desert propriety that established the positive correlation between sin and deserved punishment. In the penalty of sense, the relationship between sin and punishment was given for a pattern and logic distinct from simple unfitness for God; this logic was finite and could therefore provide the basis of differential treatment of sinners; and it showed how the individual who tried but failed to attain salvation did indeed fare better than his more irresponsible counterpart.

NOTES

[1]S.T., I-II, 114, a. 1.

[2]Eric D'Arcy, "'Worthy of Worship': A Catholic Contribution."

[3]S.T., I-II, 114, a. 1.

[4]Joel Feinberg, "Justice and Personal Desert," in his Doing and Deserving: Essays in the Theory of Responsibility (Princeton: Princeton University Press, 1970), p. 85.

[5]S.T., II-II, 23, a. 1 ad 1.

[6]S.T., II-II, 103, a. 1. Cf. Feinberg, Doing and Deserving, Chapter 5, and C. L. Stevenson, Ethics and Language (New York: Yale University Press, 1948).

[7]Of course, there is at least one more alternative, although it may not be easy for the teacher or learner to use, and that is for the preoccupation with motivation to be set aside, and for a-type and b-type activities to be undertaken for their own sake. This will be tantamount to a liminal moratorium on moral and spiritual autonomy. In effect, a rule-deontological ethic is introduced, instilled during the period of immediate direction, until the individual emerges in A. But this is A with a difference, for the priorities with which he acts never become a matter of interior wheel-spinning, but are left at the level of unconscious habit.

For some traditions, and for some individuals, to set aside the preoccupation with motivation is to set aside the spiritual life. Yet a de facto deontology emphasizing action can be established even in these cases by turning the language of motivation against itself in paradox. This is easily done, for example, with the metaphors of path, way, journey, pilgrimage, and the like, so that the way comes to be valued over the destination, and each step comes to be taken for its own sake.

[8]S.T., I-II, 4, a. 1 ad 1.

[9]S.T., I-II, 4, a. 2 ad 3.

[10]Alan Watts, "Zen and Control," in his This Is It! (New York: Random, 1972). Compare Kant:

> [The command, "Love God above all and thy neighbor as thyself"] requires respect for a law which orders love and does not leave it to arbitrary choice to make love the principle. But love to God as inclination (pathological love) is impossible, for He is not an object of the senses. The latter is indeed possible toward men, but it cannot be commanded, for it is not possible for man to love someone merely on command. It is, therefore, only practical love which can be

understood in that kernel of all laws. To love God means in this sense to like to do His commandments, and to love one's neighbor means to like to practice duties toward him. The command which makes this a rule cannot require that we have this disposition but only that we endeavor after it. To command that one do something gladly is self-contradictory. For a law would not be needed if we already knew of ourselves what we ought to do and moreover were conscious of liking to do it; and if we did it without liking but only out of respect for the law, a command which makes just this respect the incentive of the maxim would counteract the disposition it commands. That law of all laws, like every moral prescription of the Gospel, thus presents the moral disposition in its complete perfection, and though as an ideal of holiness it is unattainable by any creature, it is yet an archetype which we would strive to approach and to imitate in an uninterrupted infinite progress. Immanuel Kant, Critique of Practical Reason, trans. Lewis White Beck (New York: Bobbs-Merrill, 1956), pp. 85-86.

[11] S.T., II-II, 44, a. 1 obj. 2.
[12] S.T., II-II, 44, a. 1 ad 2.
[13] S.T., III, 85, a. 5.
[14] Ibid.
[15] S.T., II-II, 104, a. 3.
[16] Augustine, Confessions, pp. 255-256.
[17] S.T., II-II, 44, a. 1.
[18] S.T., I-II, 6, a. 5.
[19] S.T., I-II, 72, a. 5.
[20] S.T., I-II, 87, a. 6.
[21] S.T., I-II, 87, a. 1.
[22] S.T., I-II, 87, a. 3.
[23] S.T., I-II, 87, a. 4.
[24] S.C.G., III, 145, a. 1.
[25] S.C.G., IV, 90, a. 5.

CHAPTER 5
ACTION

I

As noted in Chapter 1, the notion of a hierarchy of being was one of the controlling ideas in Aquinas's system. Like teleology, justice, and charity, its implications were evident not only in the broad outlines of his synthesis but in his treatment of specifics as well. In his theory of will and action, hierarchy played a decisive role: Aquinas held that what was more powerful was higher, and that what was higher was more inward and hidden; accordingly, the center of personal power and control was located in the inner life of the individual.

Although the sources of this view can be traced to motifs in the New Testament, in Augustine, and in Pseudo-Dionysius, Aquinas's emphasis on hierarchy is perhaps best revealed in his commentary on the Nicomachean Ethics.

Aristotle appeared congenial to the inward turn when he said, "choice...is a better criterion for judging character than actions are." Thomas offered a rationale:

> [The appropriateness of discussing choice] is clearly shown by the fact that although both inner choice and outward action flow from the habit of virtue, virtuous or vicious practices are judged rather by choice than by outward works. Every virtuous man chooses good but sometimes he does not do it because of some external hindrances. On the other hand, the vicious man sometimes performs a virtuous deed not out of virtuous choice but out of fear or some unbecoming motive, for instance, vainglory or something else of this kind. Hence it obviously pertains to our present purpose to consider choice.[1]

Here, although he introduces the language of inner and outer, Aquinas has added little to Aristotle's own introvert predilections. "Inner choice" clearly refers to something one person could judge from the behavior of another. Perhaps Aquinas has placed a slightly greater accent on the difficulty of making such judgments, but that is all.

In another passage, however, instead of underlining the introvert character of Aristotle's position, Aquinas tried to explain the importance of inwardness in terms of power or control (potestas). Grosseteste's translation may be read as follows:

> If these things seem to be the case, and we cannot reduce them to principles other than those in us, whose principles, in turn, are also in us, then they are both in us and voluntary.[2]

Thomas expanded on this in his commentary:

> He says first that if these things, that is deliberation, choice, and willing--which are in our power--are seen as principles of our operations and we cannot reduce our operations to principles other than those that are in our power (i.e., deliberation and choice) it follows that our good and bad operations are within our power. Because their principles are in our power, they themselves are in our power and are voluntary.[3]

Both Grosseteste's text and Thomas's interpretation of it went beyond what Aristotle had said. In Ostwald's rendering,

> [I]f our conclusions are accepted, and if we cannot trace back our actions to starting points other than those within ourselves, then all actions in which the initiative lies in ourselves are in our power and are voluntary actions.[4]

Where Aristotle had said that actions were in our power because their starting points are in us, the Grosseteste version said that the principles or starting points (ἀρχαί, principia) must be in us and have their own starting points in us as well.[5] Aquinas explained this by saying that the point of emphasizing inwardness was that events interior to the self were more fully controlled by it. And control was not exercised by just anything "in us"; it was exercised by the principles of deliberation and choice--principles we control, and by virtue of which we control other principles of action and external events as well.

This passage is not unique. Throughout the commentary on the Nicomachean Ethics, Aquinas fastened upon and stressed the passages in which Aristotle had leaned toward a more strongly rational, deliberative conception of voluntariness. When he read Aristotle saying that "the actions that men do according to reason seem to be their own in the most proper sense, and to be voluntary," Aquinas underlined the importance of the remark by drawing a contrast to the lower powers:

> He observes that men's reasoned actions seem to be theirs in the most proper sense and to be done voluntarily. What a man does because of concupiscence or anger he does not seem to do by his own will but under the direction of an external impulse. It is evident that a man is in a particular fashion what conforms to his intellect and reason.[6]

In this reading, Aquinas did not force the interpretation, nor was he encumbered by a misleading Latin version; the text of the Ethics really does suggest that deliberated, chosen actions are more truly representative both of man in general and of individual character in particular than those that do not involve reason.

Aquinas merely used this position to gloss the passage on the internal origination of action.

But Aristotle had not denied full voluntariness to actions done in anger or from desire, even though they did not provide criteria for judging character that were as strong as choice and the actions that proceed from it. With passages such as the one just cited, Thomas did not see how full voluntariness could be attributed to such actions unless the distinctively human powers of intellect and will were somehow involved. He therefore faced an important hard case for his interpretation when he found Aristotle saying,

> Further, what difference is there from the viewpoint of involuntariness between sins committed after reflection and sins committed on account of anger? It is our duty to avoid both. The irrational passions seem to be no less human. So too then are the actions of man proceeding from anger and sensual desire. It is unreasonable, therefore, to regard these as involuntary.[7]

Here the internal principia of action were not deliberation and choice, but passion and appetite. Thomas had to find some way to make this passage jibe with his interpretation of the summary statement on internal principles; the higher powers had to have some role if such actions were to be counted human and voluntary.

His solution had important ramifications for his own theory of responsibility. In cases of anger or desire, he said, deliberation and choice were present in a sense, for they were conspicuous by their absence. This absence in such cases was an interior omission of the intellect or will to control the lower powers:

> But as sins that are committed after reflection, that is with deliberation, are to be avoided and are blameworthy, so also sins that are committed on account of anger or another passion. A man can, by means of his will, resist passion. Hence if he does a disgraceful act because of passion, he is blamed. Therefore, they do not differ from things done by deliberation so far as they are voluntary.[8]

He continues in the same vein:

> Irrational passions, i.e., of the sensitive appetitive faculty can obey reason, as was stated before. Therefore, the actions proceeding from anger, sensual desire, and the other passions are human, for neither praise nor blame are imputed to a man who acts involuntarily. Therefore, it is unreasonable to say that things done out of passion are involuntary.[9]

This solution indicates the importance of the interior hierarchy of the soul's powers in shaping Thomas's introvert conception of responsibility. A close comparison brings out the difference between the two thinkers. Aristotle's reasoning was as follows:

1. An action that proceeds from passion or appetite is an action that proceeds from a part of the person.

2. An action that proceeds from a part of a person is an action of the person (i.e., a voluntary action).

3. Therefore, an action that proceeds from passion or appetite is an action of the person (i.e., a voluntary action).

In Aquinas's reasoning, however, there were additional steps, both explicit and implicit:

1. An action that proceeds from passion or appetite is an action that proceeds from a lower power.

2. An action that proceeds from a lower power could have been controlled by a higher power.

3. An action that could have been controlled by a higher power may be ascribed to that power as its action, since the occurrence of the action is a consequence of the higher power's omission to exercise control.

4. An action that proceeds from a higher power by action or omission proceeds from a part of a person.

5. An action that proceeds from a part of a person is an action of the person (i.e., a voluntary action).

6. Therefore, an action that proceeds from passion or appetite is an action of a person (i.e., a voluntary action).

In the passages previously cited, therefore, a hierarchical conception of power, a concept of man as distinguished by rationality, and an emphasis on interior acts of self-control emerge as general features of voluntary action in Aquinas's interpretation of Aristotle. This notion of voluntariness found its complement in the idea of interior omissions: cases in which the higher, rational, and more inward powers did not control the lower powers in their charge.

II

Thomas's strong emphases on a hierarchy of power, on the role of rationality, and on the importance of interior acts and omissions carried over into his discussion of responsibility in the <u>Summa Theologiae</u>. Indeed, the first three articles in the treatise on human acts explain how the principles of action are internal to man, specify those principles as higher and more reflexive than the corresponding principles in animals, and foreshadow the importance of interior omissions in his theory of sin. Thus, there was a complex congruence between hierarchy, rational self-control, and inwardness in Aquinas's theory of responsibility. Thomas seems to have thought that this congruence was crucial to the strategic role of interior acts in his religious ethics, but believed also that it did not jeopardize the value of his analysis for the external, public ethics of human interaction. He saw no reason why a theory of responsibility should not have an inner as well as an outer face.

The relevance of hierarchy to Aquinas's theory has been mentioned briefly in previous chapters. The individual's fitness for salvation depended upon his mode of subjection to God, and his mode of subjection to God, in turn, depended upon the condition of his soul. Yet I use "condition of the soul" here merely as a shorthand expression for the actuation of the soul's powers at a given time, and these powers were moved to actuation either by themselves or by powers higher on the ladder of being. God and the soul could move the soul, therefore, and the soul could move the body, but the body could not directly move the soul: "The higher power is not directly moved by the lower."[10]

As indicated by the concept of interior omissions, the soul not only held a position on the hierarchy, but was itself hierarchical in structure. The powers of the soul were differentiated by their functions, and, since differentiation gave rise to inequality, there was therefore a hierarchy of control in the interaction of the soul's powers. Just as the soul had sovereignty over the body, so the higher powers of reason and rational appetite had sovereignty over the irascible and concupiscible powers.

Within the chain of being, higher beings moved or controlled themselves first, and affected lower beings only by consequence. For Aquinas, any mode of self-movement beyond the level of instinctual response involved the rational capacity to grasp "the meaning of an end and of a means to an end, and the relationship of one with reference to the other."[11] Accordingly, gradations of power and rational activity were correlated in the upper echelons of the hierarchy.

But the upper links of the chain of being did not merely represent a ranked correlation of power and intelligence. The hierarchy was also one of hiddenness. To Thomas, what was higher was more important, but was not more accessible to understanding on that account. On the contrary, the higher anything was on the scale of being, the more problematic and indirect was human knowledge of it. Higher beings such as God and the angels, for example, were more intelligible in themselves, but less well-known to man than ordinary objects of food or clothing. People were most familiar with what they learned from their senses, but their senses were not proportionate in power to the knowledge of intelligibilia. Complex intellectual operations or revelation from God were needed if the higher things were to become known to a rational animal.

The same correlation between "high" and "hidden" held for the higher powers in man. Thus, human thoughts and volitions were indirectly known to third-person observers, who might reach judgments only on the basis of what the individual audibly or visibly said or did. "[M]an is not competent to judge of interior movements, which are hidden, but only of exterior acts, which are manifest."[12] Thomas's reasons for this view stemmed from a variety of sources, but the most comprehensive principle in support of it was the notion of a hierarchy of being. As man was made in the image of God, and the acts of his essence therefore resembled faintly the acts of the higher essence, so his acts, like God's, were known only by problematic inferences from visible effects. And, as we shall see, just as language based on divine effects was adapted analogically to allow talk about the inner life of God, so language based on human effects was adapted metaphorically to allow talk about the inner life of man.

"High" was "powerful," then, but real power was "intellectual" or "spiritual"; and the intellectual or spiritual powers were more "hidden," more "interior." All of this had a bearing on responsibility, because responsibility presupposed control over one's actions. In Aquinas's way of thinking, control was a matter of order and power, and hierarchy was a scale of order and power. Thus, in man, control was exercised by reason, which provided order or "form," and by will, which provided impetus or "matter"; this was the controlling self. The controlled self was the sensitive appetite, the bodily parts, and, reflexively, the reason and will as well. From the standpoint of control-as-order, therefore, it was crucial that the intellect be involved in voluntary action; from the standpoint of control-as-power, on the other hand, it was crucial that the will have its role.

III

Thomas's theory of responsibility was top-heavy and introverted, then, because he felt that this was entailed by the special status of rational animals as self-determining creatures. "Man is master of his own acts because he can deliberate about them, for when deliberating, reason is related to opposite alternatives, and the will can tend to either."[13] As discussed earlier, the difference between man and the lower animals was a difference in the degree of natural determination in soul or form, and a concomitant difference in voluntary determination as well. It was not that animals did not make judgments or have desires, but rather that their judgments and desires were instinctually restricted to a narrow range. Human beings, by contrast, were intellectually ordained to being in general, and, since the intellect specified the object to the will, human wills were broadly oriented by nature to the good in general. This natural generality and indeterminacy of rational form had to be narrowed and specified if interior or exterior voluntary actions were to occur, for "actions have to do with contingent singulars," and a universally oriented potency could not give rise to acts relating to singulars without some mediating principle.

Aquinas might have argued that learning and habituation suffice for the needed specificity of response. He could then have construed deliberation as a function of habituation; in effect, as an acquired skill in practical reasoning. But this approach would have committed Aquinas to a relatively weak position on the individual's responsibility before God and man, for it would have left much of human character to the circumstances of birth, parentage, and social environment, thereby inviting pardon or pity for wrongdoing. Instead, he opted for a conception of responsibility consistent with infinite deserts. Instead of subordinating deliberation to habituation, he subordinated habituation to deliberation. Early upbringing, though influential, did not prevent the young adult from reviewing, reflecting, and appropriating or rejecting what had thus far been made of him.[14]

To Thomas, therefore, what was most distinctive about the rational creature was that a generality of instinctual determination allowed a specificity of rational determination:

> [M]an, judging about his course of action by the power of reason, can also judge about his own decision, inasmuch as he knows the meaning of an end and of a means to an end, and the relationship of one with reference to the other. Thus he is his own cause not only in moving but also in judging. He is therefore endowed with free choice--that is to say, with a free judgment about acting or not acting.[15]

How the individual judged determined how he willed, and conversely. In Aquinas's terminology, the reason had command (imperium) over the will, while the will made use (usus) of the reason. Their interaction resulted in an ordered movement of the mind toward the fulfillment of intentions.

Deliberate action was Aquinas's norm for voluntary action, but not all voluntaria involved deliberation at the time. This was obvious in cases of culpable omission, in which the individual did not even consider the action that he failed to perform (e.g., forgetting an appointment). It also held for voluntary actions that were the result of prior habituation. An action that proceeded from a "habit of choice" (habitus electivus) was an action from a deliberated will (ex voluntate deliberata) either because habituation took place under the direction of deliberation, as in training; because habituation could have and should have taken place under such direction; or because deliberation could presently lead to withholding consent and choice from the use of the habit. Thus Aquinas emphasized deliberation, not because it was immediately involved in every voluntary action, but because it was the voluntary process by which rational animals could and did exercise control over their actions and habits.

Because of the close cooperation between intellect and will in voluntary actions and omissions--because thinking was voluntary doing and voluntary doing required thinking--to begin discussion of one of the two powers was to turn to the other almost immediately. Placing initial emphasis on the will, then, a voluntary act or omission would fall into one of three groups:

1. An <u>actus</u> <u>elicitus</u> or <u>actus</u> <u>imperatus</u> exercised by a will whose object was correctly specified by the intellect; <u>or</u>

2. An omission to perform such an <u>actus</u> where obligatory and possible; <u>or</u>

3. An <u>actus</u> <u>elicitus</u> or <u>actus</u> <u>imperatus</u> exercised by a will incorrectly specified by the intellect, where the specification was a consequence of (1) or (2).

Thus, it was a necessary but not sufficient condition for voluntariness that actions or omissions for which an individual might be held responsible could be traced back to the will as their <u>principium</u>. Voluntary actions might be mediated by other powers of the soul (<u>actus</u> <u>imperati</u> <u>a</u> <u>voluntate</u>) or they might be unmediated (<u>actus</u> <u>elicitus</u> <u>a</u> <u>voluntate</u>).[16] Voluntary omissions, on the other hand, might involve an act of the will directly, as when an individual abstained from acting, or might involve no act at all, as when his obligation simply did not occur to him.[17] But the fact that an act proceeded from the will in one of these ways did not suffice for voluntariness, for the intellect might misinform the will in some way. Acts of the will had a content, an "<u>obiectum</u>" or "<u>specificatio</u>."[18] The individual did not simply will; he willed to be moved or to be at rest, to speak or to be silent.[19] Thomas usually refers to this content as the object, and to the intellect as specifying it to the will. This object was presented to the will as an end and good in its own right, or as means to an end already intended. Since the exercise (<u>exercitium</u>) of the will toward the specified object was restricted to simple acceptance or rejection, how the intellect specified the object mattered a great deal to the voluntariness of the will's response, and to its merit or demerit as well. Thus, it was necessary for voluntariness that the action or omission be traceable to the will; it was also necessary that the object of the will be correctly specified.

Four areas of this position stand in need of clarification, and they are best discussed before addressing the acts involved in realizing an intention: the role of omissions; the meaning of "correctly specified," as I have used it above; the relation of the specified object to the exercise of the will; and the distinction between "elicited acts" and "imperated acts."

Investigating the first leads to the second, and indicates how closely Aquinas tied his framework for the psychology of action to the normative interests of his religious ethics. False specification of the object sometimes caused involuntariness and excuse, sometimes mitigation of fault, sometimes simple culpability, and sometimes aggravation of guilt.[20] Paragraph (1) above is compatible with all but involuntariness and excuse. Thomas did not rest his distinctions between types of ignorance on a general definition of "object"--perhaps because he felt that any precise philosophical elucidation would fail to allow for the vague and often confused ways that people considered themselves and their actions, perhaps because he felt that only God was "the searcher of hearts."[21] Nor did he simply lean on Aristotle's distinction between ignorance of circumstances and ignorance of ethical norms; he used it, but saw a need to discuss the theoretical and practical questions of the individual's responsibility for either type of ignorance. Because culpable ignorance of an ethical norm had to be traced to the will, the question to be asked was whether the will was at some point negligent in failing to know and apply the relevant norm. Ignorance of the norm was no excuse, but in Thomas's view, at least, this principle assumed that the individual could have known and applied it.[22]

The problem of responsibility for ignorance in the specification of the will led directly, therefore, to the problem of omitting to learn or consider. Aquinas alerted the reader to this connection early in the treatise on voluntariness:

> Just as an act of knowledge is required for voluntariness, so also is an act of the will; that is, it must be within one's power to consider, to will, and to act. Thus, just as not to will and not to act are voluntary when it is time to will or act, so also not to consider is voluntary.[23]

But if the distinction between culpable and inculpable ignorance ultimately rested on an omission to consider, this would pose a problem, for it would suggest that Aquinas's conception of positive acts of will presupposed the conception of omissions in its definition, even though a conception of omissions presupposed a notion of acts of the will: an omission, presumably, was the absence of a commission. To put the problem generally, a theory of human action in which omissions have a large role must either turn back on itself in a vicious circle, or regress to a core in which omissions have no place.

Here Thomas would have been trapped if his project had been to develop a value-free theory of action. In fact, however, he did not restrict himself to purely descriptive terms, but traced the regress to ethical norms imprinted in the practical reason and applied in the act of consent (<u>consensus</u>). These norms of the natural law were so much a part of the very structure of the will residing in reason that the will could only function with reference to them. The most incorruptible norms were highly general; the first principle of practical reason, "good is to be pursued and evil to be avoided," was simply an express formulation of the natural inclination of the will to the good in general.[24] The more corruptible norms, however, were more specific, such as the natural law against theft--and it was up to the individual whether or not he lost them through sin. The will had to act in relation to these norms, since they were inherent to its relationship to practical reason, and therefore it either used them properly or abused them culpably.

By characterizing the norms of the natural law as inherent in the will's relationship to practical reason, Aquinas blocked the regress at a point where the omission to consider the relevant moral norms was either impossible or else a direct result of previous sin.

Aquinas's emphasis on the obligation to consider relevant norms and on the culpability of omissions to fulfill that obligation was thus complemented by his doctrine that every rational creature who had not already corrupted his conscience through sin had, immediately available to him, sufficient moral knowledge to avoid sin. Aquinas argued that the capacity of conscience, or "synderesis," was a natural habit of the practical reason which provided the first principles of practical reasoning to the individual.[25] It was natural in the sense that its principles, like the first principles of theoretical reason such as the principle of contradiction, were among the eternal reasons (rationes aeternae) that belong to the rational creature as made in the image of God.[26] Yet synderesis was a habit nonetheless, for these rationes aeternae were only latent in the individual at birth, and were brought forth during the course of his upbringing through the operation of the agent intellect (intellectus agens). Accordingly, depending on the history of the individual, Thomas would speak sometimes of the corruption of the conscience and sometimes of its lack of development.

Since synderesis was not equally developed in all individuals, a corrupt or undeveloped conscience was subject to error. A double bind resulted if the erroneous act of consent concerned something that the individual was obliged to know and could have known: his will would be evil whether or not it was in accord with his erring reason.[27] For if the will followed erring reason, then it did so culpably; but if it did not, it was culpable nonetheless, since reason "sets forth its judgment as true, and consequently as being from God, from whom is all truth." As Alan Donagan says,

> It follows that the position of a man with a culpably erroneous conscience is a terrible one. If he acts in accordance with his conscience, he does something materially wrong for which he is culpable, because, although he acts from ignorance, his ignorance is culpable. Yet if, against his conscience, he does what is materially right, he is still culpable, because he has fallen foul of the second-order precept that an action against conscience is always culpable.[28]

Obviously, the individual had to do what he could to correct his erroneous conscience. If the corruption of synderesis had been minor, then learning the point of error might suffice--by discussing the decision with a priest, for example--but if the corruption was due to mortal sin, only God could repair the damage.[29]

If the object specified to the will was correct or culpably incorrect, therefore, then the immediate response of the will was voluntary. The exact character of this response, the "exercise" of the will, is difficult to ascertain.

Aquinas said, "the act of the will is nothing else than an inclination proceeding from an interior knowing principle, just as the natural appetite is a kind of inclination proceeding from an interior principle without knowledge."[30] What held for the act of the will also held for the "operation" of the will and for the "movement" of the will:

> the operation of the will is a certain inclination of the willer to the thing willed.[31]

> the movement of the will is nothing but the inclination of the will to the thing willed.[32]

On other occasions, however, he seems to imply a contrast between "inclinatio" and "actus" or "motus."

Aquinas did not define "inclinatio"; it was presented under its specific forms, such as intention, consent, and choice. Thus, examples of inclination of the rational appetite include the individual's orientation to the good in general, his interest in good health, his intention to become a kinder person, his consent to feelings of ill-will, his choice of words in speaking to an acquaintance, and so on. Inclinationes included pangs or yearnings immediately known, personal traits that the individual would acknowledge if asked, and others that he would deny or doubt that he possessed. Most important, perhaps, the fact that an agent had an inclination to an object implied only a strong possibility that he would take action to attain it as an end.

Since any particular inclination was specified by its object, the general meaning of "inclination to an object" might be sought in the notion of "object." But Thomas was only a little more explicit about "obiectum" than about "inclinatio." The object of the will in any act of the will was the good, conceived as either attainable or not, together with whatever means may have been settled upon to attain it. This is not much to go on, as Eric D'Arcy has observed:

> One may feel that there was not a sufficiently detailed study of the obiectum, and insufficiently detailed criteria provided for distinguishing between the obiectum and the finis.[33]

D'Arcy does not give reasons for these misgivings, but Donagan indicates what is at stake:

> Since a rational agent, as such, controls his actions in the light of his knowledge of what they are, to hold him answerable for his actions under descriptions he does not know they fall under is to demand that he answer for something for which, as a rational agent, he cannot answer.[34]

The goodness or badness of an act of the will was determined by its object, and, as Donagan says and Aquinas would have agreed, the agent must know or be able to know the proper description of the object. Yet the end (finis) was part of the object, even the ultimate end; for Aquinas believed that man willed all that he willed for the sake of the ultimate end.³⁵ The question that arises, therefore, is whether Aquinas's capacious conception of the object resulted in a theory of responsibility that violated the condition that Donagan describes. We will turn to this question in the next chapter, when we examine Aquinas's theory of sin.

The distinction between the elicited and the imperated acts of the will allowed Thomas to maintain that the will was free in its inclination to the object, yet sometimes constrained, interrupted, or frustrated in its subsequent direction of the soul or body. Simply stated, the elicited act (<u>actus elicitus</u>) was the act of the will proper, while the imperated act (<u>actus imperatus</u>) was less an act in its own right than a relation between two acts, one of the will and the other of some other power or member.³⁶ In the elicited act of the will, then, the object specified by the intellect called forth an inclination of the will. The act was fully attributed to the will, since it <u>was not</u> mediated by any other power or member, but presupposed only the function of the intellect in providing its content. The imperated or commanded act, on the other hand, <u>was</u> mediated by another power or member. Thus, although the <u>actus imperatus</u> could not fail through an obstruction or resistance of the will itself, it could fail through an obstruction or resistance of the power or member imperated: deliberation could be interrupted by an unexpected noise; legs could suddenly cramp.³⁷

The force of the distinction between elicited, unmediated acts and commanded, mediated acts emerges in the question, "Whether violence can be done to the will":

> There is a twofold act of the will. One is its immediate act, the one that is elicited from it, namely, willing itself. The other act of the will is the one commanded by the will and put into execution by means of some other power, as walking and speaking, which are commanded by the will to be executed by a motive power. The will can undergo violence with respect to these commanded acts insofar as violence can prevent exterior members from executing the will's command. But no violence can be done to the proper act of the will.
>
> The reason for this is that the act of the will is simply a kind of inclination proceeding from the interior knowing principle, just as the natural appetite is a kind of inclination proceeding from an interior principle without knowledge. Now what is forced or violent comes from an exterior principle. Hence to be forced or compelled to will is contrary to the very act of the will, just as any forced or violent movement is contrary to the natural inclination or movement of natural things. For a stone can be moved upward by force, but it is impossible for this violent movement to be from its natural inclination. Similarly a man can be dragged by force, but that this happen by his own will conflicts with the notion of violence.³⁸

This passage indicates the two ways that the free inclination of the will could occur and yet result in involuntariness: problems antecedent to the elicited act, and problems subsequent to it. First, the elicited act of the will could be involuntary through an inculpably false specification of the object; resultant acts, commanded by the will, would be based upon this false object and likewise be involuntary. Secondly, the imperated act of the will could be involuntary when the powers or members were prevented from following through with the direction of the will.

IV

There are two questions that any interpretation of Aquinas's theory of responsibility must face. First, what was the relevance for responsibility of the agent's capacity to examine and control his own rational processes? Secondly, what was the significance of Aquinas's use of metaphor in describing voluntary acts and excuses? Reflexivity, it seems, enabled the agent not only to have first-order, spontaneous control of himself, but also to have control of his controlling principia. Metaphors, on the other hand, drawn from external human operations, combined to depict an interior hierarchy of priorities among the soul's powers and their actuations. Both reflexivity and metaphor, therefore, seem to have been central features of introversion in Aquinas's theory.

Because the individual could reflect on his own acts of intellect and will, his not doing so might at times be a negligent omission. In Thomas's view, the capacity to think about thinking and will about willing provided the power of self-control necessary for accountability to God. Yet his vocabulary for voluntary action had its primary significance in reference to everyday courses of external action, good and bad. Present-day examples would include planning a vacation, cooking a dinner, and planting a shrub. This vocabulary therefore acquired a secondary significance in reflexive application to its own processes:

> Choice precedes use if each is referred to the same thing. But nothing prevents the use of one thing from preceding the choice of another. And because the acts of the will can turn back on themselves, in any act of the will we can find consent, choice, and use, such that we can say that the will consents to choose and consents to consent, and uses itself in consenting and choosing.[39]

To understand this aspect of Aquinas's position, it is necessary first to get a preliminary understanding of the external face of his theory of action, for this was the primary significance from which his conception of reflexive acts was derived.

In a typical case of a completed voluntary action, therefore, the order of specification by the intellect and exercise by the will, of object and inclination, can be schematized as follows:

A Complete Human Action

Acts of intellect or reason	Acts of will

I. The order of intention
    A. With regard to the end

(1) Considering	(2) "Complacentia"
	(3) Enjoying
(4) Judging	(5) Intending

    B. With regard to the means

| (6) Deliberating | (7) Consenting |
| (8) Deciding | (9) Choosing |

II. The order of execution

| (10) Commanding | (11) Using |
| | (12) Enjoying[40] |

Here Part II, the terminus of the series, was external, as in carnal sins, for example.

In other cases, the terminus might be internal, as in spiritual sins, or the process beginning with deliberation might be complicated by the contingencies involved in a long and complex series of means. In some cases, therefore, no corporeal means needed to be involved; in others, reflexive forms of using and commanding had to occur before outwardly directed forms of using and commanding could take place.

Aquinas was sensitive to the possibility of a vicious regress here, and tried to avoid it. He was aware, for example, that a second-order consent was not a first-order consent, and was interested only in the possibility of multiple levels of reflexive control; he did not imply that for any act of consent there had first to be a prior act of consent. Aquinas's reflexive use of this vocabulary was complicated, then, but by distinguishing its outwardly turned face from its introverted aspect, Aquinas believed that he could keep track of the differences and avoid circularity.

Yet the theory was still more complicated. The chart above gives the first-order vocabulary, which includes terms such as "deliberating" (consilium), "commanding" (imperium), and "using" (usus); these indicated external relations and interactions in their primary significance. Their metaphorical significance was therefore doubled, rather bewilderingly, in the reflexive aspects of Aquinas's theory of action.

A modern reader is likely to view this treatment of language with skepticism. The language of interior hierarchy, with its echelons of command and control, may appear in this light to be vacuous, if highly articulated, theorizing. Several specific objections might be raised, but perhaps the most representative would be the charge of circularity: that Thomas first reified (and in some cases personified) process and relationship, then used these pseudo-entities (and pseudo-agents) in a circular explanation, much in the way that Moliere's medical student explained that opium causes sleep because it possesses a "dormitive power." To put the objection more precisely, it seems that Thomas, looking for a way to explain human action, first divided the soul into parts, then used human agency as a model for how each part interacted with the others to produce actions. If this interpretation should prove correct, the explanans and the explanandum would presuppose each other in a vicious circle.

If Aquinas had not been aware of what he was doing, then this line of criticism would be plausible, for the error it describes is a common one. In fact, however, Aquinas was self-conscious in his use of metaphor, and recognized that his theory of responsibility was saturated with it:

> Now actions belong to supposits and wholes and, properly speaking, not to parts and forms or powers, for we do not say properly that the hand strikes, but a man with his hand, nor that heat makes a thing hot, but fire by heat.... Nevertheless, in one and the same man we may speak metaphorically of his various principles of action such as the reason, the irascible, and the concupiscible, and these obey reason; and in general in so far as each part of man is ascribed to what is becoming to it. Hence the Philosopher calls this "metaphorical justice."[41]

When he analyzed the details of voluntariness, Aquinas was of the same opinion as in the remarks above. The role of reason was "despotic" over the external members, "royal and political" over the lower powers; internal "command" (imperium) was likened to orders given in the indicative and imperative moods; "use" of parts of the self was compared to external employment of a horse or a stick:

> The use of something implies its application to some activity, and hence the activity to which we apply a thing is called its use, just as to go horseback riding is to make use of a horse, and to hit is to make use of a stick. Now we apply the interior principles of action to activity, namely the powers of the soul or the members of the body--for example, the intellect to understanding and the eye to seeing--as well as external things, such as the stick for hitting. But it is clear that we apply external things to action only by means of intrinsic principles, which are either powers of the soul, habits of the powers, or organs, which are members of the body.
>
> Now it was shown above that it is the will which moves the powers of the soul to their acts, and this is to apply them to operation. Hence it is clear that use primarily and principally belongs to the will as to a first mover, to reason as directing, and to other

powers as executing, which powers are compared to the will which applies them as instruments to the principal agent, just as building is attributed to the builder and not to his tools.

Hence it is clear that use properly is an act of the will.[42]

Such passages were not admissions that he was confused, nor were they expressions of indifference to the dangers of metaphorical usage. But if Aquinas knew what he was doing, why did he think he could do it? How could he use metaphors to such central purposes if he was aware of their limitations?

A natural explanation is the one given in his early discussion of metaphor, "that spiritual truths be expounded by means of figures taken from corporeal things, in order that thereby even the simple who are unable by themselves to grasp intellectual things may be able to understand it."[43] As he said in his Prologue to the Summa ,

Because the master of Catholic truth ought not only to teach the proficient, but also to instruct beginners (according to the Apostle: "As unto little ones in Christ, I gave you milk to drink, not meat." I Cor. 3:1-2), we purpose in this book to treat of whatever belongs to the Christian religion, in such a way as may tend to the instruction of beginners.

The difficulty with following this line of interpretation to explain metaphors of interiority, however, is that it leads to the conclusion that Thomas rarely, if ever, taught those he regarded as proficient; for he used the same types of metaphors in his other writings that he used in the Summa Theologiae.

Rather, it seems that he used metaphors, not only in spite of their limitations but because of them, as if he had attached an asterisk or other marker warning of the status of his remarks, and thus commended them to "the exercise of thoughtful minds."[44] Aquinas held that, unlike analogical usage of a term, metaphorical usage was equivocal with its literal usage, and his practice was to use metaphors that could be replaced by univocal or analogical expressions if need be. The actual subjects, or literal referents, of the metaphorical agents that appeared in his theory of action were the powers of the soul, and the actual subject of the internal, metaphorical polity was the priority of causal dependence that governed the interaction of those powers. It might be said that these powers were "dormitive" themselves, but in Aquinas's view they properly referred to ranges of possibility that became refined to probability or tendency through habituation. These habituated powers belonged to patterns of dependence and interdependence that determined which of their innumerable possibilities emerged in actu. To put it in the terms of a twentieth-century philosophical metaphor, each power defined a section of "logical space" so related to the others that the actuation of a possibility in one or more of the others cut down the number of possibilities that remained open to it.[45] In response to the demands of the moment, therefore, the powers of the soul coordinated until the possibilities in the will "reduced to act": the arm raised, or the lips moved, and the consequences followed. In Aquinas's view, this happened neither chaotically nor deterministically, but simply followed the hierarchy of dependence in the soul.

Yet it is arguable that Aquinas should have introduced some means of expressing himself other than the metaphors of internal agency, perhaps by using actual asterisks or technical jargon. It is also arguable, however, that the metaphors of miniature agents do a better job, once they are properly understood. For, in role, a human agent is himself a range of possibilities defined in relation to others; thus, just as one can imagine a social organization by imagining the roles and relationships that limit interaction within it, so Aquinas could express his sense of intrapsychic organization by depicting possibilities, processes, and relationships by the metaphors of internal agency. Also, by characterizing these internal patterns with a metaphorical chain of command, Aquinas evoked the seriousness with which he believed the soul's condition should be regarded. In any case, only the most proficient could have understood his theory if he had presented it entirely in the language of potency and act; Aquinas wanted a wider audience.

In his conception of responsibility before God, Aquinas used the second-order metaphors to explore and make vivid the processes that he developed in the introversion of justice and friendship. Just as "iustitia" and "amicitia" had primary meanings governing the relationship of the individual to God, so the language of the acts of the will had a primary significance in the genesis of observable actions, and a secondary significance in the soul's private career before God. Thus, although the outer face of Aquinas's theory of action was formidably complex in its own right, the more complicated, inner face will be the topic of the rest of this chapter.

V

Aquinas indicates that his treatise on human acts can be applied either to proximate ends or to the ultimate end. In its widest setting, therefore, the treatise bears on man's pursuit of happiness and the ordination to an end in God; in its narrowest setting, on actions as simple as reaching for a quill. Thomas divided the circular movement of the rational appetite into two arcs, two "orders": the order of intention, leading to the choice of the means; and the order of execution, leading, if all went well, to the attainment of the end intended.[46] In the order of intention were the acts listed on the chart as considering, complacentia, enjoying, judging, intending, deliberating, consenting, deciding, and choosing; in the order of execution were commanding, using, and (again) enjoying. Here I will concentrate on the ideas of principal importance for Aquinas's theory of responsibility, beginning with the order of intention.

In his discussion of complacentia, Frederick Crowe points out that Aquinas held that there was a "duplex via" or "double way" in the will, not only a "via motionis" in which the agent progressed toward his objective through intention, deliberation, consent, and the rest, but also a prior, "via receptionis" in which the will of the agent responded affirmatively but passively toward the object specified by the intellect.[47] This act, the "complacency" of the will in the object, was a necessary precondition of the acts in the via motionis. The will could only incline to what had already been received from the intellect, and because this passive aspect could occur without subsequent intention (e.g., in the visio dei itself, in ordinary pipe-dreams), it was to be regarded as a distinct act of the will. As Aquinas put it, "[T]he appetible object gives the appetite, first, a certain adaptation to itself, which consists in complacency in that object; and from this follows movement toward the appetible object."[48] In Crowe's diagram:

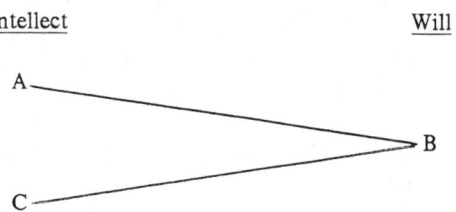

Here A designates the act of intellect specifying the end/object to the will, B the exercise of the will toward the object, and C an act of the intellect commanded by the will. Crowe comments:

> Here A and C are different acts of intellect according to a twofold order, A in via receptionis, C in via motionis. But what of B, the intervening act or acts of will? On reflection we can see that at least it does double service in the will, being at the end of one process and the beginning of another; but the duality is not immediately apparent.[49]

Thomas's own remarks support Crowe's analysis:

> Will and intellect have a mutual priority over one another, but not in the same way. Intellect's priority over will is in receiving (in via receptionis), for if anything is to move the will it must first be received into the intellect.... But in moving or acting (in movendo sive agendo) will has priority, because every action or movement comes from the intention of the good; and hence it is that the will, whose proper object is the good precisely as good, is said to move all the lower powers.[50]

Thus, in complacentia the will stood at a critical juncture, the end of the intake "from things to soul," the beginning of the outflow "from soul to things."[51]

"Complacency" in the end, then, was a favorable reception of an object resulting from an aptitude of the will to it. Aquinas used various terms to express aptitude: proportio, consonantia, coaptatio, connaturalitas, aptitudo, convenientia, immutatio.[52] In short, a preliminary fitness between the end and the will was necessary even for complacentia, the initial attraction: "nothing is favorably disposed to something unless it is like or suitable to it."[53] Crowe points out that in this first relationship of the will to the good, the distinction between self and not-self was, for the time being, beside the point. Complacentia was a love of the object that implied initial union and rest before any effort was made to seek the object or other. At this point, therefore, the individual had no need to try either to conform the end to himself or to conform himself to the end; indeed, the fact that it had not been attained in reality was not included in the object. Similarity of form between the will and the object resulted in a simple receptive act of affirmation. This primordial act of the will, then, established the foundation and possibility in the structure of the will for the transcendence of the distinction between self and other that we have already considered in the discussion of charity.

Complacentia, therefore, referred to the first "possession" of the object by the will:

> There is a twofold relationship of the will to what it wills. One comes from the willed thing's being in some way in the one who wills through some proportion or order to that willed thing. Hence things that are naturally proportioned to some end are said to desire it naturally. But to have an end in this way is to have it imperfectly. Now everything imperfect tends to what is perfect. Therefore both the natural and the voluntary appetite or desire move to possess an end really, which is to possess it perfectly. This is the second relationship of the will to what is willed.[54]

Fitness for the ultimate end, for example, was "possession," a natural aptitude for happiness, and moved through charity to the second "possession," the beatific vision itself.

Complacency in the end was accompanied by enjoyment (fruitio), which then pervaded the subsequent acts in the via motionis toward the end.[55] Initially, it was simply the pleasurable aspect of complacentia, but once intention of the end was established, it implied anticipation of the full possession of the end:

> Now a fruit enjoyable to sense is what we expect a tree to produce ultimately, and which is savored with a certain delight. Hence fruition, that is, enjoyment, seems to relate to the love or delight which one has from the thing that is ultimately expected, which is the end.[56]

At interim ends along the way to "the thing that [was] ultimately expected," the resting of the will in partial fulfillment of its goal through the stages of its means, would result also in partial fruition, except where the means involved was too unpleasant in itself: "that which is in itself not delightful, but is only desired as ordered to something else, as bitter medicine for health, in no way can be called the fruit."[57] Sorrow for past sins in penance, for example, would be a bitter medicine conducive to the health of the soul.

Enjoyment was not a distinct exercise of the will, then, but a concomitant of actual exercises. The next true exercise of the rational appetite was intention (intentio), and was made under a different specification: the good to which the will was inclined was now conceived as an attainable end, requiring further activity from the agent. In intention, therefore, the will was inclined not only to the end, but to whatever means were suitable to the attainment of it. A spiritually sick man might want to regain the health of his soul, for example, and might therefore be ready to do something to bring that end about.

As Donagan observes, because an intention could have an object as comprehensive as happiness or as narrow as the raising of an arm, its act could be so determinate in the means it presupposed that intention, consent, and choice could refer to the same actuation of the will.[58] In such cases, the deliberation that followed intention would be reduced to the simplest form of practical reasoning, recognition that the action presently available as means was also the end sought. Typically, however, intention for Aquinas was not "intention to do," but "intention with which"--not the agent's intention to act, but the point, reason, or objective for which the agent consented to means and chose to act.[59]

Intention was an elicited act toward the end, and from it the next requisite act toward the means was imperated. This commanded operation was the intellectual act, deliberation (consilium).[60] Consilium arose, therefore, from the force of intention as a direct and natural consequence. As an imperated act, however, consilium could be interrupted. The spiritually sick man's deliberation about how to regain the health of his soul could be disturbed, for example, by a bump on the head. Although Thomas's typical cases of commanded acts were external actions, then, Anthony Kenny is right when he suggests that "deliberation... is not so much an actus elicitus as an inner actus imperatus."[61] To my knowledge, Aquinas never said it was anything else.

Deliberation was an inquiry (inquisitio), but an inquiry of a distinctive kind. Aquinas emphasized three features. First, it had the end intended as its principle, analogous to a premise in theoretical reasoning;[62] secondly, it had the choice (electio) and use (usus) of means as the term of inquiry, analogous to a conclusion in theoretical reasoning;[63] thirdly, it had to do with questions that could never be settled with strict certainty, for means had to do with contingent singulars, and among contingent singulars there was no way to establish demonstratively that one course of action was the only or the best one to take.[64]

Deliberation could be as complex as the situation demanded. The comparison with theoretical reasoning was also the basis of contrast with it, for practical reasoning differed substantially:

> Now we must note in regard to singular contingent matters that various conditions or circumstances have to be taken into account in order for something to be known with a certainty; these cannot be considered easily by one person alone, but they are taken into account with greater certainty by several, for what one notices escapes the

attention of another. In necessary and universal matters, however, the consideration is more simple and more absolute, in which respect one man by himself can be sufficient.[65]

Indeed, "nothing prevents deliberation from being potentially infinite inasmuch as there can be matters for deliberation to infinity."[66] But deliberation had a principle and a term, and the process of inquiry moved between these. Although potentially infinite, therefore, deliberation was actually finite:

> The inquiry of deliberation is actually finite at both ends, on the part of the principle and on the part of the term. Now a twofold principle is taken with respect to the inquiry of deliberation. The first is a proper one, belonging to the very genus of actions, and this is the end, about which there is not deliberation but which is supposed as a principle, as we have said. The other principle is taken as it were from another genus, just as in demonstrative sciences one science assumes something from another about which it does not inquire. Now the principles taken for granted in the inquiry of deliberation are facts of sense observation, for example, that this is bread or this is iron; also taken for granted are the general principles known in some speculative or practical science, for example, that adultery is prohibited by God or that man cannot live without sufficient nourishment. No one who deliberates inquires about such matters.
>
> Now inquiry terminates in what we are able to do at once. For just as the end has the nature of a principle, so that which is done because of the end has the nature of a conclusion. Therefore, that which presents itself as first to be done stands like an ultimate conclusion, and with respect to this, inquiry comes to an end.[67]

This process was one of "resolution," by which the agent first knew a desired effect, the end, and then canvassed his knowledge of causes to determine the steps he could take to bring about means and end.

There was nothing random about the process, especially if the agent had the virtue of practical wisdom. But there was nothing apodictically certain about it, either. Thomas drew attention to the lack of demonstrative certainty in deliberation by contrasting its conclusions with those of theoretical inquiry:

> A conclusion does not always follow necessarily from principles, but only when the principles cannot be true if the conclusion is not true. Similarly, the end a man has does not necessitate the choosing of the means to the end, since not every means is such that the end cannot be attained without it, or if it is such, it is not always considered under that aspect.[68]

Donagan's exposition is helpful:

> An agent resolving the attainment of an end into its simple causes will

produce a premiss to the effect that it will be attained on a certain condition: say 'If $\underline{M}$ is adopted, $\underline{E}$ will be attained.' Quite obviously, from such a premiss, taken together with the judgement, '$\underline{E}$ is good to attain', which led to $\underline{E}$'s attainment being willed, it does not follow that '$\underline{M}$ is the suitable means to adopt.' For the conditional premiss does not exclude others: for example, 'If $\underline{N}$ is adopted instead of $\underline{M}$, $\underline{E}$ will be attained' (I-II, 13, 6 ad 2).[69]

For the spiritually sick man intending salvation as his end, conversations with both heretics and orthodox believers might come to mind as means.

The process of bringing such $\underline{M}-\underline{E}$ and $\underline{N}-\underline{E}$ connections to mind might be simple or complicated. In one way or another, the agent asked himself or an advisor, "What causes $\underline{E}$?", and, where necessary, "What causes the cause of $\underline{E}$?", and so on, until he had one or more complete causal chains. In complex deliberations, then, several causal chains might be considered; the "practical syllogism" became the "practical sorites," and might be multiplied in several series. Deliberation proceeded until a single chain was selected, and a single link, "what we are able to do at once," was settled upon as the "judgment of reason" that concluded the practical syllogism and specified the object to the will for choice.[70]

Deliberation, then, was a single process moving from the end as principle to the first or only means as a conclusion. In the simplest case, it involved no intervening acts of the will, as when a physically sick man concluded immediately, "I should see a doctor."

Since this process moved from intention to choice, it comes as something of a surprise to find that between these acts, occurring at the stage where one or more chains have been identified, there appeared an additional act of the will, consent (<u>consensus</u>).

> To consent implies the application of sense to something. Now it is proper to sense to know things as present, for the imagination apprehends the likenesses of corporeal things even in the absence of the things whose likenesses they are, whereas the intellect apprehends universal notions, which it can grasp with no concern as to the presence or absence of the singulars. Now because the act of an appetitive power is a sort of inclination to the thing itself according to a certain likeness, the very application of the appetitive power to the thing, inasmuch as it adheres to it, takes on the name "sense" since it acquires, so to speak, an experience of the thing to which it adheres, inasmuch as it finds satisfaction in it. Hence it is said in Scripture, "Think (<u>sentite</u>) of the Lord in goodness" (Wisdom 1:1). Accordingly, to consent is an act of the appetitive power.[71]

Aquinas otherwise avoided the implication that deliberation involves two stages, and since he followed Aristotle in many other ways in these pages, it is curious that deliberation, before terminating in choice, first involved a prior act of the will, consent.

Although there are hints in the question on consent, his reasons for introducing consensus must be sought elsewhere, in his theory of sin. Sin was an inordinate voluntary act, and for an act to be inordinate, a higher good had to be subordinated to a lower, thereby rejecting the order represented in the hierarchy. In actions and omissions such a reversal of the proper order could not occur prior to the first elicited act of the will toward a means, and this act was consent.[72] Consent provided the first opportunity, therefore, for the will to violate natural or divine law, and for this reason Aquinas introduced moral norms at this stage in his theory of voluntary acts. The act of moral review in consent was thus a kind of parenthesis in the intentional series, introducing an ethical content extrinsic to the causal relations of means and ends. Questions of order and inordinacy could be raised at this point because the deliberation to a set of means enabled the agent to ask himself whether some or all ways of pursuing his intended end conflicted with the pursuit of other ends, and in particular with the ends of the natural and divine law.

Thus, because in the course of deliberation it was natural to reject out of hand those means that were grossly in conflict with other important projects and principles, even before reaching a choice of one means, Aquinas believed that the individual was morally responsible for his failure to exclude from consideration means that violated God's law. In order to establish full responsibility for consent, Aquinas followed Augustine in emphasizing the involvement of the superior reason (superior ratio) in the moral review:

> A final decision always belongs to the one who is superior and to whom it belongs to judge of the others, for as long as a judgment remains to be given there is not a final decision (sententia). Now it is clear that it belongs to the superior reason to judge of everything else, for we judge of sensible matters by reason and we judge of matters pertaining to human reasons according to divine reasons (rationes divinas), which belong to the superior reason. Consequently, as long as one is uncertain whether he should resist or not according to divine reason, no judgment of reason has the aspect of a final sentence. Now the final sentence for acting is the consent to the act. Therefore consent to the act belongs to the superior reason, yet in the sense in which reason includes the will, as we have said.[73]

Here the metaphor of interior hierarchy and the para-juridical model of ethics combine in a word-play on the notion of "sententia," a word-play that applied to decisions in general but had the special significance of a jural deposition.

But the interior act in question was of a special order, for since consent belonged to the higher reason, the consenting agent made use (or culpably omitted to make use) of his interior access to the divine law. Of course, only the agent who was in a state of grace had such direct internal access to the divine law, but if he lacked it, this was imputed to him as a culpable corruption of synderesis. The strong accent on the finality of consent, moreover, indicated that with this act, logically prior to choice and to subsequent execution, the agent was already subject to merit or demerit before God. This was Thomas's way of ensuring that personal responsibility before God was affected neither by external circumstances nor, perhaps, by differences in practical wisdom from one person to another.

The role of consent as the first possible act of sin in the intentional series is evident in the language of adhering and loving that appears in the question on consent. As in complacentia and enjoyment, in consent Thomas stressed the "likeness" or assimilation of the will to its object, the fact that it "acquires, so to speak, an experience of the thing to which it adheres, inasmuch as it finds satisfaction in it."[74] This experiential involvement in the means, if they were sinful, resulted in a stain upon the soul.

The locus classicus in the Christian tradition for such a sin is Matthew 5:25: "If a man looks at a woman to lust after her, he has already committed adultery with her in his heart." Aquinas commented:

> That a man thinking of fornication takes pleasure in the act thought of is due to his desire being inclined to this act. Wherefore the fact that a man consents to such a delectation, amounts to nothing less than a consent to the inclination of his appetite to fornication: for no man takes pleasure except in that which is in conformity with his appetite. Now it is a mortal sin, if a man deliberately chooses that his appetite be conformed to what is itself a mortal sin....[75]

Aquinas went on to point out that even tacit consent, without the actual consent of the will in consideration of the relevant moral norms, might suffice for mortal sin. Thus, a willing imaginary experience of sin was sin, and the assimilation of the object to the will in experiencing it resulted in a stain upon the soul:

> A stain is properly ascribed to corporeal things, when a comely body loses its comeliness through contact with another body, e.g., a garment, gold or silver, or the like. Accordingly, a stain is ascribed to spiritual things in like manner.
>
> Now man's soul has a twofold comeliness; one from the refulgence of the natural light of reason, whereby he is directed in his actions; the other, from the refulgence of the divine light, viz., of wisdom and grace, whereby man is also perfected for the purpose of doing good and fitting actions. Now, when the soul cleaves to things by love, there is a kind of contact in the soul: and when man sins, he cleaves to certain things against the light of reason and of the divine law, as shown above. Wherefore the loss of comeliness occasioned by this contact is metaphorically called a stain on the soul.[76]

To be drawn to something enough to act upon it, of course, is a powerful indication of attachment to it. But as these passages indicate, the attachment could be sinful even if the agent did not act upon it, simply because his will cleaved to the object in love.

Consent was followed by choice. Thomas described the relation between them as follows:

> Choice adds to consent a certain relation to something which is preferred to something else; and hence, after consent is given, there still remains choice. For it may be that through deliberation several means are found that are conducive to the end; and as long as each of these is acceptable, consent is given to each one, but among those which are acceptable we give preference to one by making a choice. However, if we find that only one means is acceptable, then consent and choice do not differ in reality but only according to reason; hence we call it consent, inasmuch as doing that thing is acceptable, and choice according as we prefer it to whatever is not acceptable.[77]

Because "consent" and "choice" sometimes denoted the same act, sometimes different acts, in the following passage Aquinas indicated the first possibility with "sententiam," the second with "iudicium":

> As we have said, choice follows upon a sentence or judgment (sententiam vel iudicium), which is like the conclusion of an operative syllogism. Hence what the operative syllogism concludes to falls under choice.[78]

When choice and consent were the same, then, the act of the will had as its object a single means settled by deliberation; when choice and consent differed, on the other hand, the act of the will in choice had as its object a judgment of reason, while the act of the will in consent had as its object a wider set, the sentence. As Donagan says,

> [A]s Aquinas remarks, it may happen that deliberation discloses several suitable means, one of which is judged most suitable, and in such cases, the agent approves and loves all the means judged suitable, while going on to choose the one judged most suitable (I-II, 15, 3 ad 3).[79]

Thus, at the completion of deliberation, the intellect specified to the will a ranked set of suitable means, toward which the will acted by either inclining to or rejecting the first. Donagan seems correct in his interpretation, since he makes it clear that he has in mind as his paradigm the simplest possible case for each type of act he discusses. For more complex cases, it seems that consent would occur from time to time during the process of deliberation, and not only at the conclusion of the decisive practical syllogism.

VI

In the order of intention, Aquinas used a comparison between a theoretical and practical inquiry to organize his discussion. The intention established the first principle; deliberation then considered means of attaining the end; consent accepted or rejected means that might promote or jeopardize other ends; and choice was the terminus of the inquiry at the most suitable means.

Although deliberation and consent were partially described in metaphors drawn from the external world, these metaphors did not cohere neatly with the comparison of deliberation to theoretical inquiry, nor was this comparison compact enough to be interpreted as a metaphor or simile. At most it was a formal analogy that Aquinas used to bring out similarities and differences between the two types of inquiry. In interpreting the acts of reason and will in the order of intention, then, it is possible to move quickly to their literal significance as actuations of potentialities, without pausing to puzzle over the metaphorical suggestiveness of his remarks.

The same cannot be said of command (imperium) and use (usus), for these are metaphorical both in their first-order usage as acts directing the body in its external movements and in their second-order usage as acts directing the reason, will, and lower appetite in their internal movements.

Command and use were a matched pair, and their extension was the same as that of the imperated acts. Since in the order of intention there were several commanded acts of the will, the second-order metaphorical usage of "command" and "use" varied according to the elicited acts that preceded them and the consequent acts they directed. Thus, because Thomas held that the reason and will had not only spontaneous but reflexive control over their own acts, the various applications of "command" and "use" collectively describe an analogy of order and instrumentality within the hierarchical structure of the soul and throughout the narrowing specification of the obiectum that occurred in the generation of external action. To put it roughly, in this second-order metaphor of self-control, "command" referred to the aspect of control that was order, while "use" referred to the aspect of control that was power or instrumentality. As such, they were not actus in the sense of stages or exercises of the will, but as threads that ran through every stage and exercise. Aquinas believed that the rational agent could be subject to infinite reward or punishment for interior acts only if he had the capability not only to control his acts through reason and will, but to control reason and will themselves; hence the remarkable scope of "command" and "use."

In their literal significance, "imperium" and "usus" referred to one person's command of another, whereby the other was used as his instrument. Since commands were usually given verbally, the role of command as a mental act could be depicted differently according to different modes of the external act of speech:

Now command is essentially an act of reason, for the one commanding, by enjoining or declaring orders the one who is commanded to do something, and to order by way of enjoining or declaring belongs to reason. But reason can enjoin or declare something in two ways. In one way simply, and then the enjoining is expressed by a verb in the indicative mood, as when one says, "This is what you should do." Sometimes, however, reason orders someone to do something by way of impelling him to it, and then it is expressed by a verb in the imperative mood, as when one says, "Do this."[80]

The indicative mood held for commands directing the intellect or the will; in other words, imperium could call for an elicited act from the intellect or will, but it could not dictate the content of that act. A person of heterodox views might deliberate to the conclusion that it would serve his purposes to accept the authority of the Church and believe its teachings, but the intellect maintained its independence of his interests; he could not force himself to believe. A similar point held for the will. A person might try hard to concentrate on a boring conversation, but fail nonetheless.

The imperative mood held for reason's dominion over the external members, which were "tools of the soul's powers."[81] Aquinas cited Augustine: "The mind commands a movement of the hand, and so ready is the hand to respond that command can scarcely be distinguished from obedience."[82] The imperative mood also held for the reason's command over the lower powers, but there was no guarantee of their compliance. In this connection, Aquinas invoked Aristotle:

> As the Philosopher says, reason, in which the will resides, moves the irascible and concupiscible powers by its command--not by a despotic rule, as a slave is ruled by a master--but by a royal or political rule, as free men are ruled by a governor and yet can act against his commands.[83]

To the extent that one person could command another, he could use the other to his own ends. In the case of "usus," however, the literal significance was most readily seen, not in the manipulation of other persons, but in the handling of an animal or tool; hence Thomas began his discussion of usus with these literal examples, then went on to talk about "use" in the figurative sense as having the same range as "command":

> The use of something implies its application to some activity, and hence the activity to which we apply a thing is called its use just as to go horseback riding is to make use of a horse, and to hit is to make use of a stick. Now we apply the interior principles of action to activity, namely, the powers of the soul or the members of a body, for example, the intellect to understanding and the eye to seeing, as well as external things, such as the stick for hitting. But it is clear that we apply external things to action only by means of intrinsic principles, which are either powers of the soul, habits of the powers,

or organs, which are members of the body.[84]

Since the obedience of powers to the command of reason differed both in general and according to circumstances, so command could occur without resultant use.

The metaphors of "command" and "use," then, were drawn from external activities, and extended in their first-order significance to the control of reason and will over the body (as in the chart in section V), and in their second-order significance to the control of reason and will over the lower appetite and over themselves.

Thus, Aquinas saw in command the power of mind to bring order to the soul and its external environment. As an act of reason, then, imperium indicated ratio not only as the movement from one intuitive understanding (intellectus) to another, but also as the form and direction--the channeling, if you will--of the movements of the soul. In the generation of action, ratio as command held together the antecedent acts that increasingly specified the obiectum; as such it was the principle of continuity and structure in the intentional series. As primarily the end but secondarily the means as well, the object that emerged in choice was the chosen act, the reason for choosing it, and the reason for choosing it over other options.

Thomas emphasized the fragile character of the continuity of actuation when he discussed the sense in which imperium was a function of reason:

> Command is an act of reason but it presupposes an act of the will. To make this evident, we must consider that since the act of the will and of reason can be brought to bear upon each other, inasmuch as reason reasons about willing and the will wills to reason, an act of the will can precede an act of reason and conversely. And because the power of a prior act carries over into the act which follows (remanet in actu sequenti), it sometimes happens that there is an act of the will which retains something from the power of the act of reason, as we noted above with respect to use and choice, and conversely, there can be an act of reason which retains something from the power of the will's act.[85]

After exploring this continuity in terms of the comparison with external commands and their verbal moods, he distinguished the interior ordering role of reason from the forceful and empowering role of will:

> Now among the powers of the soul, the first mover in regard to the doing of an act is the will, as we have pointed out above. And since the second mover moves only in virtue of the first mover, it follows that it is due to the power of the will that reason moves by way of command. Hence to command is an act of reason, presupposing an act of the will in virtue of which reason moves, by commanding, to the doing of the act.[86]

The interior role of use, like that of command, was to define relations between stages in the generation of action, not to mark a stage in its own right. "Use," in cases such as the will's use of reason in deliberation, referred to the successful completion of an imperated act of the will. To understand use and command, therefore, it is important to see that the actus imperatus was not a second exercise of the will after the actus elicitus--I am not first inclined to speak, and then direct my tongue to its act--but a direct effect of the actus elicitus on another power. To employ Crowe's diagram again, the actus imperatus referred neither to B nor to C, but to both, and to the relation between them:

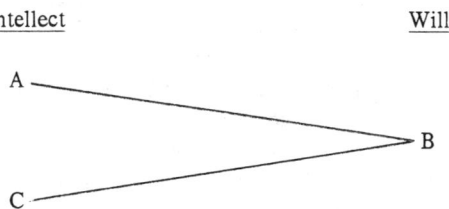

Thus, the term "use" picks out the successful instrumentality of the subordinate or directed power in fulfilling the inclination of the actus elicitus; the term "command" analytically isolates the order and continuity in that instrumentality.

"Consent," "command," and "use" are the oddest and most difficult conceptions in Aquinas's theory of human acts. But as viewed from the perspectives developed in previous chapters, this is not surprising; for these were the conceptions that did double duty, serving both the external and the internal aspects of his theory. Because it looked outward, consent was a natural feature for Thomas to isolate in connection with deliberation, for it was important for the agent to ask himself whether the means under consideration include some that would jeopardize other projects, ends, or interests. (The rational agent could not, for example, adopt means that would require him to be in one place when he had another, equally important commitment to be somewhere else at the same time.) Since this kind of reflection attached naturally to deliberation, and could be given special attention as an act of consent, Aquinas felt justified in indicating that the ultimate end was among the ends that were to be considered, and in pointing out that the attainment of the end would be jeopardized if the will of God was not observed by the higher reason.

But consent had an introvert significance as well, for as the first act of the will in relation to the means, consent was the first possibility of tacitly or explicitly subordinating a higher end to a lower by accepting means for attaining the lower that placed the higher at risk. In Thomas's own language,

> But since we have said above that the cause of sin is some apparent good as motive, yet lacking the due motive, viz. the rule of

reason or the divine law, this motive which is an apparent good appertains to the apprehension of the senses and to the appetite; while the lack of the due rule appertains to the reason, whose nature it is to consider this rule; and the completeness of the voluntary sinful act appertains to the will, so that the act of the will, given the conditions we have just mentioned, is already a sin.[87]

Further acts of the will, elicited or commanded, added to the sin already committed their willingness to retain sinful means as a live option for action. Consent, therefore, was the early, inward, and critical moment in the individual's responsibility before God. Aquinas's use of the imagery of the court and the stain upon the soul underlined the gravity of this moment in the inner life.

"Command" and "use" were more complex. The simplest way to interpret them is to concentrate on their outward face as acts directing the body in externally observable action. But the reflexive and introvert usage of these terms—coextensive with the commanded acts in the order of intention—complicated their meaning considerably and cannot be overlooked. Aquinas may have had several reasons for positing this second-order control, but the principal explanation seems to be tied to the seriousness of the human condition before God, its characterization in the language of responsibility, and the assumption that a just God who held people eternally responsible for mortal sin must have provided full means of self-control. On these grounds, it seems, Thomas envisioned a mode of self-control that was not merely spontaneous in its own movement and direction of the lower powers and the body, but capable also of second-order direction of its own powers of self-control.

In Thomas's view, then, the spontaneity and reflexivity of the will combined to assure individual responsibility for interior movements of the soul. Actuations of the soul's powers were either directly controlled in a manner analogous to the control of external events, or, if not, then they were often to be interpreted as the result of negligence to develop, maintain, or exercise available means of control. In some cases, of course, internal control was difficult to sustain, and responsibility was proportionately diminished. Just as sudden emergencies in the external world could catch the agent by surprise, so, for example, could sudden movements of the lower appetite upset the normal hierarchy of control, since the reason and will had strict control only over the bodily members.

Feinberg's work points up a strong identification between the person, on the one hand, and the behavior that serves as a desert base for favorable or unfavorable treatment, on the other. In Aquinas's discussion of acts of the will, the theoretical basis for such an identification was developed for the order of intention, and was reinforced by the reflexivity of reason and will. Each stage progressing toward the attainment of an end was a representative, internal expression of the character of the agent. The end was freely adopted in intention, since, although there was only one true ultimate end for man, the orientation of the will to the good in general allowed the individual the freedom to seek his happiness in particular goods such as wealth or fame. And, although intention per se was neither consent nor choice, it was nonetheless a manifestation of the basic character of the individual, of the inclinationes seated in his will: "As a man is so does the end seem to him."[88] Moreover, any end short of the summum bonum itself might be considered as a means to the happiness of the agent, and therefore reviewed morally in consent and selected in preference to others in choice. In this way the capacity of the rational creature to reflect on his own means and ends provided a basis for personal responsibility even at the initial stage in the generation of action.

In the normal case, acts consequent to intention were no less one's own. The deliberation of the means was imperated by the will, and, through the act of consent, the results of deliberation could be assessed in relation to other personal interests and in consultation of the natural and divine laws. Next, in choice the option was left to the will even to reject the conclusion drawn by the practical syllogism. And, finally, command and use combined to extend the control of the mind either outward upon the external world or inward, recursively, upon subsequent internal movements. Thus, for every waking moment in the life of the individual, Aquinas believed that God had provided the basic conditions for responsible control over the inner life, and for adequate, if often uncertain, control over external affairs as well.

NOTES

[1] S.L.E., p. 132, ll. 18-29.
[2] S.L.E., p. 149, ll. 19-21.
[3] S.L.E., p. 150, ll. 11-13.
[4] Aristotle, Nicomachean Ethics, 1113 b19-22.
[5] S.L.E., p. 530, ll. 1-4.
[6] S.L.E., p. 531, ll. 56-65.
[7] S.L.E., p. 130, 1111a 33-63.
[8] S.L.E., p. 130, ll. 89-97.
[9] S.L.E., p. 130, ll. 97-107.
[10] S.T., I-II, 77, a. 1 ad 2; I-II, 9, a. 2; 10, a. 3.
[11] Q.D.V., 24, a.1.
[12] S.T., I-II, 91, a. 4.
[13] S.T., 6, a. 2 ad 2.
[14] S.T., I-II, 89, a. 6.
[15] Q.D.V., 24, a. 1.
[16] S.T., I-II, 6, a. 4.
[17] S.T., I-II, 6, a. 3; 71, a. 5; II-II, 79, a. 3.
[18] S.T., I-II, 9, a. 1; 10, a. 2.
[19] S.T. I-II, 8, a. 1 ad 2.
[20] S.T., I-II, 6, a. 8; 76, aa. 1-4; 78, a. 1.
[21] S.T., II-II, 103, a. 1; I, 20, a. 3 ad 2; II-II, 83, a. 13.
[22] S.T., I-II, 6, a. 8.
[23] S.T., I-II, 6, a. 3 ad 3.
[24] S.T., I, 79, aa. 11-13; I-II, 94, a. 2. Cf. Germain G. Grisez, "The First Principle of Practical Reason," in Aquinas: A Collection of Critical Essays, ed. Anthony Kenny (New York: Anchor, 1969), pp. 340-382.
[25] S.T., I, 79, aa. 11-13. Cf. Eric D'Arcy, Conscience and Its Right to Freedom (New York: Sheed and Ward, 1961), pp. 3-48.
[26] S.T., I-II, 79, a. 12; 15, a. 4.
[27] S.T., I-II, 19, aa. 5, 6.
[28] Alan Donagan, The Theory of Morality (Chicago: University of Chicago Press, 1977), p. 136.
[29] S.T., I-II, 87, a. 3.
[30] S.T., I-II, 6, a. 4.
[31] S.T., I, 106, a. 2
[32] S.T., I, 105, a. 4.

[33] Eric D'Arcy, "'Worthy of Worship': A Catholic Contribution," in Religion and Morality, ed. Gene Outka and John P. Reeder, Jr. (New York: Anchor, 1973), p. 202. Cf. S.T., I-II, 7, a. 4 ad 3.

[34] Alan Donagan, The Theory of Morality, p. 121.

[35] S.T., I-II, 1, a. 6; 10, a. 1.

[36] S.T., I-II, 17, a. 4.

[37] S.T., I-II, 6, a. 4.

[38] Ibid.

[39] S.T., I-II, 16, a. 4 ad 3.

[40] Compare Alan Donagan, "Thomas Aquinas on Human Action," in N. Kretzmann, A. Kenny, and J. Pinborg, eds., The Cambridge History of Later Medieval Philosophy, Chapter 33, p. 653.

[41] S.T., II-II, 58, a. 2.

[42] S.T., I-II, 16, a. 1.

[43] S.T., I, 1, a. 9.

[44] S.T., I, 1, a. 9 ad 2.

[45] Cf. Ludwig Wittgenstein, Tractatus Logico-Philosophicus, trans. D. F. Pears and B. F. McGuinness (New York: Humanities Press, 1961), pp. 7, 15, 17, 35, 69.

[46] S.T., I-II, 1, a. 1 ad 1; 18, a. 7 ad 2.

[47] Frederick Crowe, "Complacency and Concern in the Thought of St. Thomas," Theological Studies, 20 (1959), pp. 1–39.

[48] S.T., I-II, 26, a. 2.

[49] Crowe, "Complacency and Concern," p. 12.

[50] Q.D.V., 14, a. 5; in Crowe, "Complacency and Concern," p. 10.

[51] Crowe, "Complacency and Concern," p. 10.

[52] Crowe, "Complacency and Concern," p. 29.

[53] S.T., I-II, 8, a. 1.

[54] S.T., I-II, 16, a. 4.

[55] S.T., I-II, 11. Alan Donagan, "Thomas Aquinas on Human Action," p. 646.

[56] S.T., I-II, 11, a. 1.

[57] S.T., I-II, 11, a. 3.

[58] Alan Donagan, "Thomas Aquinas on Human Action," pp. 648–49.

[59] S.T., I-II, 14.

[60] S.T., I-II, 14.

[61] Anthony Kenny, Will, Freedom and Power (London: Blackwell, 1974), p. 25.

[62] S.T., I-II, 14, aa. 2, 5, 6.

[63] S.T., I-II, 14, a. 1; 13, a. 3.

[64] S.T., I-II, 10, a. 2 ad 3; 13, a. 6 ad 1; 14, a. 4 ad 3.

[65] S.T., I-II, 14, a.3.

[66] S.T., I-II, 14, a. 4.

[67] Ibid.
[68] S.T., I-II, 13, a. 6 ad 1.
[69] Alan Donagan, "Thomas Aquinas on Human Action," p. 648.
[70] S.T., I-II, 13, a. 3; 13, a. 1 ad 2.
[71] S.T., I-II, 15, a. 1.
[72] S.T., I-II, 15.
[73] S.T., I-II, 15, a. 4.
[74] S.T. I-II, 15, a. 1.
[75] S.T., I-II, 74, a. 8.
[76] S.T., I-II, 86, a. 1 ad 1.
[77] S.T., I-II, 15, a. 3 ad 3.
[78] S.T., I-II, 13, a. 3.
[79] Alan Donagan, "Thomas Aquinas on Human Action," p. 649.
[80] S.T., I-II, 17, a. 1.
[81] S.T., I-II, 17, a. 9.
[82] S.T., I-II, 17, a. 9, c.e.
[83] S.T., I-II, 9, a. 2 ad 3; 17, a. 7.
[84] S.T., I-II, 17, a. 1.
[85] Ibid.
[86] Ibid.
[87] S.T., I-II, 75, a. 2.
[88] S.T., I-II, 9, a. 2.

CHAPTER 6
SIN

I

It is necessary now to bring the preceding discussion to bear on the question of how acts elicited or commanded by the will affected the individual's relation to God. Since merit has been discussed above, I will focus here only on Aquinas's theory of sin. In contrast to the concept of merit, Thomas found in the concept of sin no difficulty in disentangling the relative contributions of the individual and God; rather, problems arose in explaining how the agent could withdraw from divine direction to the extent that he did.

The goodness or badness of a human action was principally determined by its object--but, as noted above, Aquinas's conception of the <u>obiectum</u> was not entirely clear. Central to the <u>obiectum</u> was the end, together with whatever was ordered to it as means. Accordingly, Thomas explained that an end was good or bad in kind (i.e., materially) if, by its nature, it accorded with or opposed the principal ends to which man had been ordained by God: God, self, and neighbors or community. In addition to this materially good or bad object, there was the formal object actually willed by the agent in the circumstances of his act. For example, in the case of a robbery committed for the sake of revenge, the material object would be "taking the goods of another"; the formal object would be "getting even with him."[1] In this example, both formal and material objects would have the neighbor as the proximate end affected by the act, but the act would also be opposed to the self (since it would foster habituation in sin), and to the Deity (since it would be contrary to his will as ruler, father, and friend).

In good and bad acts alike, then, the weight of the act depended upon the end or ends that "attached" to the material and formal <u>obiecta</u>.[2] The higher the end that attached to an inordinate act, the more grave the sin.

> Now the object of an act is its end, as stated above; and consequently the difference of gravity in sins depends on their objects. Thus it is clear that external things are directed to man as their end, while man is further directed to God as his end. Wherefore, a sin which is about the very substance of man, e.g., murder, is graver than a sin which is about external things, e.g., theft; and graver still is a sin committed directly against God, e.g., unbelief, blasphemy, and the like: and in each of these grades of sin, one sin will be greater than

another according as it is about a higher or lower principle. And forasmuch as sins take their species from their objects, the difference of gravity which is derived from the objects is first and foremost, as resulting from the species.[3]

The weight of the material goodness of an act of will, therefore, depended on the end it <u>normally</u> promoted; the weight of the material badness of an act, on the end it <u>normally</u> demoted. The weight of the formal goodness of an act, on the other hand, depended on the end or ends the agent <u>intended</u> to promote; the weight of the formal badness, on the end or ends the agent <u>knew or should have known</u> that it demoted.

The lack of symmetry in this account is evident. In material goodness or badness, the weight of a voluntary act followed from its promotion or demotion of an end as this would normally have occurred in the order of things. And in the formal goodness of an act, similarly, the weight of the act followed from the end the agent intended to promote, based on his knowledge of normal causation, together with whatever knowledge he had of the special circumstances within which he acted.

The criterion of the formal badness of an act, however, was more complex. In Aquinas's view, the sinfulness of an act was not part of the intention with which the agent acted, but was beside the intention (<u>praeter intentionem</u>). His end, if not actually good, appeared good to him, and "it is the end that is willed in the willing of the means." Although the badness of an act was not part of an agent's intention, it was nevertheless necessary that the agent be able readily to know, recognize, or infer the end demoted from the end intended, or from the means to which he consented in order to realize that intention. That is, he must be able to know it, without difficulty, from the object he did know and will. Donagan's condition is worth citing again here, for, as we shall see, it is a modern expression of the condition that Aquinas himself held:

> Since a rational agent, as such, controls his actions in the light of his knowledge of what they are, to hold him answerable for his actions under descriptions he does not know they fall under is to demand that he answer for something for which, as a rational agent, he cannot answer.[4]

The most important way that Thomas met this condition was by explaining the sense in which God, as the ultimate end, "attached" (<u>contingit</u>) to the object of the will in sin, for this explains the sense in which his sin was inordinate. In meritorious acts, the ultimate end was part of the object of the will itself, part of its "turning" toward God in an act informed by charity. In sinful acts and omissions, however, the "turning" of the will was toward some mutable good and away from God: "Two things are to be observed in sin, conversion to a mutable good...and aversion from the immutable good...."[5] How, then, did the <u>obiectum</u> in "turning toward" relate to its sinfulness in "turning away," and how was the agent cognizant of this relation when he sinned?

At the level of the material sinfulness of an act, Aquinas suggested that the end to which it stood opposed was immediately connected with the end it affirmed. In the case of theft, for example, the gain to self through the deprivation of another was directly opposed to the good of the other. Similarly, in the case of suicide, the loss of the burdens of life was attained through the loss of life itself. In effect, in the attempt to attain his end through a means, the sinner jeopardized his relation to a higher end, thereby subordinating a higher good to a lower. In sins in which the connection was not so readily apparent, the express precepts of human and divine law were necessary to make the inordinacy of such acts explicit. In this way, Aquinas's conception of the material sinfulness of an act could be seen as an attempt to meet the same condition Donagan describes.

Aquinas's position may appear to amount to a form of cost-benefit analysis, with spiritual costs and benefits overriding all others. If this were the case, then the opposition between object and end might be resolved into a more basic principle, a principle of harm. Yet although Thomas agreed that harm to self or other aggravated a sin, he denied that it was the sole principle of gravity in sin. The order of ends gave priority first to God, next to self, and third to others.[6] A harm principle would reverse this priority in many cases that involve conflicts between self and others; but more importantly, it would reverse it in all cases involving conflicts between self and God--for God could in no sense be harmed. Accordingly, Thomas preferred to see harm as a form of inordinacy rather than the other way around. In a special sense, however, we can say that harm was indeed his principle, for damage to a relationship to a proper end was the common property of all forms of inordinate act, and certainly held for sin as harm to the proper mode of subjection to God.

Thus, Thomas's distinction between mortal and venial sin rested on the harm or lack of harm to the individual's relationship to God as his ultimate end:

> Now disturbance of an order is sometimes reparable, sometimes irreparable: because a defect which destroys the principle is irreparable, whereas if the principle be saved, defects can be repaired by virtue of that principle. For instance, if the principle of sight be destroyed, sight cannot be restored except by divine power; whereas, if the principle of sight be preserved, while there arise certain impediments to the use of sight, these can be remedied by nature or by art. Now in every order there is a principle whereby one takes part in that order. Consequently, if a sin destroys the principle of the order whereby man's will is subject to God, the disorder will be such as to be irreparable, considered in itself, although it is possible to repair it by the power of God. Now the principle of this order is the last end, to which man adheres by charity. Therefore whatever sins turn man away from God, so as to destroy charity, considered in themselves, incur a debt of eternal punishment.[7]

Viewed in light of the analogies of ruler-subject, father-child, and friend-friend, this passage implies that mortal sin caused irreparable damage to the friendship with God. At times, therefore, Aquinas wrote of the aversion to God as if it were only indirectly interpersonal; at other times, however, he stressed the relation to the Other by emphasizing the roles of pride, contempt, and even hatred in the breach of the relationship.

From the interpersonal perspective, venial sin emerged as the type of act or omission that was pardonable (venialis), because it was not directly opposed to the Other, to his definition of the relationship, or to his measure of control over it. Like minor offenses or irritations to any relationship, then, venial sins did not call the relationship itself into question, but occurred within it. Mortal sin, by contrast, caused irreparable harm to the very basis or "principle" of the relationship, for it was directly opposed to the Other, to his definition of the relationship through natural and divine law, and to his control over it through grace.

Inordinate acts were mortal, then, when the opposition between "turning to" and "turning from" did not involve matters external to the two parties, but was "about their very substance." The insubordination between "turning to" and "turning from" in mortal sin was thus an affirmation of self that directly implied a rejection of God--a "love of self to the contempt of God," as Augustine had put it.[8] To use the example of a mortal sin ending a state of charity, the shared activity or inward communicatio between the two friends was destroyed by an act of will denying the mutual love and benevolence on which it was based. The means represented by the obiectum of a sin of this type, such as blasphemy or unbelief, immediately indicated the aversion involved: "let not thy will but mine be done," the antithesis of the exemplary love expressed at Gethsemane, and thus a direct, fundamental, and evident reversal of the proper hierarchy of goods.

Aquinas's analysis of the material nature of sin, then, described how, in some acts, the end to which the object of the consenting will was opposed was immediately evident from the object itself, while in others express prescriptions and prohibitions filled in the steps of inference necessary for the potential sinner to recognize the relation between "turning to" and "turning from" in his consent to means. As a sinner, therefore, the agent either had some sense of his act as a "turning from" the end, or else was culpably responsible for lacking that sense, due to corruption of or failure to develop the natural habit of synderesis.

Aquinas's analysis of the material object and the ends that attach to it was designed to help the agent assess his own actions, and thereby to inform his consent to formal objects. Nevertheless, the problem of the relation between conversion and aversion arose in a second, and more acute form. For, given Thomas's analysis of the relation between the material object and the end opposed to it, one may wonder that sin ever occurred at all. Since the knowledge that an act was inordinate was--or once had been--immediately available to the potential sinner, how could he sin? By arguing that God had made ample provision for the individual to avoid sin, Aquinas also made the question, "Whence comes evil?" all the more acute.

II

Thus, in relating the knowledge necessary for responsibility to the culpable ignorance necessary for sin, Aquinas needed to draw a fine line. In drawing it, he offered a solution to the Socratic paradox that no one sins knowingly.[9] To restate the paradox in Thomas's own terms, it seems that voluntary sin was a contradiction in terms, since the knowledge required for voluntariness precluded the ignorance presupposed by sin. For if the agent fulfilled the conditions of voluntariness, and therefore knew what he was doing, then it seems that he would not have sinned; just as sinfulness was sufficient reason against performing an act, so an agent who performed such an act must somehow have lacked the knowledge that it was sinful. If, on the other hand, the agent lacked the knowledge that his act was sinful, then it seems he did not know what he was doing, and his sin was therefore involuntary. Therefore, either the individual acted voluntarily and did not sin, or he sinned and did not act voluntarily. Posed in this way, the problem appears to have required a solution that would distinguish different senses of "knowledge" and "ignorance," and that was how Aquinas approached it.

In Aquinas's view, sin was voluntary but not intentional. No one intended evil, for the object of the will was an apparent good. Yet people did consent to or choose evil knowingly, when their interest in the end they intended overrode their concern that the means were inordinate. Aquinas thereby removed sinfulness from the object as intended, and even from the object as consented to and chosen, but not from the actual or potential awareness of the agent in affirming the means.

This, in outline, was Aquinas's solution, but it can be clarified further. Thomas did speak of sinful intentions, and when he did so he can be interpreted in one of two ways.[10] First, he may have meant that ignorance of the difference between a true but limited good like honor and a false good like vainglory was culpable ignorance of moral knowledge that was available to everyone. This interpretation relies heavily on a role for omissions, and would have left Thomas open to the objections that attach to such reliance.[11] Secondly, he may have meant that intention, consent, and choice were conflated because the end was attained through a single means known without deliberation. For example, if the individual intended the death of his neighbor, then he also consented to the act of murder and chose it as his means. It seems, however, that the first interpretation could always be subsumed under the second, since Thomas sometimes spoke of consent to an end, and generally reserved the application of moral norms to the act of consent. Thus, to expand the scope of the second interpretaton, the individual who intended vainglory as his end should have paused to consider that this end was less than ultimate, and reflected that it was not compatible with but rather opposed to his ultimate end.

To interpret Aquinas's position in this second way places the onus of moral responsibility almost entirely on consent, but this seems to have been where Thomas placed it himself, both in the question on consent in the treatise on human acts, and in the treatise on sin. Sin consisted in the inordinacy of a voluntary act, and if an act was inordinate, then a higher good was subordinated to a lower. In actions and omissions such a reversal could not occur prior to the first act of the will toward the means, and this act was consent. Consent provided the first opportunity, therefore, for the will to violate natural, human, or divine law, and Aquinas therefore introduced moral norms at this point in his theory of human acts.

Yet if this interpretation is correct, then Socrates' hydraheaded paradox appears again: for if in consent the agent had considered the means in the clear light of the eternal reasons, then presumably he would not have consented to means that were sinful, and hence there would have been no sin; but if the agent did not consider the means in the light of these norms, then the conclusion of his moral reasoning would lack a crucial premise. Again, either there was no sin, or the sin was involuntary. In a notable passage, Thomas simply denied both horns of the dilemma; direct contempt of the eternal reasons was not impossible, and omission to consider them was not inculpable:

> The higher reason is said to consent, from the very fact that it fails to direct the human act according to the divine law, whether or not it advert to the eternal law. For if it thinks of God's law, it holds it in actual contempt: and if not, it neglects it by a kind of omission.[12]

This seems unsatisfactory; a statement of fact rather than an analysis that resolves the difficulty. The problem can be pursued further, but Bernard Lonergan has argued that Aquinas cannot be shown to have explained the act of sin, for he believed that even God did not understand it. Sin, as Lonergan puts it, was "an absolute objective falsity," for in it the sinner actually withdrew from the ordinance of the divine intellect (<u>subducere se ab ordinatione divini intellectus</u>):

> For, obviously, the possibility of our understanding anything is ultimately due to the object's commensurability to the divine intellect; and in absolute objective falsity it is precisely this commensurability that is lacking. We can know sin as a factor; we cannot place it in intelligible correlation with other things except <u>per accidens</u>; that is, one sin can be correlated with another, for deficient antecedents have defective consequents; but the metaphysical surd of sin cannot be related explanatorily or causally with the integers that are objective truth; for sin is really irrational, a departure at once from the ordinance of the divine mind and from the dictate of right reason.

The rational and the irrational cannot mix, except in fallacious speculation. And this precept is not merely relative to man; it is absolute. The mysteries of faith are mysteries only to us because of their excess of intelligibility; but the <u>mysterium iniquitatis</u> is mysterious in itself and objectively, because of a defect in intelligibility.[13]

Thus, Aquinas's way of fulfilling the condition Donagan states was to say that the privative character of the <u>obiectum</u> as demoting a higher end could be immediately known to the agent by consulting his lower and higher reason in consent. The will might be so inclined that this knowledge made no difference, in which case the agent held God's law in contempt, or the agent might omit to bring this knowledge to mind, in which case he was negligent. In either case, the act of the will in demoting a higher good in favor of a lower was a "metaphysical surd."

III

In light of the problem of evil, it is not hard to say why Aquinas treated sin as an absolute objective falsity: as an act of withdrawal from the ordinance of the divine intellect, sin fell outside that ordinance, and therefore could not be ascribed to God. But Lonergan's interpretation should not be read as denying that Aquinas could diagnose motives for sin, nor as asserting that Thomas commonly excused himself from this task. On the contrary, Aquinas was at least as thorough in his accounts of sinful actions as he was in his analysis of meritorious ones. Indeed, he came close to exculpating sinners as victims of the extreme difficulty of the call to a supernatural end.

Conceived as an act against a personal deity, mortal sin was modelled on the familiar phenomena that appear during a crisis in a relationship. Because the relationship between the soul and God was so unstable, it was in crisis or potential crisis more often than not. A mortal sin, then, was an apparently irrational act done in the context of some mode of subjection to God, involving withdrawal from that relationship (<u>subducere se ab ordinatione divini intellectus</u>) by an act expressing aversion to and contempt of him. But why would anyone want to withdraw from a relationship to God in the first place? Gratitude had somehow given way to ingratitude, reverence to contempt, even love to hatred-- but how?

Aquinas gave the initial answer: such an act had to be done in pursuit of some good or apparent good. In other words, just as human relationships often go bad through interest in a good impossible within the context of the relationship, so the individual's relationship to God reached a crisis through acts that were destructive of the relationship <u>praeter intentionem</u>. By virtue of some good or apparent good, the agent withdrew from the relationship.

Aquinas had no difficulty identifying the goods intended by a will already hardened in sin. "As a man is, so does the end seem to him," and therefore a man with multiple debts of eternal punishment saw the end and ruler of the universe only in a prohibitive and punitive role; for that was the whole of God to an intellect commanded by a disordered will. The Deity was known to the rational animal by his effects, and although some of those effects could not be repugnant to anyone (e.g., to be, to live, to understand),

> Some...are contrary to an inordinate will, such as the infliction of punishment, and the prohibition of sin by the divine law. Such like effects are repugnant to a will debased by sin, and as regards the consideration of them, God may be an object of hatred to some, in so far as they look upon him as forbidding sin, and inflicting punishment.[14]

The God-hater, then, was simply a person too badly warped in spirit to conceive of God properly. Within its limitations, however, his response was an understandable aversion to constraint and harm.

The more difficult case, however, was that of a mortal sin committed by a person who was not biased against the ultimate end, but properly converted to it. Thomas's remarks on charity and mortal sin make the change only partially intelligible:

> Charity by reason of its actus excludes every motive for sinning. But it happens sometimes that charity is not acting actually, and then it is possible for a motive to intervene for sinning, and if we consent to this motive, we lose charity.[15]

For example, suppose someone in a state of charity underwent a sudden movement of lust; this would have been an intervening motive for sinning. But what was the motive to consent to this motive, and thus to begin to fantasize sinfully (delectatio morosa)? Aquinas gave no answer to this, and it therefore appeared that the search for an explanation had already been blocked at the mysterium iniquitatis.

Thomas's comment on the charity of the blessed, however, suggested that to do so would limit prematurely the intelligibility that could be attained:

> [I]t is natural for a form to be in its matter in such a way that it can be lost, when it does not entirely fill the potentiality of the matter.... Hence the one form may be lost by the other being received.
>
> On the other hand, the form of a celestial body which entirely fills the potentiality of its matter, so that the latter does not retain the potentiality to another form, is in the subject inseparably. Accordingly, the charity of the blessed, because it entirely fills the potentiality of the rational mind, since every actual movement of the mind is directed to God, is possessed by its subject inseparably: whereas the charity of the wayfarer does not fill the potentiality of its subject, because the latter is not always actually directed to God: so that when it is not always actually directed to God, something may occur whereby charity is lost.[16]

Here, without denying personal responsibility for mortal sin, Aquinas was suggesting that part of the explanation for the occurrence of mortal sins among those in a state of grace had to do with the existential situation of the individual. Even the person in a state of charity was a pilgrim in transition through a world to which he could not fail to give some attention. And this world, it might be added, had given him his basic conceptions of what it was to be in a relationship to another.

Characteristically, Aquinas did not follow up the latter possibility; a sense of the comprehensive context of human action before God was used only to bind, never to loose the individual from his responsibility. As in the case of the God-hater, he explored the situation and perspective of the sinner just far enough to give his act a commonsense intelligibility, never so far as to lead to pardon or pity.

Here the notion of hierarchy had a major role. To demonstrate this, I would like to pursue a contemporary and anachronistic line of argument against Aquinas, then to show the role of hierarchy and inwardness in precluding it.

The friendship of the individual and God in charity might be described, ideally, as a closed circuit. God first infused the habitus of charity into the soul, then the individual responded in love; God responded favorably in turn, "so that man obtains from God, as a reward of his operation, what God gave him the power of operation for." The ideal give-and-take between the individual and God in temporal friendship, therefore, was a recurrent cycle or spiral, moving the individual gradually but increasingly toward deiformity, and thus toward eternal friendship with the Deity.

But this supernaturally empowered cycle of interaction, although it was an attractive ideal, was rarely realized; nor was this solely the fault of the human agent. A wayfarer had more to do in life than interact with God, and God had some responsibility for this, for he gave the will its dual orientation. Other, worldly aspects of the individual's life fed into the cycle, therefore, and however much he might try through charity to refer his acts to God, his charity could not always be in actu.

Yet not only was interaction with God interrupted by the day-to-day distractions of life; the individual's understanding of that very interaction was modelled on his experience of interaction with other human beings. The individual's understanding of his friendship to God was based on the analogy of temporal attributes, and these in turn drew upon his worldly experience of the roles, relations, and rules that governed interaction between equals and unequals. In these social contexts the individual had acquired his sense of personal dignity and honor. It was as likely that this pride would be included as lost in his analogical use of asymmetrical relationships to understand his interaction with God. The margin of error in the common man's version of temporal analogy, therefore, was simply too great for his pride not to come into play from time to time and disrupt the spiral of grace.

As noted in Chapter 3, Aquinas argued that obligation between any subordinate and his superior was a one-way street: the subordinate as such was obligated to his superior, not conversely. Yet he also noted that it was rare that one person was subordinate to another in all respects, and noted too that the two parties usually stood as equals under higher-order laws.

A similar point held for favor: the superior friend as such could act favorably toward the subordinate, not the other way around. Yet here too the mixture of superior and inferior qualities that came with being human always allowed room for an exchange of favors between the two parties. With these qualifications, then, Aquinas mitigated his conception of justice between unequals.

These qualifications, however, were totally absent from the asymmetrical relation of the individual to God. God was superior in every respect, and therefore had only favors to give and obligations to exact; he could no more receive favors than he could fulfill obligations. This was his nature as a perfect being, and in itself, said Aquinas, it entailed no defect or privation.

But the individual, conceiving his various modes of subjection to God on analogy with the relationships that defined his worldly identity, experienced this difference as a problem of intellect and will. From his birth, nothing had been in his intellect unless it had first been in his senses. His senses had seen the effects of God, and he knew God by analogy from these effects. In his relationship to God as ultimate end he was ordered to him "as to an end that exceeds the grasp of reason." But all this was just another way of saying that, even in a state of charity, the individual had very little sense of the ordinatio divini intellectus. He was informed of it through natural reason, divine revelation, and divine grace, but his understanding of it remained grounded analogically in relationships that misled his will. For in any human relationship he knew, patterns of interaction as one-sided as those in the spiral of grace would leave no place for personal honor and dignity, and would therefore readily give rise to ingratitude and contempt, and perhaps even to hatred.

The argument above, then, might be constructed using present-day sociological conceptions of language and social context, or, more simply, using an analogical appropriation of Aquinas's own style of commonsense: too much help to a friend could harm the friendship by increasing rather than reducing inequality, and by infringing on rather than respecting the independence of the friend. Aquinas's spiral of grace undercut the basic conceptions upon which worldly gratitude, reverence, and love were based: the conceptions of self, one's own, control over what was one's own, and a discernable quid pro quo. Whatever its logical viability, therefore, it may be argued that the practical bearing of Aquinas's use of temporal analogy was bound to lead to a prideful reaction in many people, due simply to their understandable inability to drop the unwanted elements from the meaning of the analogy. Given the radical asymmetry of the relationship, the pride of the individual naturally asserted itself. The individual might withdraw from the relationship, then, through a simple desire for some measure of personal dignity and independence.

Thomas's most obvious resources for responding to such a brief for the sinner amount to a cold-eyed realism about the way things were: God was perfect, man was grossly imperfect, and therefore the individual had to undergo some very substantial changes in attitude if he was to become fit for the ultimate end in God. Pride was understandable, to be sure, but it had no place in the relationship to God.

The point I wish to make, however, is that Aquinas's approach to personal responsibility systematically avoided the use of external explanations of internal movements, and did so through the belief in hierarchical order and its corollary that higher is more inward. Thus, explanation by appeal to externals held only for half of the dual orientation of the will. Reference to externals allowed Aquinas to make sense of sinful acts only insofar as the sinner was oriented to the external world and rested his will in it; they did not allow him to make them fully intelligible, however, because that orientation itself could not be explained by the influence of the external world.

In this defense against the argument given above, Aquinas's decisive assumption was the conception of hierarchy. By virtue of the notion of a hierarchy of being, Thomas could define the spiritual context of human action in double-binding ways that directed the individual to his end in God, while at the same time denying that binds in the temporal context excused failures to attain that end. The higher was more powerful than the lower, the inner more powerful than the outer, and the inclination to the universal good more powerful than the inclination to particular goods. The therapeutic and favorable interpretation of any bind on the will was always the dominant and proper one.

Apparent counterexamples to this role for hierarchy were the external conditions that excuse the agent from sin or mitigate his guilt. In cases of excuse or mitigation, the temporal context of a voluntary, inordinate act did contribute to its inordinacy, and in a way that diminished the gravity of the act. Yet cases of excuse or mitigation, in Aquinas's view, were quite different from failures to interpret properly the condition of the rational creature as existing in the world yet subject to God. Because they failed to observe the hierarchy of control in the soul, actions that resulted from extrinsic conditions also failed to engage the intellect and will in their proper function, and to that degree were less voluntary. Excusing conditions either failed to communicate the obiectum properly to the will or else constrained the acts commanded by it; mitigating factors communicated in part, but also deluded or eluded the will to some degree.

Now since the individual's mode of subjection to God was built on the natural tendencies of intellect and will, and was altered only in keeping with those natural orientations, influences that did not fully engage these potencies did not substantially affect the relationship to God. By contrast, the individual in charity, whose pride emerged because he had nothing of his own to contribute to the relationship, performed (or accountably omitted to perform) an interior act of the will in which both intellect and will were fully involved. Conditions of excuse and mitigation, therefore, were quite unlike the conditions that might be adduced in explanation of the breach of friendship with God.

Hierarchy, therefore, supported Thomas's emphasis on independence from the external world and dependence on the Other within, and in a way that kept responsibility on the individual and placed him in a double bind. As he put it,

> As stated above, the internal cause of sin is both the will, as completing the sinful act, and the reason, as lacking the due rule, and the appetite, as inclining to sin. Accordingly something external might be a cause of sin in three ways, either by moving the will itself immediately, or by moving the reason, or by moving the sensitive appetite. Now, as stated above, none can move the will inwardly save God alone, who cannot be a cause of sin, as we shall prove further on. Hence it follows that nothing external can be a cause of sin, except by moving the reason, as a man or devil by enticing to sin; or by moving the sensitive appetite, as certain external sensibles move it. Yet neither does external enticement move the reason, of necessity, in matters of action, nor do things proposed externally, of necessity move the appetite, except perhaps it be disposed thereto in a certain way; and even the sensitive appetite does not of necessity move the reason and will. Therefore something external can be a cause of moving to sin, but not so as to be a sufficient cause thereof: and the will alone is the sufficient completive cause of sin being accomplished.[17]

In short, "nothing external is a cause of sin, except through the medium of the internal cause, as stated."[18] Thomas did not have in mind general features of man's experience of the external world, but the same principle held. The notion of hierarchy ruled out the possibility of substantial influence flowing up through the structure of the soul to turn the human spirit against God. Responsibility was thereby preserved internally.

Thus, Aquinas gave to the sinful act the most complete causal explanation possible given his commitment to the hierarchical structure of the soul, but that belief in hierarchy was the principal bulwark against an interpretation of the human condition as a situation in which contingencies of personal experience and temperament could excuse the agent from sin. Hierarchy, then, was central to his theory of human responsibility, and it gave him the conception he needed to sustain the perfectionist tension between justice and love. With it, responsibility was not only a backward-looking conception that belonged to the bestowal of just deserts, but also an integral part of the conceptual framework that directed the individual in fear and love to his ultimate end in God. Granting Aquinas his conception of a hierarchy of being and its application to the human soul, it follows that the sinner had to hold himself responsible for his escape from the double binds that defined his condition, and this acceptance of responsibility appears to have been an indispensable condition for his forward motion out of the bind and toward the vision of God.

NOTES

[1] S.T., I-II, 18, a. 6.
[2] S.T., I-II, 73, a. 3.
[3] Ibid.
[4] Alan Donagan, The Theory of Morality, p. 121.
[5] S.T., II-II, 162, a. 6.
[6] S.T., I-II, 73, a. 8.
[7] S.T., I-II, 87, a. 3.
[8] Augustine, The City of God, trans. Gerald G. Walsh, Demetrius B. Zema, Grace Monahan, and Daniel J. Honan (Garden City, New York: Doubleday, 1958), p. 321.
[9] Plato, Protagoras, trans. W. K. C. Guthrie, in Plato: Protagoras and Meno (Penguin Books: Harmondsworth, 1956). See G. W. Mortimore, ed. Weakness of Will (New York: Macmillan, 1971).
[10] S.T., I-II, 78, a. 1 ad 2.
[11] Q.D.V., 24, a. 1.
[12] S.T., I-II, 74, a. 7 ad 2.
[13] Bernard Lonergan, Grace and Freedom (New York: Herder and Herder, 1971), p. 113.
[14] S.T., II-II, 34, aa. 1, 2.
[15] S.T., II-II, 24, a. 11 ad 4.
[16] S.T., II-II, 24, a. 11.
[17] S.T., I-II, 75, a. 3.
[18] S.T., I-II, 75, a. 3 ad 2.

CHAPTER 7
EPILOGUE

Aquinas's religious ethics was governed by three models: teleology, justice, and friendship. He presented them as similar in structure--so much so, indeed, that he felt that he could move without explanation between their different terminologies. He described the individual who was fit for salvation as proportionate to the ultimate end, deserving of eternal reward, and suited for divine friendship.

There is nothing in the concepts of teleology, justice, and friendship that called for the introversion of responsibility. In Thomas's system, the grounds for introversion were found elsewhere, implicit in his conception of God, in his idea of God's presence to the human soul, and in his understanding of the hierarchical structure of the soul. As he saw it, the individual's mode of subjection to God was defined and redefined only at the nether term, through changes effected by grace or by the higher, more inward powers of intellect and will. The inward face of human action determined the relation to God, much as its outward face affected relations to other people.

In consequence, the relations to God expressed by using the notions of teleology, justice, and friendship were conceived as inward relations, inwardly changed. This inward turn added to Aquinas's already existing problems in reconciling the three models, but it also contributed to the solution he proposed. One important question that Aquinas had to settle was the relation between the self-regarding character of teleology and the other-regarding character of justice. A partial resolution was achieved in charity or friendship, for in charity the fulfillment of the self was attained through the love of another, and the distinction between lover and beloved was blurred by the fact that the beloved was regarded as "another self." Introversion added to this argument the idea that in relation to God the other is, in a sense, within the self, thereby further confounding the distinction between self and other.

Thus, although he adopted from Aristotle the secular ethical language of teleology and justice, Aquinas implied that, in the last analysis, the separation of self and others that these conceptions presupposed was merely worldly. They could certainly be used when emphasizing the sinner's estrangement from God, but they were far less helpful in commending a close and loving relationship with him. In the latter instance, Aquinas turned to Aristotle's analysis of friendship and stressed the possibility of identifying the self with the divine Other. In doing so, he presented a vision of the inner life in which the worldly conflicts between self-regarding and other-regarding considerations were overcome, and with them the distinctions between self and other which those conflicts presupposed and reinforced.

In this way, Aquinas brought together three powerful ethical models and focused them directly on the life of the spirit. The result was at times paradoxical, but in interpreting and evaluating the paradoxes that arose it is important to recall the transformative intention of Christian ethics. Classical Christian ethics has never been merely a system of moral rules, but always a way of salvation as well. Accordingly, the stages of the soul's journey back to God and the critical transitions between them are built into it as the paradoxes of teleology, justice, and love. Thomas gave them more fine-grained articulation in his use of Aristotle, and, in doing so, he enables us to see their outlines more clearly. Notably, the backward-looking character of justice, which binds the individual to the sins of his past, conflicts with the forward-looking character of teleology, which directs him away from that past toward his future end. Likewise, the precept of charity, which brings love under the aegis of justice, conflicts with the spontaneous nature of love.

Aquinas addressed these paradoxes as theoretical problems in the consistency of Christian doctrine, but by arguing for that consistency he helped to keep the onus of responsibility on the believer. These apparent inconsistencies (or practical impossibilities), he implied, were not to be viewed as flaws in the Christian way of salvation, but rather to be accepted as what we might now call existential problems on the way. As in any classical Christian ethics, in Aquinas's moral theology the individual lives a life in transition, conceiving himself as being in the world but not of it. Accordingly, in expressing and encouraging this liminality, Aquinas reworked a tradition in which the language of the world was placed at odds with itself. His predecessors in the tradition, such as Paul and Augustine, had put the external world at a distance by putting its discourse at a distance. Instead of an alternative language, they had used the worldly language against itself in paradox. Aquinas, of course, believed that their paradoxes were not contradictions, but could in principle be resolved in keeping with his doctrine of analogy. But the force of this position was at once to keep the pressure on the believer and to reassure him that there was a path of salvation that could consistently be followed.

The basic paradox was "Be independent, but return to me through my help." Aquinas thought it through in his account of the dual orientation of the will. This was a bind that lasted a lifetime, defining the long transition from birth to salvation or damnation. Yet there was also the brief, decisive transition in which the individual moved from mortal sin to charity, and this passage was fraught with paradoxical injunctions such as the precept of charity, tantamount to the command, "Love me or I will damn you." As in the double binds analyzed by Bateson and others, the paradox was not a contradiction, but before the sinner could find his way between the levels of meaning and see the need to turn to God, he went through the painful process of discovering that he had no viable alternative.

As noted in Chapter 5, the notion of the hierarchy of being is a crucial conception in setting the bind, and thus in contributing to the transformation of the sinner. In Thomas's system, the paradoxical injunctions through which spiritual change may be effected presuppose that the individual accept responsibility for his interior acts and states. Accordingly, if the pressure of the bind was to be kept on the sinner, it could not be deflected by blaming God or pointing to the influences of the external world. Aquinas's theodicy was addressed to the former way of escape; the notion of hierarchy allowed him to close off the alternative route of claiming that circumstances outside the sinner's control had brought him to his sorry state. In Aquinas's conception of the hierarchy, the chain of command was from top to bottom, from internal to external, from spiritual to material. Although Aquinas granted that there could at times be upward influence, he admitted very few cases in which external events and conditions could reach through the lower powers to usurp the control of intellect and will. The hierarchical structure of the soul, therefore, helped to sustain his introvert conception of responsibility, held the sinner in the double bind, and thereby played a major role in the transformations through which the soul made its return to God.

BIBLIOGRAPHY

Abbreviations

Q.D.C.: Quaestio Disputata de Caritate
Q.D.V.: Quaestio Disputata de Veritate
S.C.G.: Summa Contra Gentiles
S.L.E.: Sententia Libri Ethicorum
S.T.: Summa Theologiae

Abelard, Peter. Peter Abelard's Ethics. Trans. by D. E. Luscombe. Oxford: Clarendon Press, 1971.

Anderson, James F. An Introduction to the Metaphysics of St. Thomas. Chicago: H. Regnery, 1953.

_____. "Bergson, Aquinas, and Heidegger on the Notion of Nothingness." Proceedings of the American Catholic Philosophical Association 41 (1967) 143-8.

_____. Reflections on the Analogy of Being. The Hague: Martinus Nijhoff, 1967.

Anscombe, G. E. M., P. T. Geach, Three Philosophers. Ithaca: Cornell University Press, 1961.

Anscombe, G. E. M. Intention. Ithaca: Cornell University Press, 1957.

Anselm of Canterbury. St. Anselm: Basic Writings. Trans. by S. N. Deane. La Salle: Open Court, 962.

_____. Why God Became Man. Trans. by Joseph M. Colleran. Albany: Magi, 1969.

Aquinas Septicentenary Commemoration: The New Scholasticism 48, 1 (1974).

Aristote et Saint Thomas D'Aquin. Louvain: Publications Universitaires de Louvain, 1955.

Aristotle. L'Ethique à Nicomaque. Ed. René Gauthier and Jean Yves Jolif. Louvain: Publications Universitaires, 1959.

_____. Nicomachean Ethics. Trans. by Martin Ostwald. Indianapolis: Bobbs-Merrill, 1962.

Armstrong, A. Hilary. Aristotle, Plotinus, and St. Thomas. London: Blackfriars, 1946.

_____, ed. The Cambridge History of Later Greek and Early Medieval Philosophy. London: Cambridge University Press, 1967.

Armstrong, Ross. Primary and Secondary Precepts in Thomistic Natural Law Teaching. The Hague: Martinus Nijhoff, 1966.

Ayers, Robert Hyman. Language, Logic, and Reason in the Church Fathers: A Study of Tertullian, Augustine, and Aquinas. New York: Olms, 1979.

Augustine. Confessions. Trans. by John K. Ryan. Garden City, New York: Doubleday, 1960.

_____. The City of God. Trans. by Gerald G. Walsh, Demetrius B. Zema, Grace Monahan, and Daniel J. Honan. Garden City, New York: Doubleday, 1958.

Austin, J. L. How to Do Things with Words. New York: Oxford University Press, 1970.

_____. Philosophical Papers. Oxford: Oxford University Press, 1970.

Baker, Richard Russell. The Thomistic Theory of the Passions and their Influence upon the Will. Notre Dame: Ph.D. thesis, University of Notre Dame, 1941.

Bars, Henry, ed. Jacques Maritain: Oeuvres 1912-1939. Bruges: Desclée, 1974.

Bastable, P. K. Desire for God: Does Man Aspire Naturally to the Beatific Vision? London: Burns, Oates, and Washbourne, 1947.

Bateson, Gregory. Steps to an Ecology of Mind. New York: Chandler, 1972.

_____, Don D. Jackson, Jay Haley, and John Weakland, "Toward a Theory of Schizophrenia." Behavioral Science, I, 1956.

Bellah, Robert N. "Religious Evolution." In Reader in Comparative Religion: An Anthropological Approach. Ed. William A. Lessa and Egon Z. Vogt. New York: Harper and Row, 1972. 45–55.

Berger, Peter. The Sacred Canopy. New York: Doubleday, 1969.

Binyon, Millard Pierce. The Virtues: A Methodological Study in Thomistic Ethics. Chicago: Ph.D. thesis, University of Chicago, 1948.

Blumberg, Harry. "The Problem of Immortality in Avicenna, Maimonides, and St. Thomas." In Harry Austryn Wolfson Jubilee Volume. Ed. by Saul Lieberman. Jerusalem: American Academy for Jewish Research, 1965.

Bohannon, Paul. Justice and Judgment Among the Tiv. New York: Oxford University Press, 1957.

Bonaventure. The Mind's Road to God. Indianapolis. Bobbs–Merrill, 1953.

Bond, Leo M. "A Comparison between Human and Divine Friendship." Thomist 3 (1941) 54–94.

Boulogne, Charles D. S. Thomas d'Aquin. Paris: Nouvelle editions latines, 1968.

Bourke, Vernon J. Aquinas' Search for Wisdom. Milwaukee: Bruce, 1965.

_____. "The Nicomachean Ethics and Thomas Aquinas." In St. Thomas Aquinas 1274–1974. Toronto: Pontifical Institute of Mediaeval Studies, 1974. I, 239–59.

_____. St. Thomas and the Greek Moralists. Milwaukee: Marquette University Press, 1947.

_____. Thomistic Bibliography: 1920–1940. St. Louis: Modern Schoolman, supplement to 21 (1945).

_____. Will in Western Thought. New York: Sheed and Ward, 1964.

Boyle, Joseph M., Jr. "Praeter Intentionem in Aquinas." The Thomist 42 (1978) 649–65.

Bradley, Denis J. M. "Rahner's Spirit in the World: Aquinas or Hegel?" The Thomist 41 (1977) 167–99.

Brecher, Bob. "Aquinas on Anselm." Philosophical Studies 23 (1975) 63-6.

Brehier, Emile. The History of Philosophy: The Middle Ages and the Renaissance. Trans. by W. Baskin. Chicago: University of Chicago Press, 1965.

Brennan, Robert E., ed. Essays in Thomism. New York: Sheed and Ward, 1942.

_____. "The Thomistic Concept of Imagination." The New Scholasticism 15 (1941) 149-61.

Brennan, Rose E. The Intellectual Virtues According to the Philosophy of St. Thomas. Washington: Catholic University of America Press, 1941.

Broad, Charlie D. "Some Basic Notions in the Philosophy of St. Thomas." Philosophy Today) 3 (1959)199-211.

Brown, Brendan F., ed. The Natural Law Reader. New York: Oceana Publishers, 1960.

Bruening, William H. "Aquinas and Wittgenstein on God-Talk." Sophia 16 (1977) 1-7.

Burke, Kenneth. The Rhetoric of Religion: Studies in Logology. Berkeley: University of California Press, 1970.

Burrell, David B. Analogy and Philosophical Language. New Haven: Yale University Press, 1973.

_____. Aquinas: God and Action. Notre Dame: University of Notre Dame Press, 1979.

_____. "Beyond the Theory of Analogy." Proceedings of the American Catholic Philosophical Association 46 (1972) 144-21.

_____. "Religious Language and the Logic of Analogy." International Philosophical Quarterly 2 (1962) 643-62.

Busa, Roberto. Index Thomisticus: S. Thomae Aquinatis Operum Omnium Indices et Concordantiae. Stuttgart: F. Fromm Verlag, 1979-80.

Cajetan, Thomas de Vio. The Analogy of Names and the Concept of Being. Trans. by E. A. Bushinski. Pittsburgh: Duquesne University Press,

1953.

Carlson, Sebastian. "The Virtue of Humility." The Thomist 7 (1944) 135-78; 8 (1944) 363-414.

Carrè, Meyrick H. Realists and Nominalists: Augustine, Abelard, Aquinas, Ockham. London: Oxford University Press, 1946.

Cavarnos, Constantine. The Classical Theory of Relations: A Study in the Metaphysics of Plato, Aristotle, and Thomism. Belmont: Institute for Byzantine and Modern Greek Studies, 1975.

Centenary of St. Thomas Aquinas, 1274-1974: The Thomist, 38. Washington: Thomist Press, 1974.

Centore, F. F. "Aquinas on Inner Space." Canadian Journal of Philosophy 4 (1974) 351-63.

Chapman, Thomas. "Analogy." The Thomist 39 (1975) 137-41.

Chenu, Marie-Dominique. "L'Originalitè de la morale de s. Thomas—Morale et Evangile." In Initiation Thèologique, III, Thèologie Morale. Paris: 1955. 7-12.

_____. "Les passions verteuses: L'anthropologie de s. Thomas." Journal Philosophique de Louvain 72 (1974) 11-18.

_____. "Ratio superior et inferior: un cas de philosophie chrètienne." Revue des Sciences Philosophiques et Thèologiques 29 (1940) 84-9.

_____. Toward Understanding St. Thomas. Chicago: H. Regnery, 1964.

Clark, Mary T., ed. An Aquinas Reader: Selections from the Writings of Thomas Aquinas. Garden City, New York: Doubleday Image, 1972.

Clark, Ralph W. "Aquinas on Intentions." The Thomist 40 (1976) 303-10.

_____. "Saint Thomas Aquinas's Theory of Universals." The Monist 58 (1974) 163-72.

Clarke, W. Norris. "Analogical Talk of God: Two Views: An Affirmative Rejoinder." The Thomist 40 (1976) 61-96.

Coffey, Reginald M. The Man from Rocca Secca. Milwaukee: Bruce, 1944.

Colish, Marcia L. The Mirror of Language: A Study in the Mediaeval Theory of Knowledge. New Haven: Yale University Press, 1968.

Condit, Ann. "The Increase of Charity." The Thomist 17 (1954) 367-86.

Congar, Yves. Thomas d'Aquin: sa vision de théologie et de l'eglise. London: Variorum, 1984.

Conley, Kieran. A Theology of Wisdom: A Study in St. Thomas. Dubuque: Priory Press, 1963.

Conway, P., tr. St. Thomas Aquinas on Aristotle's Love and Friendship. Providence: Providence College Press, 1951.

Copleston, F. C. Aquinas. Harmondsworth: Penguin, 1955.

_____. A History of Philosophy, Vol. II. Westminster, Md.: Newman Press, 1950.

Corbin, Michel. Le Chemin de la Théologie chez Thomas d'Aquin. Paris: Beauchesne, 1972.

Cranz, F. Edward. "The Publishing History of the Aristotle Commentaries of Thomas Aquinas." Traditio 34 (1978) 157-92.

Crowe, Frederick. "Complacency and Concern in the Thought of St. Thomas." Theological Studies, 20 (1959) 1-39, 198-230, 343-395.

Crowe, Michael Bertram. "On Re-Writing the Biography of Aquinas." Irish Theological Quarterly 41 (1974) 255-273.

_____. "Synderesis and the Notion of Law in St. Thomas." Actes du Premier Congrès International de Philosophie Médiévale. Louvain: 1958. 601-609.

_____. "The Term Synderesis and the Scholastics." Irish Theological Quarterly 23 (1956) 151-64, 228-45.

Curran, John W. "The Thomistic Concept of Devotion." The Thomist 2 (1940) 410-43, 546-80.

Daley, Mary C. The Notion of Justification in the Commentary of St. Thomas

Aquinas on the Epistle to the Romans. Milwaukee: Ph.D. thesis, Marquette University, 1971.

Daly, Jeanne Joseph. *The Metaphysical Foundations of Free Will as a Transcendental Aspect of the Act of Existence in the Philosophy of St. Thomas Aquinas.* Washington: Catholic University of America Press, 1958.

D'Arcy, Eric. *Conscience and its Right to Freedom.* New York: Sheed and Ward, 1961.

──────────. *Human Acts.* Oxford: Oxford University Press, 1963.

──────────. "'Worthy of Worship': A Catholic Contribution." In *Religion and Morality.* Ed. Gene Outka and John P. Reeder, Jr. Garden City, New York: Anchor, 1973. 173-203.

D'Arcy, Martin C. *Thomas Aquinas.* Westminster, Md.: Newman, 1944.

Deck, John N. "St. Thomas Aquinas and the Language of Total Dependence." *Dialogue* 6 (1967) 74-88.

De Ferrari, Teresa Mary. *The Problem of Charity for Self: A Study of Thomistic and Modern Theological Discussion.* Washington: Catholic University of America Press, 1963.

Deferrari, Roy J. *A Latin-English Dictionary of St. Thomas Aquinas.* Boston: St. Paul Editions, 1960.

Deferrari, Roy J. and M. Inviolata Barry. *A Complete Index of the Summa Theologica of St. Thomas Aquinas.* Baltimore, 1956.

──. *Lexicon of St. Thomas Aquinas.* Washington: Catholic University of America Press, 1948-1953.

DeLetter, P. "Hope and Charity in St. Thomas." *The Thomist* 13 (1950) 204-48; 325-52.

──────────. "Merit and Prayer in the Life of Grace." *The Thomist* 9 (1956) 446-80.

──────────. "Original Sin, Privation of Original Justice." *The Thomist* 17 (1954) 469-509.

_____. "Reciprocal Causality: Some Applications in Theology." The Thomist 25 (1962) 382-418.

_____. "The Reparation of Our Fallen Nature." The Thomist 23 (1960) 564-83.

_____. "Theology of Satisfaction." The Thomist 21 (1958) 1-28.

_____. "Venial Sin and Its Final Goal." The Thomist 16 (1953) 2-70.

Dennehy, Raymond. "The Case for Natural Law Re-examined." Natural Law Forum 1 (1956) 5-52.

_____. "The Ontological Basis of Human Rights." The Thomist 42 (1978) 434-63.

Derrida, Jacques. "Structure, Sign, and Play." In Writing and Difference. Trans. Alan Bass. Chicago: University of Chicago, 1978.

Destrez, Jean. Etudes critiques sur les oeuvres de saint Thomas d'Aquin d'àpres la tradition manuscrite. Paris: J. Vrin, 1933--.

Dienstag, Jacob I., ed. Studies in Maimonides and St. Thomas Aquinas. New York: Ktav Publishing House, 1975.

Diggs, Bernard James. Love and Being: An Investigation into the Metaphysics of St. Thomas Aquinas. New York: S. F. Vanni, 1947.

Doherty, Kevin F. "St. Thomas and the Pseudo-Dionysian Symbol of Light." The New Scholasticism 44 (1970) 69-100.

Doig, James C. Aquinas on Metaphysics: A Historico-Doctrinal Study of the Commentary on the Metaphysics. The Hague: Nijhoff, 1972.

Donagan, Alan. "St. Thomas on the Analysis of Human Action." Chapter 2.6 of The Cambridge History of Later Medieval Philosophy, ed. N. Kretzmann, Anthony Kenny, and Jan Pinborg. New York: Cambridge University Press, 1982.

_____. The Theory of Morality. Chicago: University of Chicago Press, 1977.

Donnelly, P. T. "St. Thomas and the Ultimate Purpose of Creation." Theological Studies 2 (1941) 53-83.

Donohue, J. W. Thomas Aquinas and Education. New York: Random House, 1968.

Douglas, Mary. Natural Symbols: Explorations in Cosmology. New York: Pantheon, 1982.

_____. Purity and Danger: An Analysis of the Concepts of Pollution and Taboo. London: Routledge and Kegan Paul, 1966.

Doyle, John J. "The Summa in Symbols: A Reply." The Thomist 32 (1968) 238-44.

Dubay, Thomas. "An Investigation into the Thomistic Concept of Pleasure." The New Scholasticism 36 (1962) 76-99.

Dunphy, William. "The Quinque Viae and Some Parisian Professors of Philosophy." In St. Thomas Aquinas 1274-1974. 2, 73-104.

Eckert, Willehad, ed. Thomas von Aquin: Interpretation und Rezeption, Studien und Texte. Mainz: Matthias Grünewald, 1974.

Eglise et Théologie: Saint Thomas Aquinas Commemorative Colloquium, 1274-1974. Ottawa, Canada: Université Saint-Paul, 1974.

Emmet, Dorothy M. The Nature of Metaphysical Thinking. London: Macmillan, 1945.

Engelmann, Paul, ed. Letters from Ludwig Wittgenstein. New York: Horizon, 1967.

Eschmann, I. T. "A Catalogue of St. Thomas's Works: Bibliographical Notes." In E. Gilson, The Christian Philosophy of St. Thomas Aquinas. New York: Random House, 1956.

_____. "Studies in the Notion of Society in St. Thomas Aquinas." Medieval Studies 18 (1946) 1-42; 19 (1947) 19-55.

_____. "A Thomistic Glossary on the Principle of Pre-eminence of a Common Good." Mediaeval Studies 5 (1943) 123-65.

Evans, Donald. "Preller's Analogy of 'Being'." The New Scholasticism 45 (1971) 1-37.

Farley, Margaret A. "Fragments for an Ethic of Commitment in Thomas Aquinas." In <u>Celebrating the Medieval Heritage</u>. Chicago: University of Chicago Press, 1978.

Farrell, Walter. <u>A Companion to the Summa</u>. New York: Sheed and Ward, 1941.

Feinberg, Joel. <u>Doing and Deserving: Essays in the Theory of Responsibility</u>. Princeton: Princeton University Press, 1970.

Figurski, Leszek. <u>Final Cause and Its Relation to Intelligence in St. Thomas Aquinas</u>. New York: Ph.D. thesis, Fordham University, 1977.

Fingarette, Herbert. <u>The Self in Transformation</u>. New York: Basic Books, 1963.

Flanigan, Thomas Marguerite. "Secondary Causality in the <u>Summa Contra Gentiles</u>." <u>The Modern Schoolman</u> 36 (1958) 31-9.

Flew, Antony. "Theology and Falsification." In <u>New Essays in Philosophical Theology</u>. London: SCM Press, 1955.

Foster, Kenelm, ed. <u>The Life of St. Thomas Aquinas: Biographical Documents</u>. London: Longmans, Green, 1959.

Fraasen, B. C. "Theoretical Entities: The Five Ways." <u>Philosophia</u> 4 (1974) 95-109.

Frankena, W. K., <u>Ethics</u>. Englewood Cliffs, New Jersey: Prentice-Hall, 1973.

Frankl, Viktor. "Paradoxical Intention: A Logotherapeutic Technique." In <u>Psychotherapy and Existentialism</u>. New York: Touchstone, 1967.

Franz, Edward Quinlisk. <u>The Thomistic Doctrine of the Possible Intellect</u>. Washington: Catholic University of America Press, 1950.

Gallagher, Donald A. "St. Thomas and the Desire for the Vision of God." <u>The Modern Schoolman</u> 26 (1949) 159-73.

Gardner, Martin. <u>Aha! Gotcha: Paradoxes to Puzzle and Delight</u>. San Francisco: W. H. Freeman, 1982.

Garrigou-Lagrange, Reginald. <u>Grace: A Commentary on S.T. I-II, qq. 109-114</u>. Trans. by Dominican Nuns, Corpus Christi Monastery, California. St. Louis: B. Herder, 1952.

_____. _Le sens du mystère et le clair-obscur intellectuel; natural et surnaturel_. Paris: Desclèe, de Brouwer, et cie, 1934.

_____. _The Theological Virtues_. St. Louis: B. Herder, 1965.

_____. _The Three Ages of the Interior Life, Prelude of Eternal Life_. Trans. by Sister M. Timothea Doyle. St. Louis: B. Herder, 1947-48.

Geach, Peter. _Mental Acts_. New York: Humanities Press, 1957.

_____. "Ascriptivism." In Richard Rorty, ed. _The Linguistic Turn_. Chicago: University of Chicago Press, 1967.

Geertz, Clifford. _Islam Observed_. New Haven: Yale University Press, 1968.

_____. _The Interpretation of Cultures_. New York: Basic Books, 1973.

Gerstein, Louis C. _On the Conception of God in the Philosophy of Maimonides and St. Thomas Aquinas_. New York: Ph.D. thesis, New York University, 1943.

Gesick, Lorraine, ed. _Centers, Symbols, and Hierarchies: Essays on the Classical States of Southeast Asia_. New Haven: Yale, 1983.

Gilleman, G. _Primacy of Charity in Moral Theology_. Trans. by W. F. Ryan and André Vachon. Westminster, Md.: Newman Press, 1959.

Gilson, Etienne. _The Christian Philosophy of St. Thomas Aquinas_. London: Victor Gollancz, 1957.

_____. _Wisdom and Love in St. Thomas Aquinas_. Milwaukee: Marquette University Press, 1951.

_____, et al. _St. Thomas Aquinas, 1274-1974: Commemorative Studies_. Toronto: Pontifical Institute of Mediaeval Studies, 1974.

Girard, Renè. _Deceit, Desire, and the Novel_. Baltimore: Johns Hopkins University Press, 1965.

_____. _Violence and the Sacred_. Baltimore: Johns Hopkins University Press, 1977.

Glenn, Paul J. A Tour of the Summa. St. Louis: B. Herder, 1960.

Glover, Jonathan. Responsibility. New York: Humanities Press, 1970.

Goffman, Erving. Stigma: Notes on the Management of Spoiled Identity. Englewood Cliffs: Prentice-Hall, 1963.

Golding, Martin. "Aquinas and Some Contemporary Natural Law Theories." Proceedings of the American Catholic Philosophical Association 48 (1974) 238-47.

_____. Philosophy of Law. Englewood Cliffs, New Jersey: Prentice-Hall, 1975.

Goldman, Alvin. A Theory of Human Action. Princeton: Princeton University Press, 1970.

Goulet, Denis A. "Kierkegaard, Aquinas, and the Dilemma of Abraham." Thought 32 (1957) 165-88.

Grabmann, Martin. Introduction to the Theological Summa of St. Thomas. Trans. by John S. Zybura. St. Louis: B. Herder, 1930.

_____. Thomas Aquinas: His Personality and Thought. Trans. by Virgil Michel. New York: Russell and Russell, 1963.

Grenet, Paul B. Thomism. Trans. by James F. Ross. New York: Harper and Row, 1976.

Grisez, Germain G. "The First Principle of Practical Reason." In Aquinas: A Collection of Critical Essays. Ed. Anthony Kenny. New York: Anchor, 1969. 340-382.

_____. "Kant and Aquinas: Ethical Theory." The Thomist 21 (1958) 44-78.

Gulley, Anthony E. The Educational Philosophy of St. Thomas Aquinas. New York: Pageant, 1964.

Guzie, Tad W. "St. Thomas and Learning Theory: A Bibliographical Survey." The New Scholasticism 34 (July 1960) 275-96.

Harley, Katherine Rose. "Freedom and Fault." The New Scholasticism 51 (1977) 494-512.

Hayner, Paul C. "Analogical Predication." Journal of Philosophy 55 (1958) 855-861.

Hardie, W. F. R. Aristotle's Ethical Theory. Oxford: Clarendon Press, 1968.

Hart, H. L. A. "Ascription of Rights and Responsibility." In Logic and Language, Second Series, ed.A. G. N. Flew. Oxford: Basil Blackwell, 1963.

_____. Punishment and Responsibility: Essays in the Philosophy of Law. New York: Oxford University Press, 1968.

Henle, Robert J. "Existentialism and the Judgment." Proceedings of the American Catholic Philosophical Association 21 (1946) 40-53.

_____. "St. Thomas and the Definition of Intelligence." The Modern Schoolman 53 (1976) 335-46.

_____. Saint Thomas and Platonism: A Study of the Plato and Platonici Texts in the Writings of Saint Thomas. The Hague: Martinus Nijhoff, 1956.

Hinnebusch, W. A. The Early English Friars Preachers. Rome: Institutum historicum FF. Praedicatorum, 1951.

Hislop, Ian. The Anthropology of St. Thomas. London: Blackfriars, 1950.

Hollis, Martin. Models of Man. Cambridge: Cambridge University Press, 1977.

Horvath, T. Caritas est in Ratione: Die Lehre des hl. Thomas über die Einheit der Intellektiven und Affektiven Begnadung des Menschen. Münster: Aschendorff, 1966.

Hughes, Patrick, and George Brecht. Vicious Circles and Infinity: An Anthology of Paradoxes. Harmondsworth: Penguin, 1975.

Hyman, Arthur, and James J. Walsh. Philosophy in the Middle Ages: The Christian, Islamic and Jewish Traditions. New York: Harper and Row, 1967.

Jaffa, Harry V. Thomism and Aristotelianism: A Study in the Commentary by Thomas Aquinas on the Nicomachean Ethics. Westport, Conn.: Greenwood Press, 1979.

Junkersfeld, Julienne, Sr. The Aristotelian-Thomistic Concept of Chance. Notre Dame: Ph.D. thesis, University of Notre Dame, 1945.

Kainz, Howard P. Active and Passive Potency in Thomistic Angelology. The Hague: Martinus Nijhoff, 1972.

Kearney, R. J. "Analogy and Inference." The New Scholasticism 51 (1977) 131-41.

Kelly, Matthew J. "Action in Aquinas." The New Scholasticism 52 (1978) 261-7.

_____. "Agency in Aquinas." Laval Théologique et Philosophique 33 (1977) 33-7.

Kendzierski, Lottie. "Object and Intention in the Moral Act." Proceedings of the American Catholic Philosophical Association 24 (1950) 102-10.

Kenny, Anthony. The Anatomy of the Soul. New York: Harper and Row, 1973.

_____. Aquinas. New York: Hill and Wang, 1980.

_____. Aquinas: A Collection of Critical Essays. New York: Anchor, 1969.

_____. Aristotle's Theory of the Will. New Haven: Yale, 1979.

_____. The Five Ways: St. Thomas Aquinas's Proofs of God's Existence. New York: Schocken Books, 1969.

_____. Will, Freedom and Power. Oxford: Blackwell, 1975.

Klubertanz, George Peter. The Discursive Power: Sources and Doctrine of the Vis Cogitativa According to St. Thomas. St. Louis: The Modern Schoolman, 1952.

_____. Habits and Virtues: A Philosophical Analysis. New York: Appleton-Century-Crofts, 1965.

_____. "The Root of Freedom in St. Thomas' Later Works." Gregorianum 42 (1961) 709–21.

_____. St. Thomas Aquinas on Analogy: A Textual Analysis and Systematic Synthesis. Chicago: Loyola University Press, 1960.

_____. "St. Thomas and the Knowledge of the Singular." The New Scholasticism 26 (1952) 135–66.

Kluge, E.-H. W. "Abstraction: A Contemporary Look." The Thomist 40 (1976) 337–65.

Knauer, Peter. "The Hermeneutic Function of the Principle of Double Effect." Natural Law Forum 12 (1967) 132–62.

Knowles, David. The Evolution of Medieval Thought. New York: Vintage, 1962.

_____. The Historical Context of the Philosophical Works of St. Thomas Aquinas. London: Blackfriars, 1958.

Kreyche, Gerald F. "The Soul-Body Problem in St. Thomas." The New Scholasticism 46 (1972) 466–84.

_____. "Virtue and Law in Aquinas: Some Modern Implications." Southwestern Journal of Philosophy 5 (1974) 111–40.

Lambert, Richard Thomas. Man's Knowledge of His Soul in St. Thomas Aquinas. Notre Dame: Ph.D. thesis, University of Notre Dame, 1971.

Langevin, Gilles. "Capax Dei": La creature intellectuelle et l'intimitè de Dieu. Paris: Desclèe de Brouwer, 1966.

Leclercq, Jean. "Tradition patristique et monastique dans l'enseignement de la S.T. sur la vie contemplative." In Studi Tomistici, I, 129–53.

Lisska, Anthony J. "Aquinas' Use of 'Phantasia'." The Thomist 40 (1976) 294–302.

_____. "Deely and Geach on Abstractionism in Thomistic Epistemology." The Thomist 37 (1973) 548–68.

Lonergan, Bernard. Grace and Freedom. New York: Herder and Herder, 1971.

_____. Verbum: Word and Idea in Aquinas. Ed. by David Burrell. Notre Dame: University of Notre Dame Press, 1967.

Lottin, Odon. Morale fondamentale. Tournai: Desclèe, 1954.

_____. "Le pèchè originel chez Albert le Grand, Bonaventure, et Thomas d'Aquin." Recherches de thèologie ancienne et medièvale 12 (1940) 275-328.

_____. "Pour une rèorganisation du traitè Thomiste de la moralitè." In Acta Congressus Scholastici Intern. Romae. Roma: Antonianum, 1951.

_____. Psychologie et morale aux XIIe et XIIIe sièkcles. 6 tomes. Gembloux: Duculot, 1942-1960.

_____. "Saint Thomas à la facultè des arts de Paris aux approches de 1277." Recherches deThèologie Ancienne et Mèdièvale. 16 (1949) 292-313.

Luyten, N. A., ed. L'Anthropologie de Saint Thomas. Confèrences...du 7e centenaire.... Fribourg: Editions Universitaires, 1974.

Mackey, Louis. "Entreatments of God: Reflections on Aquinas' Five Ways." Franciscan Studies 37 (1977) 103-19.

McCormick, Richard A. Ambiguity in Moral Choice. Milwaukee: Marquette University Press, 1973.

_____ and Paul Ramsey, eds. Doing Evil to Achieve Good: Moral Choice in Conflict Situations. Chicago: Loyola University Press, 1978.

McGinn, Bernard. "Development of the Thought of Aquinas on the Reconciliation of Divine Providence and Contingent Action." The Thomist 39 (1975) 741-52.

McGinnis, R. R. The Wisdom of Love: A Study in the Psychometaphysics of Love According to the Principles of St. Thomas. Rome: Ag. del Libro Catholica, 1951.

McInerny, Ralph. "The Analogy of Names is a Logical Doctrine." In Tommaso d'Aquino VI, 647-53.

_____. St. Thomas Aquinas. Boston: Twayne Publishers, 1975.

_____. Ethica Thomistica: The Moral Philosophy of Thomas Aquinas. Washington: Catholic University of America Press, 1982.

_____. "The Logic of Analogy." The New Scholasticism 31 (1957) 149-71.

_____. The Logic of Analogy. The Hague: Martinus Nijhoff, 1961.

_____. "Prudence and Conscience." The Thomist 38 (1974) 291-305.

_____. Rhyme and Reason: St. Thomas and Modes of Discourse. Milwaukee: Marquette University Press, 1981.

_____. "Some Notes on Being and Predication." The Thomist 22 (1959) 315-35.

_____. Studies in Analogy. The Hague: Martinus Nijhoff, 1968.

_____. "The Teleological Suspension of the Ethical." The Thomist 20 (1957) 295-310.

McKian, J. D. "The Metaphysics of Introspection According to St. Thomas Aquinas." The New Scholasticism 15 (1941) 89-117.

Maurer, Armand A. St. Thomas and Historicity. Milwaukee: Marquette University Press, 1979.

_____, ed. St. Thomas Aquinas 1274-1975: Commemorative Studies, 2 vols. Toronto: Pontifical Institute of Mediaeval Studies, 1974.

_____. "St. Thomas on the Sacred Name Tetragrammaton." Mediaeval Studies 34 (1972) 275-86.

Meagher, Robert E. "Thomas Aquinas and Analogy: A Textual Analysis." The Thomist 34 (1970) 230-53.

Melanges offerts à Etienne Gilson. Paris: J. Vrin, 1959.

Melanges offerts à M.-D. Chenu, Maitre en thèologie. Paris: J. Vrin, 1967.

Meyer, Charles R. The Thomistic Concept of Justifying Contrition. Mundelein, Ill.: Seminary of St. Mary of the Lake, 1949.

Miethe, Terry L., and Vernon J. Bourke. Thomistic Bibliography, 1940-1978. Westport, Conn.: Greenwood Press, 1980.

Miller, Clyde L. "Maimonides and Aquinas on Naming God." The Journal of Jewish Studies 28 (1977) 65-71.

Mondin, Battista. The Principle of Analogy in Protestant and Catholic Theology. The Hague: Martinus Nijhoff, 1963.

―――――――. St. Thomas Aquinas' Philosophy in the Commentary to the Sentences. The Hague: Martinus Nijhoff, 1975.

Montagnes, Bernard. La doctrine de l'analogies de l'etre d'après saint Thomas d'Aquin. Louvain: Publications universitaires, 1963.

Mortimore, G. W., ed. Weakness of Will. New York: Macmillan, 1970.

Morris, Herbert. "Persons and Punishment." In Theories of Punishment, ed. Stanley E. Grupp. Bloomington: Indiana University Press, 1971.

Mullane, Donald Thomas. Aristotelianism in St. Thomas. Washington: Ph.D. thesis, Catholic University Press of America, 1929.

Mulligan, Robert W. "Ratio Superior and Ratio Inferior: The Historical Background." The New Scholasticism 29 (1955) 1-32.

―――――――. "Ratio Inferior and Ratio Superior in St. Albert and St. Thomas." The Thomist 19 (1956) 339-67.

Mundhenk, Johannes. Die Seele im System des Thomas von Aquin. Hamburg: Meiner, 1980.

Murdoch, John Emery and Edith Dudley Sylla, eds. The Cultural Context of Mediaeval Learning. Boston: Reidel, 1975.

Myers, Joseph R. Social Distance According to St. Thomas Aquinas. Washington: Catholic University of America Press, 1955.

Naus, John. The Nature of the Practical Intellect According to St. Thomas Aquinas. Rome: Gregorian University, 1959.

Nemetz, Anthony A. "The Meaning of Analogy." Franciscan Studies 15 (1955) 209-23.

Niebuhr, H. Richard. Christ and Culture. New York: Harper and Row, 1951.

Nielsen, Kai. "Analogical Talk of God: Two Views: A Negative Critique." The Thomist 40 (1976) 32-60.

_____. "An Examination of the Thomistic Theory of Natural Moral Law." Natural Law Forum 4 (1959) 44-71.

Noonan, John T., Jr. "Maxima Amicitia." In Tommaso d'Aquino 5, 344-51.

Numèro commemoratif...saint Thomas d'Aquin: Laval Thèologique et Philosophique. 30, 3 (1974). Quèbec: Universitè Laval, 1974.

O'Brien, Thomas C. "Sacra Doctrina Revisited: The Context of Medieval Education." The Thomist 41 (1977) 475-504.

O'Connor, D. J. Aquinas and Natural Law. London: Macmillan, 1967.

O'Connor, William R. The Eternal Quest: The Teaching of St. Thomas Aquinas on the Natural Desire for God. New York: Longmans, 1947.

O'Donnell, J. Reginald, ed. Essays in Honor of Anton Charles Pegis. Toronto: Pontifical Institute of Mediaeval Studies, 1974.

Oesterle, John A. "Conscience and Contingency." In XIII Congreso Internacional de Filosofia 7 (1964) 369-75.

_____. "St. Thomas, Moral Evil, and the Devil." In Tommaso d'Aquino 5, 510-15.

_____. "St. Thomas as a Teacher: A Reply to Professor Pegis." The New Scholasticism 39 (1965) 451-66.

O'Meara, Thomas F. "Paris as a Cultural Milieu of Thomas Aquinas' Thought." The Thomist 38 (1974) 689-722.

O'Neil, Charles, ed. An Etienne Gilson Tribute. Milwaukee: Marquette University Press, 1959.

_____. "The Notion of Beauty in the Ethics of St. Thomas." The New Scholasticism 14 (1940) 340-78.

_____. "Prudence, the Incommunicable Wisdom." In Essays in Thomism, R. E. Brennan, ed. New York: Sheed and Ward, 1942.

187-204.

Ouwerkerk, C. A. J. van. Caritas et Ratio: Etude sur le double principe de la vie morale chrétienne d'après s. Thomas d'Aquin. Nijmegen, 1956.

Outka, Gene. Agape: An Ethical Analysis. New Haven: Yale University Press, 1972.

Owens, Joseph. "Analogy as a Thomistic Approach to Being." Mediaeval Studies 24 (1962) 303-22.

_____. "Aquinas as Aristotelian Commentator." In St. Thomas Aquinas Commemorative Studies. Toronto: Pontifical Institute of Mediaeval Studies, 1974. 1, 213-38.

_____. "Aquinas: 'Darkness of Ignorance' in the Most Refined Notion of God." Southwestern Journal of Philosophy 5 (1974) 93-110.

_____. "Soul as Agent in Aquinas." The New Scholasticism (1974) 40-72.

_____. St. Thomas Aquinas on the Existence of God: Collected Papers of Joseph Owens, C.Ss.R. Ed. by John R. Catan. Albany: State University of New York Press, 1980.

Palmer, H. Analogy: A Study of Qualification and Argument in Theology. New York: St. Martin's Press, 1973.

Passerin D'Entreves, A. Natural Law. London: Hutchinson, 1951.

Peghaire, Julien. Intellectus et ratio selon Thomas d'Aquin. Paris: J. Vrin, 1936.

Pegis, Anton C. "Nature and Spirit: Some Reflections on the Problem of the End of Man." Proceedings of the American Catholic Philosophical Association. 23 (1949-1950) 3-20.

_____. "St. Thomas and the Nicomachean Ethics: Some Reflections on Summa Contra Gentiles III, 44, 5." Mediaeval Studies 25 (1963) 1-25.

_____. St. Thomas and Philosophy. Milwaukee: Marquette University Press, 1964.

_____. St. Thomas and the Problem of the Soul in the Thirteenth Century. Toronto: Pontifical Institute of Mediaeval Studies, 1976.

_____. "St. Thomas Aquinas," in Encyclopedia of Education. New York: Macmillan, 1971.

Peifer, John F. The Concept in Thomism. New York: Bookman Associates, 1952.

Penelhum, Terence. "The Analysis of Faith in St. Thomas Aquinas." Religious Studies 13 (1977) 133-54.

Pepler, C. The Basis of the Mysticism of St. Thomas. London: Blackfriars, 1953.

Perinelle, Georges. L'attrition d'après le Concile de Trente et d'après saint Thomas d'Aquin. Le Saulchoir, Kain: Revue des sciences philosophiques et théologiques, 1927.

Pfürtner, Stephanus. Luther and Aquinas on Salvation. Trans. by Edward Quinn. New York: Sheed and Ward, 1964.

Phelan, Gerald B. Saint Thomas and Analogy. Milwaukee: Marquette University Press, 1948.

Pieper, Josef. "The Contemporary Aquinas." Philosophy Today 3 (1959) 73-5.

_____. The Four Cardinal Virtues. Notre Dame: University of Notre Dame Press, 1966.

_____. Guide to Thomas Aquinas. Trans. by Richard and Clara Winston. New York: Pantheon, 1962.

_____. "The Meaning of 'God Speaks'." The New Scholasticism 43 (1969) 205-28.

_____. The Silence of St. Thomas. Trans. by John Murray and Daniel O'Connor. New York: Pantheon, 1957.

Plato. Meno. In Plato: Laches, Protagoras, Meno, Euthydemus. Trans. W. R. M. Lamb. London: William Heinemann, 1924.

_____. Protagoras and Meno. Trans. W. K. C. Guthrie. Harmondsworth: Penguin, 1956.

Platt, John. "Social Traps." American Psychologist, 8 (1973) 641-651.

Preller, Victor. Divine Science and the Science of God: A Reformulation of Thomas Aquinas. Princeton: Princeton University Press, 1967.

Principle, Walter H. "Thomas Aquinas' Principles for Interpretation of Patristic Texts." In Studies in Medieval Culture, 7-8. Kalamazoo: Western Michigan University, 1976. 111-22.

Przywara, Erich. "Der Grundsatz: 'Gratia non destruit sed supponit et perficit naturam.' Eine ideengeschichtliche Interpretation." Scholastik 17 (1942) 178-86.

Quine, W. V. "The Ways of Paradox." In The Ways of Paradox and Other Essays. Cambridge: Harvard University Press, 1966.

Rahner, Karl. "Aquinas: The Nature of Truth." Trans. by Andrew Tallon. Continuum 2 (1964) 60-72.

_____. Spirit in the World. London: Sheed and Ward, 1968.

_____. "Thomas Aquinas on the Incomprehensibility of God." In Celebrating the Medieval Heritage. Chicago: University of Chicago Press, 1978.

Randall, John Herman, Jr. Aristotle. New York: Columbia University Press, 1960.

Ramsey, Ian T. Religious Language. London: SCM Press, 1957.

Rassam, Joseph. La métaphysique de saint Thomas. Paris: Presses universitaires de France, 1968.

Rawls, John. A Theory of Justice. Cambridge: Harvard University Press, 1971.

Redpath, Peter A. The Moral Wisdom of St. Thomas: An Introduction. Lanham: University Press of America, 1983.

Regis, Louis Marie. St. Thomas and Epistemology. Milwaukee: Marquette University Press, 1946.

Reilly, Richard. "Weakness of Will: The Thomistic Advance." In Thomas and Bonaventure: Proceedings of the American Catholic Philosophical Association.

Reyna, Ruth. "On the Soul: A Philosophical Exploration of the Active Intellect in Averroes, Aristotle, and Aquinas." The Thomist 36 (1972) 131-49.

Richards, I. A. Philosophy of Rhetoric. New York: Oxford University Press, 1936.

Ricoeur, Paul. The Symbolism of Evil. Boston: Beacon, 1967.

Riesenhuber, Klaus. "The Bases and Meaning of Freedom in Thomas Aquinas." In Thomas and Bonaventure: Proceedings of the American Catholic Philosophical Association. 99-111.

Rioux, Bertrand. L'etre et la vèritè chez Heidegger et saint Thomas d'Aquin. Montreal: Presses de l'Universitè de Montreal, 1963.

Robinson, T. M. "Averroes, Moerbeke, Aquinas and a Crux in the De Anima." Mediaeval Studies 32 (1970) 340-44.

Roensch, Frederick J. The Early Thomistic School. Chicago: Priory Press, 1954.

Rorty, Amelie Oksenberg. The Identities of Persons. Berkeley: University of California Press, 1976.

Ross, James F. "Analogy as a Rule of Meaning for Religious Language." International Philosophical Quarterly 1 (1961) 468-502.

_____. "Aquinas and Philosophical Methodology." Metaphilosophy 1 (1970) 300-17.

_____. "A New Theory of Analogy." Proceedings of the American Catholic Philosophical Association 44 (1970) 70-85.

_____. Philosophical Theology. Indianapolis: Bobbs-Merrill, 1969.

Rossner, William L. "An Inclination to an Intellectually Known God: The Question of the Existence of Intellectual Love." The Modern Schoolman 52 (1974) 65-92.

_____. "The Process of Human Intellectual Love, or Spirating a Pondus." The Thomist 36 (1972) 39-74.

_____. The Theory of Love in the Philosophy of St. Thomas Aquinas. Princeton: Ph.D. thesis, Princeton University, 1953.

Rowe, William L. The Cosmological Argument. Princeton: Princeton University Press, 1975.

Ruane, John P. "Self-Knowledge and the Spirituality of the Soul in St. Thomas." The New Scholasticism 32 (1958) 425-442.

Ruesch, Jurgen, and Gregory Bateson. Communication: The Social Matrix of Psychiatry. New York: Norton, 1951.

John K. Ryan. "The Reputation of St. Thomas Among English Protestant Thinkers of the Seventeenth Century." The New Scholasticism. 22 (1948) 1-33, 126-208.

Ryan, Michael. The Notion and Uses of Dialectic in St. Thomas Aquinas. Notre Dame: Ph.D. thesis, University of Notre Dame, 1963.

Ryle, Gilbert. The Concept of Mind. London: Hutchinson, 1949.

Santoni, Ronald E., ed. Religious Language and the Problem of Religious Knowledge. Bloomington: Indiana University Press, 1968.

Sauras, Emilio. "Thomistic Soteriology and the Mystical Body." Thomist 15 (1952) 543-71.

Schall, James V. "The Totality of Society: From Justice to Friendship." The Thomist 20 (1957) 1-26.

Scharlemann, Robert P. Thomas Aquinas and John Gerhard. New Haven: Yale University Press, 1964.

Schleck, Charles A. "St. Thomas on the Nature of Sacramental Grace." The Thomist 18 (1955) 1-30; 242-78.

Schmidt, Robert William, The Domain of Logic According to St. Thomas Aquinas. The Hague: Martinus Nijhoff, 1966.

Schneider, Marius. "The Dependence of St. Thomas' Psychology of Sensation Upon His Physics." Franciscan Studies 22 (1962) 3-31.

Schütz, Ludwig. Thomas-Lexicon. Paderborn: F. Schoningh, 1895.

Schwartz, Herbert T. "Analogy in St. Thomas and Cajetan." The New Scholasticism 28 (1954) 127-44.

Schwartzman, Helen B. Transformations: The Anthropology of Children's Play. New York: Plenum, 1978.

Schwartzman, John. "Symptoms and Rituals: Paradoxical Modes and Social Organization." Ethos 10 (1982) 3-25.

Sertillanges, A. D. La Philosophie morale de s. Thomas d'Aquin. Paris: Aubier, 1942.

Shahan, Robert W. and Francis J. Kovach. Bonaventure and Aquinas: Enduring Philosophers. Norman: University of Oklahoma Press, 1976.

Sheehan, Robert J. The Philosophy of Happiness According to St. Thomas Aquinas. Washington: Catholic University of America Press, 1956.

Sheehan, Thomas J. "Notes on a 'Lovers' Quarrel': Heidegger and Aquinas." Listening 9 (1974) 119-36.

Smith, Raymond. "The Virtue of Docility." The Thomist 15 (1952) 572-623.

Steenberghen, Fernand van. Aristotle in the West: the Origins of Latin Aristotelianism. Trans. by Leonard Johnston. Louvain: E. Nauwelaerts, 1955.

_____. The Philosophical Movement in the Thirteenth Century. Edinburgh: Nelson, 1955.

_____. Psychology, Morality, and Education. London: Burns and Oates, 1958.

Steger, Evelyn E. The Verbum Cordis According to St. Thomas Aquinas. Washington: Ph.D. thesis, Catholic University of America, 1967.

Stengren, George L. "Connatural Knowledge in Aquinas and Kierkegaardian Subjectivity." In Kierkegaardiana. København: Reitzels, 1977.

Stevenson, C. L. Ethics and Language. New Haven: Yale University Press, 1948.

Stock, Michael. "A Thomistic Analysis of the Concept of Repression." The Thomist 25 (1962) 463-94.

Stockhammer, Morris. *Thomas Aquinas Dictionary*. New York: Philosophical Library, 1965.

Streng, Frederick J. *Emptiness: A Study in Religious Meaning*. Nashville: Abingdon, 1967.

Sullivan, John J. *Commandment of Love: The First and Greatest of the Commandments Explained According to the Teachings of St. Thomas Aquinas*. New York: Vantage, 1956.

Sullivan, Robert P. *Man's Thirst for God*. Westminster, Md.: Newman Press, 1952.

_____. "Natural Necessitation of the Human Will." *The Thomist* 14 (1951) 351–399.

Sweeney, Leo. "Preller and Aquinas." *The Modern Schoolman* 48 (1971) 267–73.

Symposium in Honor of St. Thomas and St. Bonaventure: 1274–1974. International Philosophical Quarterly. 14 (December 1974).

Thomas and Bonaventure: A Septicentenary Commemoration. Proceedings of the American Catholic Philosophical Association, 48. Washington: Catholic University of America Press, 1974.

Thomas Aquinas. *De Anima, in the Version of William of Moerbeke, and the Commentary of St. Thomas Aquinas*. Trans. by Kenelm Foster and Sylvester Humphries. New Haven: Yale University Press, 1951.

_____. *Aristotle: On Interpretation. Commentary by St. Thomas and Cajetan*. Trans. by Jean T. Oesterle. Milwaukee: Marquette University Press, 1962.

_____. *Basic Writings of St. Thomas Aquinas*, ed. by Anton C. Pegis. New York: Macmillan, 1945.

_____. *On Being and Essence*. Trans. by Armand A. Maurer. Toronto: Pontifical Institute of Medieval Studies, 1968.

_____. *On Charity (De Caritate)*. Trans. by Lottie H. Kendzierski. Milwaukee: Marquette University Press, 1960.

_____. *Commentary on the Metaphysics of Aristotle*. Trans. by

John P. Rowan. Chicago: H. Regnery, 1961.

_____. <u>Commentary on the Nicomachean Ethics</u>. Trans. by C. I. Litzinger. Chicago: H. Regnery, 1964.

_____. <u>Compendium of Theology</u>. Trans. by Cyril Vollert. St. Louis: B. Herder, 1952.

_____. <u>An Introduction to the Metaphysics of St. Thomas Aquinas</u>. Trans. by James F. Anderson. Chicago: H. Regnery, 1953.

_____. <u>Philosophical Texts</u>. Trans. by Thomas Gilby. Oxford: Oxford University Press, 1951.

_____. <u>S. Thomae Aquinatis Opera Omnia iussu Leonis edita</u>, 48 vols. Rome, 1882-1971.

_____. <u>Selected Writings</u>. Ed. by M. C. D'Arcy. New York: Dutton, 1964.

_____. <u>Sententia Libri Ethicorum</u>, in <u>S. Thomae Aquinatis Opera Omnia iussu Leonis edita</u>, 48 vols. Rome, 1882-1971.

_____. <u>On Spiritual Creatures</u>. Trans. by Mary C. Fitzpatrick and John J. Wellmuth. Milwaukee: Marquette University Press, 1949.

_____. <u>On St. Paul's Epistle to the Ephesians</u>. Trans. by M. L. Lamb. New York: Magi, 1966.

_____. <u>On St. Paul's Epistle to the Galatians</u>. Trans. by R. F. Larcher. New York: Magi, 1966.

_____. <u>On St. Paul's Epistle to the Philippians and First Thessalonians</u>. Trans. by R. F. Larcher. New York: Magi, 1969.

_____. <u>Summa Contra Gentiles</u>. Trans. by Anton C. Pegis, James F. Anderson, and Vernon J. Bourke. Notre Dame: Notre Dame University Press, 1975.

_____. <u>Summa Theologiae</u>. Trans. by Blackfriars. New York: McGraw-Hill, 1964--

_____. <u>Summa Theologica</u>. Trans. by Fathers of the English Dominican Province. New York: Beringer, 1947-48.

_____. *Treatise on Happiness*. Trans. by John A. Oesterle. Englewood Cliffs, New Jersey: Prentice-Hall, 1964.

_____. *The Trinity and the Unicity of the Intellect*. St. Louis: Herder, 1946.

_____. *Truth*. Trans. Robert W. Mulligan, James V. McGlynn, and Robert W. Schmidt. Chicago: H. Regnery, 1952-53.

_____. *On the Unity of the Intellect Against the Averroists*. Trans. by Beatrice H. Zedler. Milwaukee: Marquette University Press, 1968.

Thomas Aquinas, 1274-1974: The Monist 58, 1 (1974).

The Thomist Reader. Washington: The Thomist Press, 1957.

Toulmin, Stephen. *The Place of Reason in Ethics*. Cambridge: Cambridge University Press, 1953.

Tracy, David, ed. *Celebrating the Medieval Heritage: A Colloquy on the Thought of Aquinas and Bonaventure*. Chicago: University of Chicago Press, 1978.

_____. "St. Thomas Aquinas and the Religious Dimension of Experience: The Doctrine of Sin." In *Thomas and Bonaventure: Proceedings of the American Catholic Philosophical Association*.

Tranøy, K. E. "Thomas Aquinas." In *A Critical History of Western Philosophy*. Ed. by D. J. O'Connor. New York: St. Martin's Press, 1964.

Turner, Victor. "Betwixt and Between: the Liminal Period in *Rites de Passage*." In *Reader in Comparative Religion: An Anthropological Approach*. Ed. William A. Lessa and Egon Z. Vogt. New York: Harper and Row, 1972. 338-347.

_____. *The Ritual Process: Structure and Anti-Structure*. Ithaca: Cornell, 1969.

Tyrrell, Francis M. "Concerning the Nature and Function of the Act of Judgment." *The New Scholasticism* 26 (1952).

_____. *The Role of Assent in Judgment*. Washington: Catholic University of America Press, 1948.

Unknown. The Cloud of Unknowing. Trans. by Clifton Wolters. Harmondsworth: Penguin, 1961.

Van Buren, Paul M. The Edges of Language: An Essay in the Logic of a Religion. New York: Macmillan, 972.

Van Gennep, Arnold. The Rites of Passage. Chicago: University of Chicago Press, 1960.

Van Roo, William. Grace and Original Justice According to St. Thomas. Rome: University Gregoriana, 1955.

Vann, Gerald. Saint Thomas Aquinas. London: J. M. Dent and Sons, 1940.

Velecky, Lubor C. "Flew on Aquinas." Philosophy 18 (1968) 213-30.

Vella, Arthur G. Love is Acceptance: A Psychological and Theological Investigation of the Mind of St. Thomas Aquinas. Malta: Malta University Press, 1959.

Verbeke, G., and D. Verhelst, ed. Aquinas and the Problems of His Time. Louvain: Leuven University Press, 1976.

Vicaire, M.-H. L'Anthropologie de saint Thomas: confèrences organisèes par la facultè de thèologie et la sociètè philosophique de Fribourg a l'occasion du 700e anniversaire de la mort de saint Thomas d'Aquin. Fribourg: Editions universitaires, 1974.

Wade, Francis C. "St. Thomas Aquinas and Teaching." In Some Philosophers on Education. Donald Gallagher, ed. Milwaukee: Marquette University Press, 1956.

Wallace, W. A. and James A. Weisheipl. "Thomas Aquinas, Saint." The New Catholic Encyclopedia 14 (1966) 102-15.

Walz, Angelus Maria. Saint Thomas Aquinas: A Biographical Study. Trans. by Sebastian Bullough. Westminster: Newman Press, 1951.

Watzlawick, Paul. The Language of Change: Elements of Therapeutic Communication. New York: Basic, 1978.

_____, Janet Beavin, and Don D. Jackson. Pragmatics of Human Communication. New York: Norton, 1967.

Watzlawick, Paul, John Weakland, and Richard Fisch, Change: Principles of Problem Formation and Problem Resolution. New York: Norton, 1974.

Weber, Max. "Objectivity in Social Science and Social Policy," trans. R. E. Rogers. In R. E. Rogers, Max Weber's Ideal Type Theory. New York: Philosophical Library, 1969.

Weisheipl, James A., ed. The Dignity of Science. Washington: The Thomist Press, 1961.

_____. Friar Thomas d'Aquino: His Life, Thought, and Work. Garden City: Doubleday, 1974.

_____. "The Meaning of Sacra Doctrina in Summa Theologiae 1. q. 1." The Thomist 38 (1974) 49-81.

_____. Thomas d'Aquino and Albert His Teacher. Toronto: Pontifical Institute of Mediaeval Studies, 1980.

_____. "Thomas' Evaluation of Plato and Aristotle." The New Scholasticism 1974, 100-24.

White, Alan ed. The Philosophy of Action. Oxford University Press, 1968.

White, Hayden. Metahistory: The Historical Imagination in Nineteenth-Century Europe. Baltimore: Johns Hopkins, 1973.

White, Victor. Holy Teaching: The Idea of Theology According to St. Thomas Aquinas. London: Aquin Press, 1958.

Williams, Bernard. Problems of the Self. Cambridge: Cambridge University Press, 1973.

Wilson, Bryan R., ed. Rationality. New York: Harper and Row, 1970.

Wippel, John F. "Thomas Aquinas and Avicenna on the Relationship between First Philosophy and the Other Theoretical Sciences: A Note on Thomas's Commentary on Boethius's de Trinitate, Q. 5, art. 1 and 9. The Thomist 37 (1973) 133-54.

Wisdom, John. Paradox and Discovery. Berkeley: University of California, 1970.

_____. Philosophy and Psychoanalysis. Berkeley: University of

California, 1969.

Wittgenstein, Ludwig. "A Lecture on Ethics." In Philosophy Today 1. Ed. Jerry Gill. New York: Macmillan, 1968. 3-14.

_____. The Blue and Brown Books. New York: Harper and Row, 1958.

_____. Philosophical Investigations. Trans. G. E. M. Anscombe. New York: Macmillan, 1953.

_____. Tractatus Logico-Philosophicus. Trans. D. F. Pears and B. F. McGuinness. New York: Humanities Press, 1961.

Wojtyla, Karol. "The Personal Structure of Self-Determination." In Tommaso d'Aquino...VII Centenario 1976. 379-90.

Wolfer, M. Vianney. The Prayer of Christ According to the Teaching of St. Thomas Aquinas. Washington: Catholic University of America Press, 1958.

Wulf, Maurice De. System of Saint Thomas Aquinas. Trans. by Ernest Messenger. New York: Dover, 1960.

Wyser, Paul. Thomas von Aquin. Bern: A. Francke, 1950.

Yarz, Francis J. "Order and Right Reason in Aquinas' Ethics." Mediaeval Studies 37 (1975) 407-18.

_____. "Virtue as Ordo in Aquinas." The Modern Schoolman 47 (1970) 305-20.

INDEX

Actus purus   4
Complacentia   38
habitus, disposition, habit   65, 66, 91, 94
Obiectum, object   72, 73, 92, 94, 95, 112, 119
Praeter intentionem   123, 125
Synderesis   94, 122
Virtus dormitiva   99

Action, description of   69, 95, 120
Action, principles or starting points of   86, 97
Activity   72, 73
Acts, exterior   85
Acts, interior   5, 8, 30, 67, 85
Acts, interior and exterior   88, 101
Acts, moral   5
Agent Intellect   28, 94
Aggravation   92, 119
Altruism   72
Analogy   3, 69, 100, 127, 128
Angels   36
Approval-seeking, paradox of   69, 72, 73
Aristotle   26, 57, 85, 111
Augustine   14, 16, 26, 32, 34, 77, 111
Autonomy   72
Aversion   120

Being Itself   28

Charity   37, 39, 59, 130
Charity, fitness for friendship   1, 2, 5, 7, 10, 13, 35, 54, 55, 57, 63, 65, 67, 68, 73, 76
Charity, precepts of   74, 76
Child, children   12, 48, 53, 57, 59
Choice   29, 85, 95, 97, 101, 109, 123
Command   91, 96, 101, 110, 113
Communication   59, 62, 67
Community   50, 59, 62, 67

Complacency   101, 102
Concupiscence   9
Conscience   94
Consent   93, 95, 97, 101, 106, 113, 123
Considering   101
Consistency   15
Contemplation   27
Contempt   25, 31, 76, 80, 125
Control   77, 85, 89, 90, 115, 129
Conversion   37, 75, 120
Counterparadox   11, 77
Court   114
Creditor   55

Debtor   55
Deciding   101, 107
Deliberation   86, 90, 91, 101, 104, 123
Desert   24, 51, 57, 63, 65, 67
Dignity   127, 128
Double bind   10, 11, 13, 14, 15, 16, 24, 31, 43, 68, 72, 74, 75, 94, 129

Egoism   69, 72
End   119
Enemies   59
Enjoyment   72, 73, 101, 103
Entitlement   51, 65, 67
Equality   7, 12, 14, 47, 49, 51, 52, 53, 54, 55, 57, 58, 59, 65, 68, 127, 128
Excellence   52
Excuse   92
Exercise   92, 94
Externals   49

Faith   34, 75
Father   3, 48, 51, 53, 57, 59, 119, 122
Fault   92, 94
Fear, servile and filial   73, 75
Feinberg   114
Fifth Way   2
Fitness   1, 8, 102
Freedom   74
Freedom of choice   29
Friend   122
Friend, friendship   4, 5, 9, 10, 12, 13, 14, 48, 51, 53, 54, 55, 57, 63, 65, 73, 76, 119, 130

Grace   56, 122, 127, 128
Gravity   92, 119

Happiness   27, 31, 34
Harm   121
Hatred   125
Heteronomy   72
Hidden   85, 89, 90
Hierarchy   5, 58, 66, 67, 85, 87, 88, 89, 101, 127, 129
High   90
Honor   51, 52, 53, 70, 127
Hope   75
Humility   76

Ignorance   92, 123
Imitation   17
Immanence   14, 40
Inclination   5, 9, 10, 25, 29, 30, 66, 79, 93, 95
Independence   7, 13, 22, 25, 31, 32, 43, 90, 128
Independence, paradox of   71
Inequality   7, 12, 14, 47, 49, 51, 52, 53, 54, 55, 57, 58, 59, 65, 68, 127, 128
Inequality of persons   7
Inordinacy   121
Inquiry   104
Intellect   25, 28, 31, 73, 87, 90
Intention   66, 78, 95, 101, 104, 120, 123, 125
Internals   49
Introversion   11, 46, 49, 60, 67, 85, 87, 88, 98
Inwardness   5, 6, 46, 60, 67, 90, 114, 127, 129

Judge   12
Judging others   90
Judgment   29, 91, 101
Justice   51
Justice, communicative function of   70
Justice, commutative   48, 49, 55, 65
Justice, distributive   46, 47, 49, 51, 55
Justice, divine   49, 51
Justice, fitness for reward or punishment   1, 2, 5, 6, 46, 49, 52, 53, 54, 63, 64, 66, 67, 72, 78, 121, 130
Justice, legal   46, 47, 50, 51
Justice, metaphorical   67, 90, 97, 98, 99
Justice, potential parts   46, 48, 51, 63, 68
Justification   56

Knowing   31, 33

Language   68, 90, 97, 98, 100, 111, 127, 128
Law   47, 50, 52, 67, 107, 122
Law, divine   53
Law, natural   93
Learning   17, 31, 33, 35, 43, 91
Light of glory   33, 35
Liminality   11, 60
Lord   2, 3
Love   11, 38, 57, 63, 65, 66, 73, 76, 125, 130
Love, commandment to   13, 74, 76
Luther   14

Maturation   15, 48, 53, 57
Merit   48, 51, 57, 63, 65, 76, 119
Metaphor   100
Mitigation   92
Mystification   16

Obedience   51, 52, 76
Obligation   51, 52, 53, 55
Omissions, interior and exterior   87, 88, 93, 123
Order   1, 79, 102, 121
Other-regarding   4, 10, 46, 60

Paradox   10, 11, 13, 14, 15, 16, 24, 30, 31, 43, 68, 72, 94, 123, 129
Paradox, pathogenic and therapeutic   75
Paradox, veridical and falsidical   15, 72, 74
Parent   12
Paternalism   37, 39
Penalty of loss   78
Penalty of sense   78, 80
Penance   40, 75
Performance   65
Plato   31
Play   11, 60
Presence   7, 40
Presumption   76
Price   65, 66
Pride   76, 127
Proportion   1, 8
Providence   28, 79
Punishment   78

Rationality   88
Reason, practical   29, 51, 93, 94
Reason, theoretical   94
Reasoning, practical   104
Reasoning, theoretical   104
Reflexivity   29, 89, 97, 98
Relations   3
Responsibility   97
Responsibility, introvert conception of   5, 11, 46, 49, 60, 67, 85, 87, 88, 130
Reverence   51, 52, 70
Reward   48, 66
Right   53, 65
Roles   3, 4, 12, 48
Ruler   2, 3, 28, 47, 48, 52, 53, 57, 119, 122

Science, practical   26, 51
Science, theoretical   26
Self-love   9, 69
Self-regarding   4, 10, 46, 60
Servant   3, 48
Sin   119
Sin, irrationality of   125
Sin, mortal   4, 25, 31, 37, 39, 56, 59, 76, 80, 94, 122, 125
Sin, venial   122
Socrates   31
Son   12, 51, 59
Specification   9, 92
Spontaneity   13
Spontaneity, paradox of   71, 77
Stain   108, 114
Status, standing   47, 49, 52, 59, 63
Subject, subjection   3, 4, 31, 47, 52, 57, 60, 76, 89, 122, 128
Supererogation   76
Syllogism, practical   106, 109

Teacher   6, 12, 17, 33, 43, 48
Teleology   26
Teleology, fitness for an end   1, 2, 5, 24, 25, 27, 34, 46, 63, 68, 72, 78
Theological Virtues   10
Theology   26

Universal Good   28
Use   91, 96, 97, 100, 101, 110, 113

Violence, constraint 96
Virtue 50, 64
Vision of God 15, 27, 34, 54, 65, 72
Voluntariness 13, 41, 78, 85, 90, 91, 123
Vows 76

Wage 65, 66
Will 9, 25, 31, 34, 55, 73, 86, 87, 90, 119
Will, free choice of the 56
Will, mediated and unmediated acts 92, 96
Will, necessitation of 36
Will, rectitude of 27
Will, turning of 28, 37, 38, 75, 80, 120
Wisdom, practical 2, 105
Wishing 7
Withdrawal 11